JOHN B.

First published as *John B. - The Real Keane* by Mercier Press in 1992
This edition with new material published in 2002 by Mercier Press
Douglas Village Cork
Tel: (021) 4899 858 Fax: (021) 4899 887
Email: books@mercierpress.ie
16 Hume Street Dublin 2
Tel: (01) 661 5299; Fax: (01) 661 8583
Email: books@marino.ie
www.mercierpress.ie

Trade enquiries to CMD Distribution
55A Spruce Avenue
Stillorgan Industrial Park
Blackrock County Dublin
Tel: (01) 294 2560; Fax: (01) 294 2564
Email: cmd@columba.ie

ISBN 1 85635 403 2
10 9 8 7 6 5 4 3 2 1

Cover design by Mercier Design
Cover photographs by Gillian Buckley

Printed by Creative Print and Design Group Harmondsworth Middlesex UK

A CIP record for this title is available from the British Library

JOHN B.

GUS SMITH AND DES HICKEY

MERCIER PRESS

This book is dedicated to the memory of co-author Des
Hickey, who most regrettably died before
the publication of *John B. – The Real Keane* in 1992.

CONTENTS

A Real Presence

There comes a time when words have said their say,
You rise and walk, alone, the banks of your loved river
Surrendering to the music God has sent your way
Beyond the mouthings of the smug and clever.

This music flows from silence before words are born,
Wings at home in freedom, a bright unpoisoned sky,
Heard later when bells tell of thoughts forlorn
And words are found for all who have to live and die.

You found words for love and lust and cunning greed
And polished men whose hearts and minds are power
And lonely men and women in their bypassed need
And gentle souls who see, and try to care.

The stars above the Feale became your words
And you see waiting now for what the night may bring
And while you see the death that you are moving towards
You raise your head to heaven and begin to sing.

I think that you were most at home in song
Clear and ringing through the Atlantic night
Where, for a moment, right defeated wrong
And stoneblind ignorance became sympathetic sight.

Late August evening near the cliffs. You're there with Mary,
You're flying, singing to the merciless, generous sea,
You're gone beyond your pain into a no-words-needed beauty
And a hushed place cherishes a real presence,
Laughing, lovable and free.

BRENDAN KENNELLY

Acknowledgements

In preparing this biography, we are indebted to John B. Keane for his cooperation and patience during our lengthy interviews with him in Listowel and Dublin. Without his assistance, we could not have proceeded with such a comprehensive book.

Equally, we are grateful to his wife, Mary, for her kindness and cooperation at all times, and to all the Keane family: John B.'s sons, William (Billy), Conor and John; daughter Joanne; brothers Michael and Denis; and sister Peg (Keane) Schuster.

Our special thanks to James N. Healy for making available his memorabilia relating to the Southern Theatre Group productions and Theatre of the South productions, to Michael Keane for writings relating to the Keane family, to Daniel Hannon for photographs of John B. Keane from his album, and to photographer Brendan Landy for photographs taken of the Keane family in Listowel.

For their generous recall we wish to thank: Ben Barnes, Kathleen Barrington, Beatrice Behan, Barry Cassin, Pan Collins, Adrian Cronin, Cyril Cusack, Tim Danaher, Martin Dempsey, Dónal Donnelly, Dan Donovan, Kevin Donovan, Joe Dowling, Flor Dullea, J. Patrick Duffner, Donall Farmer, Bernard Farrell, Mary Feehan, John Finegan, Andrew Flynn, Brenda Fricker, Charles Ginnane, Tony Guerin, Kay Healy, Tom Honan, Carmel Honan, John Hurt, Joe Kearns, Frank Kelly, Éamon Kelly, Brendan Kennelly, Pádraig Kennelly, Patrick Laffan, Mick Lally, Peadar Lamb, Arthur Lappin, Joe Lynch, Gerry Lundberg, Bryan MacMahon, Tomás MacAnna, James McGlone, Virginia McGlone, Proinsias MacAonghusa, Anna Manahan, Patrick Mason, Ronnie Masterson, Christopher Morris, Máirín Morrish, Des Nealon, Jim Norton, Maurice O'Doherty, Phyl O'Doherty, Hugh O'Lunny, Dónal Ó Móráin, Denis O'Shea, Father Kieran O'Shea, Noel Pearson, Brian Quinn, Nóra Relihan, Martin Reynolds, Phyllis

Ryan, Frank Sanquest, John Schuster, Jim Sheridan, Raymond Smith, Noel Smith, John Spillane, Gerry Sullivan, Maureen Toal, Michael Twomey, Marie Twomey and Barbara Walsh.

We wish to thank the editors of the following newspapers for their permission to quote from reviews of plays and special features: the Kerryman Group, Tralee, the *Irish Independent*, *Evening Herald*, *Sunday Independent*, *Irish Times*, *Irish Examiner*, *Evening Echo*, *Sunday Tribune*, *Times* of London, *Daily Telegraph*, *London Evening Standard*, *Sunday Express*, *Financial Times*, *New York Times*, *Kerryman*, *Limerick Leader*, *Kerry's Eye*, *Limerick Chronicle* and Clonmel *Nationalist*. We would also like to thank Kerry County Library, Tralee.

Our grateful acknowledgement also to the following authors and their publications: *Festival Glory in Athlone* by Gus Smith (Aherlow Publishers), *Self-Portrait* by John B. Keane (Mercier Press), *The Celebrated Letters of John B. Keane* (Mercier Press), *Death Be Not Proud and Other Stories* by John B. Keane (Mercier Press), *Remembering How We Stood* by John Ryan (Lilliput Press), *The Abbey, Ireland's National Theatre* by Hugh Hunt (Gill & Macmillan), *The Highest House on the Mountain*, *Sharon's Grave* and *Sive* (Progress House) and *The Field*, *The Year of the Hiker* and *Big Maggie* (Mercier Press).

INTRODUCTION

When *John B. – The Real Keane* was published a decade ago, the Listowel playwright was still busy producing short stories, essays and novels – and, less so, plays – on his old typewriter in his office room above the pub in William Street – his retreat, as he called it, from the world around him. It was the first biography of his engaging life and included interviews with most of the people who had helped to shape his career as a dramatist. Indeed, for the launch of the book at the Gaiety Theatre, Dublin, he travelled with his wife, Mary, from Listowel and was happy to renew acquaintance with friends from both inside and outside the theatre.

In subsequent years, some of these producers and actors regrettably passed on, notably James N. Healy, Martin Dempsey, Ray McAnally, Joe Lynch, Éamon Kelly, Eamonn Keane and others. All of them without question were outstanding interpreters of Keane's racy plays and admired his craft as a playwright. Their contributions, therefore, were not only essential to the story itself but vital for future generations of playgoers – a fact acknowledged during his lifetime by the dramatist himself.

When John B. died at his home after a long illness on 30 May 2002, a nation grieved. This response was to be expected, and the funeral crowds testified to his popularity. For one thing, his first great success in the theatre, *Sive*, had been staged at one time or other in almost every parish in the land and, it was said, had proved to be a huge fund-raiser for hard-up church and school committees. In addition, television had made him a national figure and he became a well-loved panellist. On his death, his biography became a valuable source of information for obituary writers, and this inevitably prompted the question of whether it should be updated.

The publisher's answer was an emphatic yes, mainly so as

to include the copious tributes voiced at his funeral and subsequently by such as Joe Dowling, current director of the Guthrie Theatre in Minneapolis and former artistic director of the Abbey Theatre; playwright Bernard Farrell; producers Barry Cassin, Patrick Mason and Tomás MacAnna. Hugh Leonard, Anthony Cronin, Jim Sheridan, Noel Pearson, Garry Hynes and James McGlone also remembered the man who had contributed so much to Irish theatre.

This new edition of the biography, entitled *John B.*, which we have no doubt will be greatly welcomed, provides a fuller picture of the legendary Kerry playwright and a fresh perspective on his work and achievements. Undeniably, he had triumphed over the early apathy shown towards him by the artistic elite in Dublin by later having productions of his plays mounted in the capital's largest theatres and becoming a fashionable Abbey Theatre playwright. Above all, however, this new edition explores Keane's Listowel roots; the voices of the region echo through the book, primarily those of Brendan Kennelly, Gabriel Fitzmaurice, Jimmy Deenihan, Danny Hannon and Tony Guerin.

John B.'s countless friends will be consoled by the knowledge that he died personally fulfilled, happy in himself, and with Mary and his children around his bedside. He is buried, as is his brother Eamonn, in his native Listowel.

September 2002

PART ONE

LISTOWEL – AND SIVE

1

The Publican's Dream

Walsh's Ballroom stands silent today. It is a 1950s symbol of a forgotten age. Once it echoed to the music of Mick Delahunty's Orchestra and the Clipper Carlton, the popular bands of the era, attracting thousands of dancers to this mecca in the market town of Listowel in County Kerry.

On three successive evenings during February 1959, Walsh's 'ballroom of romance' was transformed into a theatre for the production of *Sive*. It was expected that this play by John B. Keane, presented by the Listowel Drama Group, would draw too many theatregoers to be accommodated in any of the town's smaller venues. Furthermore, large audiences would bolster the group's fund-raising activities.

John B. Keane was a Listowel publican, by then acquiring a local reputation as a poet. He had written sketches for shows and a few months earlier Radio Éireann had broadcast his play *Barbara Shearing*. Listowel already had an established playwright in Bryan MacMahon, whose plays were staged in Dublin by the Abbey Theatre. The popular novelist Maurice Walsh, who had also had a play produced, came from nearby, while the earlier playwright George Fitzmaurice had also helped put north Kerry on the theatrical map. Keane admired Fitzmaurice's imaginative writing and dreamed of becoming a playwright, yet until now he had seen few plays on the stage.

It was a visit to a play in the winter of 1958 that inspired Keane to begin writing his own play. He had gone with his wife to a performance of Joseph Tomelty's *All Souls' Night*. The work made a profound impression on him. Walking home to his public house in William Street, he turned to Mary and said, 'You know, I could write a play like that.'

That night he sat up late in the kitchen at the back of the

bar. Fortified with a pint of Guinness, he began to jot down the first scene of a play in a threepenny notebook. The opening directions read: 'The kitchen is poorly furnished, with an open hearth on its left wall. A door leads to a bedroom at the left side of the hearth. On the wall facing the audience there is a small window, and a door leads to the yard at the front of the house.' In his imagination he saw his characters – a young girl who is to be married off to a lecherous old man from the mountains, her young lover, and the woman who has helped make the bizarre match, the girl's avaricious aunt. There would be two tinkermen who would relate news and gossip through their words and songs, just as he had seen them do as a boy in the Stacks Mountains.

He began to live with his characters late into the night, adding a new dimension to his life. By day he worked in the public house, sometimes tired after his night's writing. He had got to know the members of the Listowel Drama Group, among them a young nurse, Nora Relihan. When he told Nóra he believed he could write a play as good, if not better, than *All Souls' Night*, she showed no surprise; she knew he had written poems and short stories and wanted to be a writer. She had recently returned from London, having qualified as a nurse, and was working in Listowel District Hospital. With an interest in literature and drama, she found that in Ireland writers were regarded as extraordinary people. In England, by contrast, people would simply say, 'He's a writer', and no more. In America they didn't hold writers in awe. But in County Kerry, writers held a special place.

Mary Keane, whose hands were full looking after their eighteen-month-old son Billy – and the grocery side of the public house – quietly encouraged her husband and did not argue with him when he wrote into the small hours. It was something she knew he wanted to do, and was content doing.

Among those who called into the public house was Denis O'Shea, Keane's one-time English teacher. At night, O'Shea and his friends drank a pint or two in the back kitchen of the bar, and chatted. One night John B. said to him, 'Denis, I'm writing a play.' Having made the announcement, he took out the notebook and read a few lines aloud. O'Shea was not too

16

surprised, for he knew the young man had written poetry. However, he could scarcely read Keane's handwriting; it was precise and very small, with the minimum of space between the lines, as though he wanted to conceal from others what he was writing. Keane would joke later, 'I suppose you could say I was a cute Kerry hoor even then.'

Alone after midnight, the young publican wrote rapidly and was seldom at a loss for words. With no distractions, his concentration was good and occasionally he would pause to drink from his pint of Guinness.

As the weeks passed, he became completely caught up in the fate of his play's heroine, Sive; he had decided to call the play *Sive* after his sister Sheila, who had recently married in Cahirciveen. 'Sive' is the old Irish form of 'Sheila'.

He confided to a friend how he had found the theme for his play: 'Years ago a man from west Limerick came to tell me he was going to get married and asked me if I could get a cheap ring. Someone had told him I knew a jeweller in Listowel who gave discounts on rings. I sent him along to the shop, where he got the discount he wanted on a ring – the cheapest ring in the shop. The next time I met him, he was with a girl. She was seventeen; he was about sixty-five, but he was older-looking than his years and he struck me as incapable of any kind of satisfactory relationship. The girl was a labourer's daughter and her family approved of the match because they felt she was rising above her social status. I remember I was appalled by the difference in ages. Of course, the marriage was a disaster. To me, the man was nothing but a sorry old dotard.'

By December 1958, he had almost completed the play. It was proving to be, on his own admission, an emotional experience. Mary noted how utterly engrossed he had become in his characters. As he wrote down the words of the final song, slowly and deliberately, tears welled in his eyes, and a few tears dropped onto the page of his notebook. The song is sung after the discovery of Sive's body in the bog:

Oh, come all good men and true,
A sad tale I'll tell to you
All of a maiden fair, who died this day.
Oh, they murdered lovely Sive,
She would not be a bride,
And laid her dead to bury in the clay.

Years later, Keane would affirm that he had put his soul into *Sive*, explaining that, 'I put everything into the writing of the play. For me, writing the final scene was one of the most profound moments of my life, and I found myself overwhelmed by emotion. It drained me; it drained me completely.'

In the play, Sive, frightened by Thomasheen Seán Rua, the corrupt matchmaker, dashes from her house into the fog and drowns in a bog-hole. Her body is placed on the kitchen table, arms folded on her breast, and the tinker musician sings his haunting dirge.

Denis O'Shea knew that John B. had completed the play, because he no longer saw him at night jotting down lines in the notebook.

'I see you've finished your play?' he remarked casually over a pint.

'That's right, Denis.' There was unmistakable pride in the young publican's voice.

'So what are you going to do with it, John?'

'I suppose I'll send it to the Abbey.'

It was the inevitable step; the majority of aspiring Irish playwrights submitted their work to the national theatre. Keane seemed satisfied with the finished play and Mary was relieved that her husband was catching up on his lost sleep. She could see he was enthusiastic about the play. For his own part, he would later say, 'I realised I was on to something very dramatic in content. I had high hopes of success.' He gave the handwritten manuscript to Dan Hanrahan to type, and when the copy was ready he posted it to the 'Managing Director, Abbey Theatre, Dublin'.

Ernest Blythe, who ruled the Abbey with an iron fist – and in the process made his share of enemies – had been a full-time organiser of the Irish Volunteers for the Kerry area and in 1915 had visited Listowel, where he found a well-organised Volunteer company. He would have known John B. Keane's mother's people, who were prominent in the republican movement, but he himself had never met the young man, although his name 'struck a bell', as he put it.

A pragmatic Northerner, Blythe was not taken by the melodramatic content of *Sive*; nor was Tomás MacAnna, then a set designer at the Abbey. Only one of the other directors, Séamus Wilmot, a native of north Kerry, spoke up in favour of the play and said he wanted to see it staged at the Abbey. 'Séamus fought tooth and nail for it,' said MacAnna, 'but he was outvoted.' The Abbey's decision was a deep disappointment to Keane, who felt certain that *Sive* was an Abbey play and had thought the novelty of the tinkers at least would appeal to the directors, including Gabriel Fallon.

There is some confusion about the next step taken by the playwright. He claims he submitted *Sive* to the drama department at Radio Éireann and that it was not accepted but was returned with an accompanying letter which suggested he send his play to a local amateur group. Micheál Ó hAodha, head of drama at Radio Éireann at the time, recalled that Bill Kearney of the Listowel Drama Group had sent him the manuscript and asked him to read it as a possible choice for the group's next production.

'Knowing the mettle of the players, I did so willingly,' said Ó hAodha. 'After some forthright criticism of fairly obvious faults, such as weak lines and an excess of contrivance, I wrote to Bill Kearney that I would be most disappointed if Listowel did not stage the play, as it would give a great lift to amateur drama, which was then becoming a new social phenomenon of rural Ireland in those pre-television days.'

In later years, Keane was to agree that Micheál Ó hAodha was the first professional theatrical producer to be sympathetic to *Sive*. To the playwright's delight, Listowel Drama Group decided to stage the play, although there was no experienced person to direct it. Brendan Carroll, who two years previously had retired from theatre to devote time to his drapery shop, was prevailed upon to return. 'I decided out of a sense of loyalty to come back,' he said. 'I was anxious also to help the play's young author.'

The group's president was Bryan MacMahon, whose play *The Bugle in the Blood* had been premièred in 1949 by the group. They had also staged an excellent production of *The Playboy of the Western World* with Éamon Kelly and Maura O'Sullivan, who by now had moved to Dublin to join the Radio Éireann Repertory Company. Although still smarting from his rejection by the Abbey, Keane had no doubt that the Listowel group would do justice to his play.

Rehearsals began in December in the old Protestant school. Finding a suitable girl to portray Sive was not easy. Brendan Carroll auditioned a number of schoolgirls, none of whom impressed him. Keane and members of the cast also searched for the ideal girl. When everyone had almost given up, John Flaherty, a local tailor who was cast as Pats Bocock, one of the tinkermen, said there was a girl living near him who seemed right for the part. Her name was Margaret Dillon.

Carroll was to agree with his judgement. A lively, pleasant girl, Margaret was still at school. She appeared to possess the qualities of innocence, sensitivity and warmth required for Sive. It was to be her first stage role, and she was naturally apprehensive.

Bill Kearney was cast as the matchmaker and Nóra Relihan would play her first character role as the loveless Mena Glavin. At the first reading, she found excitement in the language. 'I think everybody in the cast accepted the play from the word go.' she said. 'We met for rehearsals two nights a week at first and this was extended to three in January. I noticed that from time to time John B. brought friends along with him to the school, among them Dr Johnny Walsh, who was showing genuine interest in the play. Usually John B. sat quietly in a corner of the room, listening to every word. If someone suggested that a line be rewritten, he would say, "I'll write it again." He was very open to advice.'

Brian Brennan, who arrived in Listowel from Dublin as a young clerk of works for a new school in the town, was first cast as Seán Dóta, the old man who is matched with Sive, but was later given the role of Liam Scuab, the young carpenter and the girl's lover. 'I thought it was a dreadful part,' Brennan said. 'Liam was a lover without a love scene and some of his lines were very weak. When I mentioned this to John B. Keane he said, "Well, Brian, I'll write a play next time with the best love scene in Irish drama – and you'll play the lover."'

Brennan was excited by the workshop idea. 'We felt we were creating the play as much as John B.,' he recalled. 'I do remember him sitting through rehearsals and changing a line when asked. I found him very approachable, though he also seemed unpredictable. One day he'd show one face and the next day he'd be something different. Brendan Carroll was very painstaking and sensitive in his approach. He knew what he wanted and he insisted on getting it.'

Carroll cut long speeches when they did not advance either the plot or the action of the play. As rehearsals progressed, John Flaherty realised that the tinkermen might steal the show. He had discussed their significance with Brendan Carroll. 'I suppose I knew tinkers better than Brendan,' Flaherty recalled. 'There was one particular fellow called Charlie O'Brien, a terrible character for the bad language. One day I saw him with a stick raised high, pointing at someone who had said something nasty to him. The way O'Brien pointed that stick fascinated me. I mentioned this to Brendan and he listened carefully.'

Even during rehearsals the rest of the cast kept their eyes on Flaherty as he struck his stick on the floor three times, then called on his rhyming son Carthalawn for 'Your best! Your mighty best!' as he solemnly brought his stick around in a semicircle to point at the man being cursed.

The words of Pats Bocock would have been insufficient without the introductory beat of the bodhrán by his son Carthalawn, however. John B. Keane had first come across the bodhrán when holidaying as a boy in the Stacks Mountains. He remembered seeing two travelling men calling at houses and striking the table with a stick to command attention before they delivered the news and gossip of the day. He learned that the bodhrán was made from goatskin and that the best tone and strongest reverberation was produced from the skin of a she-goat.

'We got the bodhrán for rehearsals from Sonny Canavan, a noted bodhrán-maker,' Keane remembered. 'John Cahill as Carthalawn knew how to get the best out of it and he produced a fine tone.' As rehearsals proceeded, Brendan Carroll realised he might have miscalculated the impact the tinkermen were likely to make on an audience; he was now convinced it could be powerful. To Keane, it was John Flaherty's gaunt stage presence and resonant voice that made his scenes with Cahill so effective.

When Keane's friend Kieran O'Shea was invited to rehearsals, the scene had the same impact on him. O'Shea was studying for the priesthood at Maynooth College, where the rules were strict: the students, like the priests, were not permitted to attend play performances. As he went into the old schoolhouse, O'Shea could hear the beat of the bodhrán and the voice of John Cahill singing:

> Oh! Mike Glavin, you're the man,
> You was always in the van,
> With a dacent house to old man and gorsoon;
> May white snuff be at your wake,
> Baker's bread and curranty cake,
> And plinty on your table, late and soon.

To young O'Shea it was a stunning and ritualistic scene he had stumbled on as Pats Bocock, stick in hand, delivers his curse and Thomasheen Seán Rua stands helpless. 'The rest of the cast could not keep their eyes off John Flaherty as he spoke his lines,' O'Shea said. 'My own reaction was the same. I had never seen anything like it.' That night he conveyed his impressions to Keane, who was anxious to know the views of his friends. He was cautious, however, refusing to be drawn about his play. 'Go and see it for yourself,' he would say. ''Twill soon be on in Walsh's Ballroom.'

To Mary Keane, her husband seemed a new man, delighted when customers in the bar told him, 'We're going to your play, Johneen.' Most of them, she knew, had never seen a play staged. The only time she saw John B. angry was when someone suggested that a banjo should be used instead of a bodhrán. 'Nonsense,' he snapped. 'A bodhrán it is, and a bodhrán it will stay.'

Posters went up in the town announcing the première for the night of Monday 2 February 1959. Bill Kearney distributed car stickers to ensure that the population of north Kerry was aware of *Sive*.

By now, rumours were sweeping Listowel that 'Johneen' Keane had written 'a strange play'. Cousins of the Keanes announced that they would attend the première. On the opening night, crowds began making their way to the venue long before curtain-up time of eight o'clock. By seven thirty, almost five hundred people were in their seats, most of them treating the occasion as a night out.

Dressed in a neat suit, John B. Keane set out from William Street. His first stop was Mike O'Connor's public house, where he called for a whiskey.

When he had knocked it back, Mike said to him cheerfully, 'Johneen, you'll have another, for I feel there's an awful ordeal facing you tonight.'

'As you say, Mike, 'tis an ordeal, but I'm not feeling too bad.'

'There's talk that you've written a good one. Good luck to you anyway.'

'I'll need it, God knows.'

Having drunk his second whiskey, he asked for a pint of stout as a chaser. But O'Connor warned, 'If you don't go soon, Johneen, you won't be fit to see the play!'

They shook hands at the door, and Keane loped briskly down the street, accepting good wishes as he went, including a word of encouragement from a local curate. He was alone by the time he reached Walsh's Ballroom, which was well-lit. Mary Keane had gone ahead with a friend, and Keane now joined them in their seats, about a dozen rows from the stage. By now, some seven hundred people were present. Three rows from the front sat Keane's parents and his younger brother Denis, and further back sat Mary's sister and her husband. Denis Keane, a fourteen-year-old schoolboy at the time, noticed that his father was excited by the atmosphere, though his mother looked calm.

To John B. Keane, there was a carnival atmosphere about the ballroom, as though everybody was expecting to see a comedy or a farce. In the past, he had written comedy sketches which had drawn audiences, so the attitude of tonight's audience was understandable. Others had come, he knew, out of curiosity to see for themselves what the local fellow had written, and he felt that perhaps a few had come to ridicule him.

Mary Keane had been at church that morning and met the curate. 'What's this I hear about John?' he asked. 'Has he written another funny sketch or something?' His attitude had hurt her. Some people weren't taking the play seriously because it was written by a local author.

In the crowded ballroom, Bryan MacMahon sat close to the stage. He had been one of the first producers for the Listowel Drama Group after it was founded late in 1943 with the motto 'The Stage Shall Never Die'. He was anxious for the group – and the play – to do well. Denis O'Shea was seated in the centre of the hall, hoping for a success for his former pupil. Keane had come to him when he was writing the play to ask if certain phrases or words were suitable.

For Keane, the moments before the rise of the curtain were anxious ones, but the few drinks had eased his nervousness. The carnival atmosphere persisted as people laughed and exchanged stories. It made him wonder if they would take his play seriously. He had written about the 1930s, the years of the economic war in Ireland, when money was scarce, minds were stagnant and the grim spectre of the county home stared the elderly in the face. He had sought to convey this harsh reality in his play.

Silence greeted the rise of the curtain, though it was not maintained during the bitter early exchanges between Mena Glavin and her mother-in-law, Nanna (played by Siobhán Cahill). By the middle of the first act, however, Keane sensed that the audience was beginning to accept that the play was not a comedy, although some people laughed in the wrong places. When people realised that the girl, Sive, was being matched with Seán Dóta, they were visibly moved. Denis Keane noticed that his father became 'terribly annoyed' when some people got up from their seats, either to go to the toilet or to walk out of the ballroom. John B. saw them too, and wondered why they were leaving. Were they outraged at the play's language?

At the distant sound of the bodhrán, some members of the audience cheered, and there were more cheers for the arrival of Pats Bocock and his son Carthalawn. Keane grew more optimistic. The bodhrán is a popular musical instrument in north Kerry, for long synonymous with the wren boys, and the familiar sound made the audience sit up. There was even a danger that their overreaction might upset the cast. There was more applause when Carthalawn sang:

> On the road from Abbeyfeale,
> Sure I met a man with meal.
> Come near, said he, and pass your idle time;
> On me he made quite bold,
> Saying the young will wed the old,
> And the old man have the money for the child.

In the audience was a clergyman who had earlier intimated that he would have to leave for a sick call at nine thirty. Instead of giving the priest an aisle seat so as to make his departure less conspicuous, someone had placed him in the centre of the hall, eight rows from the stage. At nine thirty, the priest stood up and, to the annoyance of those in his row, pushed his way out of the hall. Nothing would convince some of the audience but that he had walked out in protest.

By the time the final curtain came down, however, the episode was almost forgotten in the enthusiastic applause and calls for the author. Keane was overjoyed. It seemed that his faith in *Sive* had been rewarded. 'I believe the play owed its immediate success to the authentic dialogue and to the fact that people were able to identify with the characters,' he recalled. John Flaherty's prediction was correct: the audience had been hypnotised by the tinkers.

The tall, lean figure of John B. Keane rose from his seat and, amid applause, climbed onto the stage. In his soft Kerry accent, he addressed the audience: 'Ladies and gentlemen, thank you all for coming tonight. Any of you who'd like to swap a black cat for a hen canary, I'm your man!' He said no more, but hurried back to his seat.

Bryan MacMahon commented, 'I knew from early on in the play that it was going to be a sensation. It had the absolute drum of the common people. We were seeing something we had known always existed here, but now it was presented on stage before us. I was gripped right through the production.'

Nóra Relihan sensed something else that first night: 'I got this feeling of shock among the audience when Mike Glavin, my husband in the play, says the word "Jesus", and again when I say to Sive, "You're a bye-child, a common bye-child – a bastard!" I could hear the intake of breath by the people out there. I think they resented the harshness of the language, and this resentment built up.'

On the following night, the words 'Jesus' and 'Jesus Christ' were omitted. While it was true, said Nóra Relihan, that the majority of the audience was excited by the play, there were others, she felt, who regarded the theme as too strong and raw: 'A rural community was seeing itself portrayed in an exposed manner on stage and people did not like what they saw. Some lines were too close to the bone.'

She was surprised when people suggested to her that a match such as that between Sive and Seán Dóta could not happen in Kerry. She tried to explain: 'I remember as a child in Killorglin seeing an old man and a young girl together on their honeymoon. When I first read *Sive*, the memory returned to me, for I do recall with horror the sight of that strange couple on honeymoon, and the memory stayed with me for years afterwards.'

Looking back, Brendan Carroll said, 'I remember most the way the production moved so many people to tears, actual tears. I remember the handkerchiefs coming out; I remember them weeping. The man who can write words that can affect people like that has a rare gift, in my view.'

Kevin Donovan, who played Mike Glavin, felt that the introduction of the bodhrán had made a tremendous impact. It was the first time the instrument had been seen on stage, and it added to the tinkers' scenes. 'The combination of the tinkers' curse and the bodhrán had a frightening effect on the audience,' he recalled. 'I could feel the reaction. I could sense it coming up from the audience. I knew the others in the cast felt it too, and that we had won them over. The tinkers' curse had made the audience cringe with terror.'

To Donovan, who had been acting in Listowel for many years, the success of *Sive* owed much to Brendan Carroll's direction. 'Brendan put a lot of work into the play,' Donovan said. He remembered that in the final scene, before Sive is carried on stage, a basin of water was thrown over the actress to suggest that she had been taken from a bog-hole. In his view, Sive's plight had captured the imagination of the audience.

He was not surprised at the power of the play's characterisation. He could pinpoint most of the play's characters in Listowel and the surrounding areas. To put them on stage, Keane had only to detail every aspect of them.

*

In the Keane public house that night, there was a buzz of excitement. Uncles, aunts, cousins, in-laws – everybody was there. The bar and the kitchen were full and Mary Keane realised that people were enthusiastic about the events of the evening. 'They felt that something special had happened,' she said. 'They didn't sing; instead they chatted and drank tea and porter and whiskey. Being generous, John B. said to me, "Mary, give everybody in the house a drink!" I nearly collapsed, for we still owed for the pub. I told him, "We'll be in debt for ever more!"'

As Keane pulled pints, one old man leaned across the bar counter and said to him, 'You made me cry tonight, Johneen, and I haven't cried for forty years.' The words heartened the young playwright. He watched his father drink a pint of stout; he seemed a proud man, though he detected a hint of anxiety. As a national-school teacher, his father wanted no scandal attached to his son's play. John B. had reassured him that all he had intended to portray in *Sive* was the absence of love on the one hand and the greed that motivated the matchmaker on the other. His mother, though equally proud of her son's achievement, told him more than once that the language in his play was strong, even crude.

Denis O'Shea was perhaps least surprised at the enthusiastic reception the play had received. He had always known that 'John Keane', as he had called him from schooldays, would write a play. He recalled one particular moment in Walsh's Ballroom that made him smile. A big man seated behind him had shouted to Nóra Relihan on stage, 'You oul' bitch! Can't you lave the child alone?' To O'Shea, that man, outraged at Mena Glavin's behaviour, was living the play.

Not surprisingly, the national papers paid no attention to the Listowel première. It was, for a time, to remain a Kerry phenomenon. The occasion was recorded by the *Kerryman*, however: its reviewer, under the initials 'M.C.', wrote, 'Prophets are seldom accepted in their own home. Not so John B. Keane. The twenty-nine-year-old publican got a tremendous reception after his play *Sive* was premièred in Walsh's Ballroom on Monday night. In fact, all through the three acts, the packed audience was highly enthusiastic – sometimes too much so – in its approval of the play and its presentation by Listowel Drama Group. *Sive* was the first of forty-odd plays by this young author to be staged anywhere. I predict that if the quality is as high, the dust of many more of his works will soon be shaken off and they will be premièred in even more exalted places than Walsh's Ballroom.'

The news that the young Listowel poet had written 'forty-odd plays' came as some surprise. No one was quite sure how much Keane had written; in Listowel they understood he had written poems, unstaged one-act plays and comedy sketches. His earliest known play was said to be titled *The Valley of Knockanure*, written when he was seventeen. While it was too early to predict a future for him as a dramatist, there was no doubt that a new talent had emerged.

Nóra Relihan considered Keane courageous to have written such a provocative and controversial play as *Sive*. Illegitimacy was a delicate issue, and exposing the greed of the matchmaker had not been done before. It took courage, too, to be single-minded in a small town like Listowel, and in this respect Relihan also admired Mary Keane. Furthermore, John B.'s arrival as a playwright would, in her view, introduce some friendly rivalry into the local drama scene, where Bryan MacMahon had his own following. MacMahon was a schoolteacher, and the profession imposed disciplines, whereas Keane, a publican, had a freer hand to express himself.

In the spring of 1959, John B. Keane was unknown outside his native Listowel. Once the local drama group began to present his play at amateur drama festivals, however, his name was to find its way into the national newspapers. Already rumours of his promise were spreading beyond the boundaries of Kerry. Naturally, people began to ask, 'Who is John B. Keane?'

2

The House in Church Street

Whenever a Keane looks back, it is invariably to the house at 45 Church Street, Listowel, where ten children were born (one child died in infancy). It was here, on 21 July 1928, that John B. Keane entered the world, weighing twelve pounds. As with his brothers and sisters, the house was to make a lasting impression on him. It could have been the setting for a novel; in time, it inspired a short story and a play.

It was in this house that William Keane, a national-school teacher, was born and later set up house with Hannah Purtill, then twenty-one, and twelve years his junior. The daughter of a small farmer in Ballydonoghue, four miles from Listowel, Hannah was apprenticed to a draper in the town. She was an attractive girl with raven hair, brown eyes and a trim figure. Her family had a strong nationalistic background, so it was no surprise when she joined Cumann na mBan and risked her life in dangerous missions for the North Kerry Volunteers. Her brother, Mick Purtill, was a founding member of the IRA's local flying squad.

In the early 1920s, Hannah attracted the attention of a Black-and-Tan officer named Darcy who occasionally visited the drapery shop where she worked. He called her 'Hannah, Maid of the Mountains' and persisted in asking her out, but to no avail. Once, as she walked alone to Mass, he stopped her at the point of a gun and demanded that she go out with him. Again, she refused. Angered, Darcy told her she had twenty-four hours to leave the town. A fearless girl, she refused to go.

It was shortly after this episode that she met William Keane, who had been teaching in Nenagh, County Tipperary, and had returned to take up an appointment at Listowel

National School. Although he was conscious of the age gap between them, Willie was an ardent admirer of Hannah and persuaded her to marry him.

Before their wedding day, Hannah received from her parents a dowry of some hundred and fifty pounds, and after the marriage William Keane took his bride home to the house in Church Street. Years later, Hannah would say that they ought to have gone to live in a house with more privacy, but at the time she did not complain. Not only did her husband's elderly parents live with them, but her husband's brother, Danny, lived in the third-floor attic, and his sister, Julianne, lived in an upstairs room.

Young Hannah was a good cook and adept with needle and thread. William Keane was a considerate man who adored his young wife. In 1924, the couple's first child was born – a son they christened Michael. There followed more sons: Eamonn, William and John. By now, Hannah was busy enough to employ a maid, but Julianne also helped by making clothes for the children and assisting with domestic chores. Julianne idolised Eamonn, who had the best looks of all the boys.

Uncle Danny cherished his privacy, and woe betide any child who climbed the steep stairs to the attic to invade his cobwebbed seclusion. On no account would he permit Julianne or Hannah to interfere in his affairs. He was five years older than William and, unlike him, placed no high regard on learning, although he read books. 'Land is the thing,' he was fond of saying, though he had none himself. He was not well off; his main source of income came from the fortnightly cattle fairs in the town. It was never clear whether he was a buyer or a drover, because he was too drunk at the end of the day to give an account of his movements. He was a good judge of cattle, and so was probably what was known as a 'go-between man'.

Michael Keane remembered that his uncle Danny carried a supply of small change and was generous with his money when the mood took him. After a time, Hannah, like the rest of the family, accepted his presence, although there were times when he did not speak to her.

William Keane filled the shelves in the room off the

kitchen with his books, and it became his library – a retreat from school and kitchen where he could read in solitude. His wife began to recognise the ascetic side to her husband and, although she sometimes accused him of walking away from domestic problems, she knew he preferred to be with his books.

At the age of four, John Keane, already sturdy, with crinkly black hair, began lessons at his father's school, though he was not taught by him. 'My father taught fifth grade at the other end of the room from Low Infants,' he recalled. 'But sometimes I managed to catch his eye and he would wink at me without changing his expression. I felt happier then.'

Soon afterwards, his father accepted the principalship of Clounmacon National School, three miles from Listowel. Because he had no car, he would cycle or walk to the school. Hannah saw to it that when he returned in the evenings he had a cosy house and a warm meal awaiting him. William had friends on the road and houses where he called and was made welcome; he occasionally paused there to chat and quaff, as his son Michael noted, from 'the jug of contentment'.

By now, two girls, Kathleen and Peg, had been added to the growing family. William was happy; 'I've enough boys in the family,' he had said. When a third girl, Sheila, was born, the house in Church Street became cramped. Young Michael was sent to his mother's family in Ballydonoghue, where he enjoyed the wide-open spaces.

Two of the children, John and Sheila, contracted diphtheria and almost died. 'It was touch and go that either of them would survive,' Peg remembered. John was an observant child who noticed that his maternal grandmother had a sweet voice and, when in a good mood, sang songs like 'Green Grows the Laurel'. The manner in which his father talked to him about characters from novels, like Sam Weller and Wilkins Micawber, made John think he must be a good teacher. John was increasingly proud of him, proud of his learning, and of the affection he displayed to the family.

It was left to Hannah to correct the boys when they got out of hand, however; they could be wild and mischievous. As the summer of 1936 approached, John, now eight, pestered his parents to let him stay with relatives in the Stacks

Mountains, where, as he was to write, 'every man, woman and child within a radius of five miles was a neighbour'.

He was sent to his cousins, the Sheehys, at Ivy Bridge. Here in the Stacks, traditional customs survived, such as the arrival of the straw boys at wedding celebrations, singing and dancing with the newly-weds.

The Sheehys' was known as a 'rambling house', where neighbours gathered to tell folk stories, often sitting up all night. John's cousin John Joe Sheehy noted that 'John would have his spake in as well.' He believed that John's parents wanted their son out of Listowel during the summer to keep him out of trouble. 'He was always wild. The Stacks was the place for him. He could run himself to death here.'

*

The holidays over, it was back to Church Street. John's now wiry and athletic frame made him a match for most boys of his age, yet he was to remark later on the 'deliberate cruelties' of boys as something he wished to forget.

A happy home life was his compensation. Earlier he had not dared to visit the attic at the top of the house where Uncle Danny lived; now he had no fears. He would go there with Eamonn to listen to Danny's stories: 'My uncle had a great imagination and he convinced both Eamonn and myself that in the field at the back of our house, the Major's Field, a major used to gallop horses at night with the hounds. So vivid was his way of telling the story that I could hear the horses' hooves outside.'

To young John, his proud and self-sufficient uncle was the first real character he knew as a child – a character who influenced him. Danny was also a pious man who disliked coarse language. John's older brother, Michael, remembered the musty attic with its pall of oily smoke and 'skeins of cobwebs hanging from the ceiling'. His uncle would be found sitting on his bed, his cap askew, his collar undone and his lips ringed with the brown stain of porter.

'Come in, come in!' Danny would call to the boys as he searched in his waistcoat pockets for tanners to give them.

After a fair day he could be generous, though he would add a rider: 'You won't spend this on the pictures? They're godless places, them picture houses. The games and the carryings-on of them actors!' Although the attic room was squalid, the boys continued to climb the narrow stairs to chat to their uncle and listen to the nonsense rhymes he recited for them.

At national school, John Keane proved a bright pupil. Bryan MacMahon remembered him as 'a black-haired, curly-headed lad, sitting down near the window in that bottom room which we had in the school. I realised he had talent. All the Keanes had talent.' John B. was to say, 'I learned a lot from Bryan MacMahon. I learned that teaching was a real vocation. He fined us ha'pennies for small sins and then at the end of term would send somebody down to the sweet shop to buy bull's-eyes.'

By the early 1940s, when war was raging in Europe, John and his brothers, like many other boys of the time in Ireland, followed the news of battles on the radio and in the newspapers. Times were not easy for the family. With so many children to feed and clothe, money was scarce. Peg recalled, 'My parents found it hard to make ends meet.' Hannah Keane made the food go around, and she knitted and patched up garments. She worried when bills were unpaid, and when her husband stayed out drinking. Sometimes she would shout up the stairs at John, 'Turn out the light!' He was less troublesome than Eamonn. 'One thing about John,' she used to say, 'is that he never gave me a back answer.' His sisters recalled John as being fiery and hot-tempered, though at the same time good-natured. He was crazy about Gaelic football and dreamed of becoming a star player. He loved watching the game or listening to big matches broadcast on the radio.

Although John was a few years older than his sister Peg, she remembered that he loved to hear stories about their legendary uncle Mick Purtill and his escapades with the flying column and how he had hoodwinked the Black and Tans. The boy looked forward to callers to the house in Church Street; he and Eamonn would waylay them for pennies. When his father's people called, they sometimes brought with them pork and puddings or a supply of black turf and bags of potatoes.

The family began to kill their own pigs; John remembered flitches of bacon hanging from the kitchen ceiling. Looking back, he remembered, 'It was a depressing time, really, for the shadow of war hung upon us and there was grinding poverty around us. Some people almost starved to death.'

Summer holidays in the Stacks helped him forget the bad times. At Ivy Bridge he first encountered the matchmakers, the best known of them being Dan Paddy Andy. In later years he recalled the story of 'the old buck of about seventy' who came across the hills in his pony and trap in search of a wife.

One of the men sitting with Dan Paddy Andy at Ivy Bridge asked, 'What does he want a woman for at that age?'

Dan Paddy retorted, 'If you saw a stallion ass coupling inside in a field with a mare, would you ask the stallion for his birth certificate? You would not, but you'd question a Christian!'

Even at Church Street, the houses were filled with characters. They all loved children, and in return John and his friends would do anything for them. 'There was no money, so the things the people valued were friendship and prowess at football and athletics,' John recalled. 'But the real test of character was how you treated the old people, whether you were kind to them and were prepared to help them. You grew up with respect for the old and this respect stayed with you.'

The Keane boys, nonetheless, earned a reputation as pranksters. Eamonn once got a bicycle, and he and John, wearing black hats and dark glasses, came riding down the street, with John ringing the bell of the bicycle as his brother shouted, 'The Germans have landed!' People rushed to their doors, some of the older folk crossing themselves in fear.

The brothers joined the wren boys, and John also took an interest in poker schools and was considered lucky at the game. 'John was never short of money,' recalled Michael. 'He always managed to think up ways of making money, even if it meant selling empty jam jars.'

It was customary by now when 'things got too hot' for him in the kitchen for William Keane to retreat to his library, leaving his hard-pressed wife the task of keeping order in the family. When he arrived home late in the evenings after his walk from Clounmacon School, Hannah sometimes scolded him for the company he kept, reminding him of his standing in the community and warning him to be wary of 'ne'er-do-well' acquaintances. But William would keep his silence. He was proud of his friends on the road, the oldest of them being Paddy Furey, a travelling man and a gifted storyteller.

Young John did not worry when he heard his mother scolding his father, for he was aware of their love for one another, even if they did not make a display of it. He was proud when people said to him, 'Your father taught me; he is a wonderful teacher.'

John became more conscious of Uncle Danny's presence in the house and felt it a duty to climb the stairs to the attic. Danny habitually went to twelve o'clock Mass on Sundays. He would stride down the street towards the church, wearing a suit a couple of sizes too big for him. He had no feeling for colour and it was not unusual to see him wearing a brown suit with a bottle-green shirt, white collar and red tie, and with a voluminous purple handkerchief protruding from his top pocket.

To John and Michael, their father and uncle were so dissimilar that they did not seem like brothers. But they had one virtue in common: their love of animals. Their father talked of Gin and Penny as though they were children. Gin was a brindled cat, and Penny a spotted, smooth-haired terrier some years junior to Gin. When William sat down to dinner, Penny, in spite of Hannah's protestations, would jump on his right knee, and Gin, with the skill of a trained gymnast, would land softly on his left knee. The boys at the table would listen to their father say, 'What'll I do with ye at all?'

Though it was a happy home, it was now obvious that the responsibility for running the household was left entirely to Hannah, who suffered from depression, despite her sense of humour. As the family grew up, the burden proved too great for her and she had a minor breakdown. 'When Mother came back from hospital,' recalled Peg Keane, 'I hugged her and asked her why she had gone away.'

In that large family, Peg and her mother were close. 'I used to love when my mother hugged me and saw me off to school,' Peg recalled. 'If I saw her upset it would worry me, for I didn't want anything to happen to her.' Her father, too, she sensed, felt the strain of having so many people under one roof. When her mother would reprimand one of the children – usually John – for leaving the light on in their bedroom as they read, her father would retort, 'Don't mind her. Read away.'

Peg accepted that her mother had to be bossy; her father had opted out of his domestic responsibilities. 'When he wouldn't pay the shop bills,' Peg remembered, 'my mother would send me out to pay them, and I'd tell the shopkeeper that we'd pay so much off a month.' She was aware too that her mother resented William's drinking if it meant leaving the family short. 'Yet they could be happy walking together and talking about their children,' Peg said. 'Their way of life was simple.'

*

In 1938, John Keane was enrolled at the local St Michael's College and began his secondary education. Though intelligent and quick-witted, he was regarded as 'a bit of a rebel' who sometimes got into trouble with his teachers. From the outset, he found St Michael's an unusual school, and no place for a boy who loved football and athletics. There were no competitions of any kind; the emphasis was solely on academic achievement. He mastered Irish and Latin without difficulty, and in Denis O'Shea he had an extremely able teacher of English and history.

O'Shea found young John 'a bright and alert student' who showed unusual promise at English. Once he asked the class to write an essay about a visit to a circus. He was surprised at the imagination displayed by John Keane, particularly as he suspected the boy had never been to a circus. The teacher wrote at the end of the page, 'You have written a very good essay from your imagination. It is full of atmosphere.' That essay became a topic of amusement between them in later years.

Generally, O'Shea found Keane attentive in class and especially good at poetry. In his essays he was able to add colour to words and phrases. He was not outstanding at history, though he had a genuine interest in the subject. O'Shea could not recall the boy causing trouble in the classroom.

Nevertheless, John was popular among his fellow rebels, smoking cigarettes and engaging in pranks. He was suspended from the school on several occasions for, as he said himself, 'smoking, speech-making, ballad-writing and play-acting'. These suspensions worried his parents. Some teachers disliked the 'rebels' and made up their minds that they were inveterate troublemakers. It might have been different if St Michael's had catered for boys who preferred to mix study with football and athletics.

John, who played football with his friends outside class, joined in poker schools in the local temperance hall, known as the Bands Room, where his brother Michael sometimes joined him. By the age of fifteen he was playing poker with adults, among them a bookie and a wholesale chemist. Once, as Michael watched him play, John whispered to him, 'Do me a favour, Michael. Will you stand somewhere else? Your face is too honest. They'll know I've got nothing when they look at your face.' Michael moved away and watched as his brother won £128.

John's confidence at the game mystified his brother. 'He had this natural poker face and never exposed his hand. On one occasion when a big pot was at stake and he had won a considerable amount, one of the players ordered a round of drinks although he had no money left. John said to him, "Excuse me, but I hope you're not paying for the round of drinks out of the money that went into the pot. I've already stood my round and I'm certainly not standing another round out of the pot I'm going to win!"'

John's confidence in winning made Michael gasp. His brother was never lost for ideas about how to make some money. John once led a gang over a wall into a disused pub in Church Street where he thought they could find empty bottles, which they could barter. Having climbed the wall, the boys drank the remnants of the alcohol from the bottles and got themselves drunk. That evening, the mothers of the neighbourhood were looking for 'Johneen' Keane's blood.

The boy persisted with his pranks. He forged a letter

purported to have been written by an aunt in America; it stated that she was returning on holiday to Listowel. His parents and all the family dressed in their Sunday best to go to the railway station to greet her. He accompanied them and was, by his own admission, 'petrified'. When all the passengers had left the train and the family stood forlornly on the empty platform, he owned up to what he had done.

To Michael, his younger brother possessed an unusual sense of humour. John once decided to try to bring the elderly bachelors and spinsters in the town together by writing letters from one to the other. When eventually he got them to meet, they discovered to their horror that the meeting had been engineered by a local prankster.

'I first got an inkling that John wanted to be a writer when he was sixteen,' Michael said. 'He would talk about writing, and he began to write poems and stories. One story was about river pirates which he had heard about from my father.'

In the crowded house in Church Street, plagued with bills, William Keane spent more time in his library. John would join his father there, and they would talk about characters in literature. William had a habit of placing a red mark on page 100 of each book, so as to be able to identify it if it were lost or stolen. Occasionally he forgot to mark a book, and when the Keane boys lent the books to their friends they were rarely returned. On one occasion, John and Eamonn were left alone in the library by their father while he joined a friend next door. He had left a few bottles of wine in a cupboard; the boys managed to prise the cupboard open and began to sample the wine. Instead of making them soporific, the drink went to their heads and they began to sing. Their father was furious.

John was proving quite versatile. Apart from his growing reputation as a fighter, poet, prankster and footballer, he could talk with youthful authority about his adventures in the Stacks Mountains in summertime, of nights passed in moving from one 'rambling house' to another, listening to stories about ghosts or about great men and their deeds. William Keane wondered what his son would do when he left school, for already he had to admit the boy had 'talents in various directions'.

*

Life at St Michael's College was unhappy for John Keane. He endured the corporal punishment and was stung by the sarcasm directed at him by teachers.

In his spare moments, he wrote poetry, and he was elated when one poem was accepted for publication by *Ireland's Own*. He was equally thrilled by the payment of five shillings he received. Like other boys who were interested in reading, he visited Dan Flavin's bookshop in Church Street and borrowed books. 'Dan lent us young fellows books because we could not afford them. You got the impression that he did not like to part with a book; he wanted to share it.'

He went to the local cinema and became a fan. While he saw travelling theatre in the form of the fit-up companies, he was not too impressed, preferring his screen heroes, such as William Boyd in the Hopalong Cassidy Westerns which he watched on Sunday nights, 'screaming and roaring for the good guys'.

Such diversions were a temporary escape from the brutality of school life and the 'beatings on countless occasions' from which other pupils suffered as much as he did. He was to ask in later years why parents had not united in the interests of their children. But the answer was self-evident: there was no other secondary school in the town. He was not to forget the brutality of the school principal. Father O'Connor was a big, blustering man with an autocratic manner. Once, after he had suspended John and two other students, William Keane met the priest in the street, and deliberately walked past him without acknowledging him.

Father O'Connor ran after him and blurted, 'Why don't you salute a priest when you see one?'

To which Keane replied, 'When I *see* one.'

In his last year at school, John, aged eighteen, had more poems published and won prizes for them. He received encouragement from his father, who began to believe in his son's talent. 'You have a good ear for poetry, boy,' he told him. 'Keep at it.' He wrote a poem about Church Street, the street he was born in and had grown to love, and was surprised how quickly the lines came to him:

I love the flags that pave the walk
I love the mud between
The funny figures drawn in chalk.
I love to hear the sound
Of drays upon their round
Of horses and their clocklike walk.
I love to watch the corner-people gawk
And hear what underlies their idle talk.

I love to hear the music of the rain
I love to hear the sound
Of yellow waters flushing in the main
I love the breaks between
When little boys begin
To sail their paper galleons in the drain.
Grey clouds sail west and silver tips remain
The street, thank God, is bright and clean again.

A golden mellow peace for ever clings
Along the little street
There are so very many lasting things
Beyond the walls of strife
In our beleaguered life
There are so many lovely songs to sing
Of God and His eternal love that rings
Of simple people and of simple things.

During elocution class at school, each boy was asked to quote a few verses from a poem. When John's turn came he chose to read his poem 'Church Street'. He delivered his lines confidently and when he had finished Father O'Connor asked him who had written the poem.

John replied, 'I did, Father.'

The priest, perhaps thinking that he was lying, lashed out with his fist and knocked him to the floor. A fellow pupil who jumped up to protest at the beating was struck across the head.

As he picked himself up, John was ordered to leave the class. Shaken, he walked to the toilets and lit a cigarette. He was hurt in mind and body, and angry that a teacher should inflict such pain on him. He could not shake off his anger for that whole day.

'A bad beating is no asset to the self-respect or dignity of an eighteen-year-old boy,' he was to write years later, when he recalled that at least one other teacher at his school believed he was stealing poems from magazines and pretending they were his own. Though the principal was more to be pitied than blamed, he thought: 'Misusing an eighteen-year-old is like baiting a three-year-old bull. He might not charge there and then, but he will explode later on and people find it hard to analyse the reasons.'

At his second attempt, he left St Michael's with an Honours Leaving Certificate. But that beating in his last year, he was to say, contributed more than anything else to his becoming a writer.

3

Finding a Job

At the age of twenty, Keane, according to himself, was 'a poet, a singer, a footballer and, I suppose, a bit of a character. I was gregarious, too, as long as the spotlight wasn't switched to me.'

He was close to his brother Michael and was influenced by him. 'There was a chemistry between us as brothers,' Michael was to recall. 'We had both spent time in the country with in-laws and we liked the country traditions.'

It was with his older brother, Billy, however, that John had his first real taste of alcohol. 'I think I was thirteen at the time and my father and some friends were coming by car from the Munster football final in Killarney and stopped at a public house,' John recalled. 'A few minutes later a fellow came into the pub and exclaimed there was an accident outside. Billy and I were left alone in the bar and proceeded to lap up the unfinished glasses. Later, as my father resumed his journey back to Listowel, we could barely speak. Billy and myself fell asleep. I'm sure my father and his friends knew what had happened.'

William Keane was becoming anxious about his son's job prospects. He said to Michael, 'Your brother is going to be a chemist, a boxer, a runner, a poet and a journalist!' He could be sarcastic when he was drinking, but he was concerned about what John intended to do with his life. John was not entirely sure himself. He tried his hand at fowl-buying and in time learned how to slaughter ducks, geese, chickens and turkeys with a deft pressure of the fingers and a swift flick of the wrists.

His months spent as a fowl-buyer he was to count as 'the happiest and most hilarious' of his life. He learned to drink, too: 'My associates taught me that porter-drinking was a scientific and ennobling art and that whiskey was a threat to industry, sanity and the sanctity of the family. I became a proficient pint-drinker and never regretted it.'

The fowl-buying job was transitory and soon he was looking for more permanent work. He was influenced by his brother Eamonn, who had earlier announced to the family that he intended to follow a theatrical career. To prove that he was serious, he adapted for the stage a scene from A. J. Cronin's novel *Hatter's Castle* and planned to play the leading part. Considering that the great actor Anew McMaster had visited William Keane's library and talked to him about Shakespeare's plays, Eamonn expected that his father would be sympathetic to his choice of career. McMaster usually stayed at the house next door in Church Street when his Shakespearean company visited the town on their tours.

John was enthusiastic about Eamonn's theatrical ambitions. His brother's Cronin sketch was to be staged as part of a nurses' fund-raising concert and he was offered the part of the moneylender. He was given one line of dialogue, which he was to keep repeating: 'I want my money, Brodie!'

In the audience at the concert were William and Hannah Keane. In her early days, Hannah had been an amateur actress and had retained her interest in drama. She had faith in Eamonn's talent and was not surprised by his decision to become an actor.

In the sketch, John, playing the moneylender, calls at Hatter's Castle and demands his debt, repeating the line, 'I want my money, Brodie!' Eamonn, as Brodie, is enraged by the demand and tries to strangle the moneylender. 'He almost did,' recalled John. 'I fell into semi-consciousness, and only recovered with the help of a nurse in the hall.'

Despite this alarming experience, John decided to form his own theatrical group, the Willie Brothers, and rented the top floor of the Carnegie Library for a matinée and evening performance. He chose a one-act play he had written, *The Ghost of Sir Patrick Drury*, and staged it in a programme that was complemented by songs and dances. The matinée was a success, but there seemed to be little money in becoming a small-town promoter.

Michael Keane suggested that Eamonn at this time was the better-known 'literary figure' in Listowel and had a vivid, if bizarre, imagination. William Keane found his son's behaviour far removed from the humdrum life of teaching in a country school, but he confided that there was perhaps some 'odd genius' at work in the family.

Eamonn packed his bags and left the town without saying a goodbye to a friend. William heard he had joined the Abbey Theatre company. Hannah breathed a sigh of relief; at least she knew where to find him. 'Eamonn has the voice of an actor,' she would say, adding that acting had helped cure his stammer. William said little; he had serious misgivings about his son's choice of career.

Hannah worried about John and was relieved when he became apprenticed to a local chemist, Keane-Stack. She looked forward to him becoming a pillar of the Listowel establishment, well-to-do and respected. Her son did not see it quite like that.

Pharmacy, however, was the only option open to him at this period. He had applied for a job as a junior reporter on the *Kerryman* but was not accepted. He was genuinely disappointed: he had quite fancied a career in journalism. Not to be outdone, he collaborated with a friend, Stan Kennelly, in launching a local paper, the *Listowel Leader*, and sold six pages of advertising. Michael Keane recalled that the paper caused a small stir in the town and that John had high hopes of its success.

Unfortunately, he allowed his imagination run away with him, and his report about a woman in Church Street with bandy legs caused an outcry. He had also inserted an advertisement which read, 'Lost, one pair of bloomers belonging to Mary O'Shea. Finder will be rewarded.'

To Michael, this was typical of his brother's humour. But the paper's outspoken attack on county councillors, blaming them for the deplorable condition of the local park, led to an uproar at the council meeting. Advertisers declared that they would no longer be prepared to contribute to the paper. Sensing trouble, John and his partner decided to quit with the small profit they had made on the first and only issue.

*

At weekends, John was a busy footballer and was considered promising at the game. Tony Guerin, who also lived in Church Street, recalled watching him. 'He was a very committed player and gave everything on the field,' Guerin said. 'He was a tall, angular fellow, and he reminded me of a plucked chicken with his elbows flying in all directions.' Guerin, who was some years younger, saw that Keane was popular with his team-mates, who looked up to him.

The rebel surfaced in John when he decided to play rugby football. For a time he was barred by the GAA from playing Gaelic games. 'That left a sour taste,' he said. 'I could see no reason for such a ban. Playing soccer or rugby didn't make one any less an Irishman.'

He once played rugby with Con Houlihan, a member of the Castleisland team who was to become a noted sports journalist. When the going got rough, Houlihan was known to remove his boots and play in his bare feet.

'It was considered a sacrilege to play rugby in Listowel at the time,' recalled Tony Guerin. 'The game was frowned on. There was hostility towards those who played it and you were labelled a West Briton. I think it was feared the game would attract Gaelic footballers.'

When not on the playing fields, or watching games, John Keane went to dances in Ballybunion, his favourite haunt in the summertime. He later wrote, 'If I had a fiver for all the sick heads and unforgettable nights I've had in Ballybunion, I could buy a racehorse . . . I did a mean quickstep, a dreamy waltz, an exuberant if aggressive "Siege of Ennis",' he boasted, 'and I could quote Byron, Shelley or Keats when cheek-to-cheek dancing was involved.'

On the dance floor when girls quizzed him about his occupation, he would tell them he was a novelist or a portrait painter and that his uncle was a parish priest or a bishop. Their reaction didn't bother him; he was only baffled when farmers' daughters refused to dance with him.

When it was quiet in the chemist's shop, he would write.

He found himself unable to concentrate on 'bottle-shaking, powder-making or tablet-counting' and gradually concluded that he did not want to qualify as a chemist. 'My mother was disappointed,' he recalled. 'She had imagined me running a prosperous chemist's shop in the town.'

The truth was that John Keane preferred to write and read books than make up prescriptions. One day Brendan Behan came into the shop to see Michael Quille, John's superior, who had spent time with him in jail on charges for IRA activities. Accompanying Behan was Tony McInerney, an Irish sprint champion. The pair were on their way to the Dingle peninsula to spend a few days with Kruger Kavanagh at Dunquin. Keane noted that the men had guns but, like himself, no money.

'Michael Quille gave a few pounds to Brendan,' Keane recalled. 'I borrowed a ten-shilling note from my mother, and we adjourned to Alphonsus Sheehy's pub, where I proceeded to drink with the others and read my poems.'

Behan listened with interest. Later, in a piece published in the *Irish Digest*, he wrote about his Listowel visit and included the name of John Keane. The chemist's apprentice was flattered.

Curly's public house was a favourite meeting place for the young poet and his friends. It was there that he became adept at poker and chess. He joined in the sing-songs and got involved in argumentative conversations. He was in search of excitement outside the dull surroundings of the chemist's shop. He was by now twenty-three, with no notion of settling down. Football, dancing and poetry filled his spare time to his satisfaction.

Still a prankster, he thought up an idea to inject fun into the general-election campaign in 1951. With his friends from Curly's, he set about organising a political skit involving a fictional politician, to be named Tom Doodle. By his own admission, the stunt was aimed at taking the bitterness out of local politics.

One of the first locals to notice that something was happening was Kieran O'Shea, the son of Denis O'Shea. On his way to Mass one Sunday morning, Kieran O'Shea noticed posters hung on telegraph poles in Church Street, proclaiming: 'Vote No. 1 Tom Doodle. Use Your Noodle and Give the Whole Caboodle to Doodle.'

The townspeople were puzzled. 'Who is Tom Doodle?' they asked. A week later, new posters appeared announcing that Tom Doodle would address a big political rally in the square in Listowel. The rally was scheduled for a Holy Day, and that evening scarcely any worshippers turned up for Benediction in the local church: everybody had gone to the railway station to greet Tom Doodle.

O'Shea knew by now that John Keane was involved in the affair. At the station, he saw him step down from the train with Doodle, who wore a top hat and a swallowtail coat, and was conspicuous by his luxuriant beard. Keane stood beside him as the election lorry proceeded, to cheers, through the crowd towards the local square.

'John was poker-faced all the time,' said O'Shea. 'I couldn't tell if he was serious or not.' The story is told that, as the lorry was coming down Church Street, an old woman looked up at Doodle and called, 'Parnell, my boy, you are back with us again!' Parnell had once addressed a meeting in the town from a window in the Listowel Arms Hotel.

The rally in the crowded square lasted an hour. When Doodle began his speech, there was loud cheering. Nobody knew the man's real identity, yet the crowd's good humour was palpable, and they seemed not to care that this was the biggest hoax perpetrated on them for many years.

Keane was later to insist that the meeting took the 'bad taste' out of local politics. 'When I introduced the speakers on the platform, including Tom Doodle, there was a great, warm spirit in the air,' he said. 'People almost believed that Doodle was real, and after the meeting they wanted his autograph. We had trouble in getting him out of the square safely.'

For some years afterwards, Keane and his friends, in what was known as the Independent Coulogeous Party, held an annual dinner to commemorate the Doodle episode. Outside the dining room, the dinner song was ceremonially chanted:

Let porter fresh from laughing barrels
Abolish life's unending quarrels;
And pray no man endure the colic
That doth attend Tom Doodle's frolic.

Keane had penned the lines and derived mischievous pleasure from the ceremony.

He was by now travelling for his employer to outlying towns and villages. Although he had no steady girlfriend, he was not short of admirers at dances and parties. The tall, lean poet and footballer had a personality that appealed to young women.

4

THE RACE-WEEK DANCERS

It was the age of the 'Ballroom of Romance', that era of Ireland's innocence when dance halls offered bright lights and soft drinks, and girls experienced their first tremulous sexual awakenings on the dance floor. 'The old and the young went to the same dances,' John B. Keane recalled, somewhat wistfully. 'Nowadays the young seem to have isolated themselves away from the older generation. It was a time, too, of the duty dance, when you were expected to take out wallflowers – or those women and girls who had failed to find dancing partners.'

There was another custom in those days. The ballrooms sold only soft drinks, so many young men made sure they tanked up with alcohol before venturing inside. To Keane, it was their way of plucking up courage, but it didn't always improve their dancing.

There were no more large-scale or more exuberant dances than in Listowel during the annual race week. In September 1951, Mick Delahunty's Orchestra supplied the music, and the Astor Cinema, converted into a ballroom for the three race nights, was thronged. For an hour, the young John Keane danced waltzes and foxtrots, and then decided to sit out the next dance. On the balcony, he noticed a very pretty girl and made up his mind to ask her to dance.

'I made straight for her and asked her to dance with me,' he recalled. Mary O'Connor accepted and the pair were swept along by the crowd. By the time they reached the dance floor, the orchestra was into a slow waltz. Deciding to wait, they sat down beside other young couples. John introduced himself as 'John Keane from Listowel'; she told him she was 'Mary O'Connor from near Knocknagoshel.' He bought her a lemonade and talked about himself, eager to tell her he wrote poetry and played football.

When the next dance was called, they moved onto the floor. It was an old-time waltz. They could scarcely hear each other above the music and the voices. Mary O'Connor moved gracefully and Keane complimented her on her dancing. By the end of the night he wasn't sure what impression he had made on the girl; all he knew was that he wanted to meet her again. She had a quiet charm, an easy sense of humour – and blue eyes that shone when she smiled. For her part, Mary O'Connor, who had danced with many young men, found Keane to be well-mannered. 'I'll walk out with you,' he told her on an impulse.

In a car outside the cinema, her brother Teddy and her sister Norrie and her boyfriend were waiting. Mary was surprised when she found out that they knew about John Keane. She promised she would try to return to Listowel on the following night for the next race-week dance. As the car pulled away, Keane lingered in the street. Then he sauntered home to Church Street, wondering why he could not get this girl out of his mind.

*

At nineteen, Mary O'Connor had a good idea of what she wanted from life. For two years she had been apprenticed to a hairdressing salon in Castleisland and lived in lodgings in the town. She worked six days a week, with a half-day off on Wednesdays, and was considered very good at her work.

Her mother had died in childbirth at the age of thirty-six, when Mary was just two years old. After she sat her Intermediate examination, her father died, and this meant her staying at home, helping to run the family grocery business while her brothers looked after their small farm. Digging potatoes from the muddy soil and milking cows on Sundays did not appeal to her. She decided instead to attend classes at the technical school in Castleisland, where she studied housekeeping and cookery. Hairstyling appealed to her, and she thought of it as a useful career. She answered an advertisement in the *Kerryman* for an apprentice hairdresser and got the job.

Like most girls of her age, she loved dancing, and whenever she could, she danced in Castleisland or Abbeyfeale, often cycling in summertime to more distant venues. Occasionally she was dated by young admirers, but avoided getting involved with them.

Now she was hoping to return to Listowel for her first date with John Keane. As the evening approached, however, she was unable to arrange for a seat in a car going to Listowel. Desperately disappointed, she hoped he wouldn't be angry. She had never felt this way about a boy; it was a curious sensation and she did not confide in her friends. She thought they might laugh at her.

Keane accepted her excuse. He was travelling as a pharmaceutical salesman between towns and villages, and he arranged to meet her in Castleisland. Her family had read a poem he had just published in the *Kerryman* and joked about it. 'Get him to write a poem for me,' her sister Norrie asked her.

When the couple met again, John Keane told Mary that her blue eyes had inspired the poem. Mary blushed and was embarrassed. She was surprised when her landlady, Julia O'Connor, told her she had read the poem and liked it. 'Young Keane is a bit of a romantic,' the landlady remarked.

With little money between them, and living twenty-six miles apart, it was not easy for John Keane and Mary O'Connor to meet regularly. Whenever there was a seat available in a car going to Listowel, she availed of it, however. On the dance floor, John would recite poetry to her. Then he would joke as he hugged and kissed her. Mary had never felt so happy in her life.

During his working visits to Castleisland, Keane was introduced to Mary's landlady, and he and Julia hit it off at once, discussing his poems, and poetry in general. As the months passed, Julia decided that the young couple ought to be thinking about marriage. When Mary arrived home after a dance or a social function, she would ask her, 'Well, did John say anything about the future?' Mary would laugh and try to shrug off the question. Julia would persist, however. 'You wouldn't want to drag it out too long, girl,' she'd say.

The couple were honest with one another. Keane told Mary that his immediate prospects in the chemist's were not bright, and she agreed that between them they would not be able to save much money. They began to discuss the idea of emigrating to America, where they both had relatives. Keane gradually lost interest in the idea, perhaps because he could not see himself progressing as a writer there. But they were both evidently in love, and trying to reach a decision caused some frustration.

'I was romantic in the loftiest sense of the word,' Keane was to claim later. 'I used to read my poems to Mary, and she always listened and said whether she liked them or not. I was proud that she believed in me, for at this time people had their own opinions about aspiring poets – and they weren't always favourable.'

They continued dancing together in spite of their increasing concern about the future. 'I've danced cheek to cheek with women in my time,' Keane later wrote, 'but none of them compared with this charming creature from Knocknagoshel.'

Mary was introduced to the Keane household in Church Street, where she was accepted as one of the family. She met Uncle Danny, who showed no surprise. William Keane was philosophical about the relationship and hoped they would have a wedding in the family; Hannah welcomed the girl warmly and told John in confidence, 'You've got a fine girl, son. Be respectful to her.'

From the outset, Michael Keane took to Mary and, being close to John, thought she was a good influence on him. 'It was a youthful affair, and I could see my brother was in love with her,' Michael recalled. Once when he went with them to a dance in Castleisland, he sensed that locals in the town resented John. 'I thought that one or two of them would have a go at him,' he said. Some men in Castleisland resented a man from Listowel taking out one of *their* young women; this wasn't the custom in Kerry at the time.

John knew that he had to decide. Secretly, he had made

up his mind to emigrate to England. The evening he broke the news to Mary, she became angry and questioned his decision. Now he knew she had a temper, and he tried to placate her as best he could. He convinced her that emigration was best for him, but that he would try hard to save enough money to come home to marry her.

She had heard stories of young men from the area who had gone away and soon forgotten the girls they had left behind. Yet the way he spoke convinced her he was sincere – though the thought of life without her young poet and dancing partner was heartbreaking.

At the time, the railway station in Listowel, a stone's throw from the Astor Cinema, was the frequent setting for emotional farewells as loved ones set out on their journeys into exile. It was no different on the morning that John Keane, suitcase in hand, bade goodbye to his parents. He had kissed Mary goodbye in Castleisland; she was by now resigned to his leaving and to his insistence that she should stay at home. 'I began to tell myself that he was right to go away for a short while,' she recalled. 'I still felt angry that he had to leave Ireland, but seeing so many others doing the same thing softened the blow for me. I believe if I had left with him, we would have married in England and perhaps would not have come back again.'

On 6 January 1952, almost five months after they had first met, John Keane took the train from Listowel to Dublin. He was greeted by his brother Eamonn in the city centre in the afternoon and, in the Tower Bar in Henry Street, the haunt of Radio Éireann employees, they began to drink to his imminent exile.

John told Eamonn about Mary and promised, 'Sure I'll come back and marry her.' At the mailboat pier at Dún Laoghaire, people hugged and kissed and said their tearful goodbyes. Eamonn urged his brother as he boarded the steamer, 'Keep up the writing.' He had faith in John's talent and feared he might abandon his literary calling.

On board the mailboat that cold night, John thought of the early Christian martyrs going out to face the terrors of the arena. 'Laugh if you like, but there was an unbelievable feeling of tragedy which embraced us all,' he said. 'It is no laughing matter to those who took part in the pilgrimage.'

In his hip pocket he fingered a naggin of whiskey, a parting gift from Eamonn. But the drunkenness of his fellow travellers, due as much he was sure to loneliness and the anguish of separation as to alcohol, appalled him. The memory of that journey would remain with him forever.

*

The three-hour voyage to the Welsh port of Holyhead was otherwise uneventful, and on the subsequent six-hour train journey to London he managed to catch some sleep, although the carriages were crowded. He had enough money to spend a few days sightseeing in London and he saw a couple of shows in the West End. After four days he took a train to Northampton, where he had arranged to meet a cousin, Denis Murphy.

'You start on Monday morning at British Timken,' his cousin told him. 'It's tough work, but it pays well.'

Keane wasn't afraid of hard work; he was young and energetic and had set his mind on making enough money to return to Ireland and settle down. The factory was three miles from the town centre and employed a workforce of some three thousand. It manufactured mainly roller bearings and enjoyed a worldwide export trade.

In his first month at British Timken, Keane swept floors without complaint. Eventually he was given a job as a furnace operator, which meant standing in front of a rotary hearth furnace in 96 degrees of heat. Into a slot he would thrust a cone-shaped steel symbol, and when it was heated he pressed it down to the nearest thousandth of an inch. He was paid piecemeal for the number of symbols he produced each day.

He was to remember the work in the furnaces as 'excruciating', although the money was 'excellent'. He found lodgings in Avingdon Avenue, counting himself lucky, as a number of boarding houses displayed notices which stated, 'No dogs, no Irish'. The Irish, he was told, were considered 'suspect because they had a reputation for drinking too much, getting into trouble, and being generally unreliable,' he recalled later. But he experienced no difficulties with Beryl, his landlady, or her husband, Henry. 'I think at first, due to my accent, they thought I was Welsh; when I told them however that I was Irish, they didn't mind at all. They judged you by your behaviour.'

Seven men were lodging with him: two Poles and five Irish – two from Northern Ireland and three from the South. Each paid two pounds five shillings a week in return for a hearty breakfast, a packed lunch to take to work and, depending on the shift hours they worked, an evening meal. Looking back after forty years, Keane remarked, 'I couldn't understand why the cabbage was boiled separately from the bacon, but it didn't worry me much, for we were well fed.' All round, he thought his landlady and her husband were wonderful people. 'I remember we had no holy-water font in the house and, without any of us knowing it, Beryl procured one from the administrator of the Catholic cathedral, a Father Gallagher from Cork.'

He discovered to his cost that the cat was the best-loved member of the household. In his innocence one morning, he found the cat sitting on his chair in the dining room and, being in a hurry to eat, swept her off the seat. Beryl looked daggers at him, and for days afterwards she scarcely spoke to him. He was advised by a fellow lodger that when he next went into the dining room he should say to the cat, 'Good morning. And how is cat this morning?' The accepted motto was, 'If you look after the cat, the landlady will look after you.'

Beryl and her husband were a friendly pair. Sometimes, when being paid John's digs' money, Henry would ask, 'How about a bottle of beer?' But John invariably refused; he was not interested in drinking in the house. He would sit at the small table in his bedroom and write stories and poems in longhand; the *Irish Press* in Dublin published one of them. Then he began work on a novel. 'I started writing out of desperation,' he recalled. 'If I hadn't, I'd have gone mad.'

After a writing stint, he sometimes joined the other men in a sing-song, with the Poles singing their folk songs and the Irish concentrating on ballads. At other times they went to

Irish pubs. In an Irish club in Northampton he got into a 'difference of opinion' and a fight ensued, in which he had to defend himself with his fists. At the best of times he had a short fuse, particularly after he drank whiskey, but on this occasion he put the fight down to his lack of experience of the clubs. 'A newcomer was vulnerable there,' he said. 'I wasn't cute enough to keep out of trouble.'

On Saturday nights, it shocked him to see mobs of Irish baiting the police or men in uniform, who included American servicemen. The bad Irish, he concluded, were very bad, but they were in the minority; most of the Irish workers in Northampton were exemplary.

During the summer months he often walked the three miles from his digs to the factory, where he would change into overalls and put on a pair of clogs. Few English, he discovered, worked in the hardening shop or the blast furnaces. The foreman was English and, in Keane's opinion, a very fair man, as were the chargehands. But the Irish were regarded as Paddies. He resented the label, and so did a workmate from Limerick, a huge fellow, who threatened to 'stuff in his furnace' anybody who called him Paddy.

To Keane, the job was a way of making money. He would emerge at dawn from a long night's factory shift, dreaming of Ballybunion, with the Atlantic lapping the black cliffs and the panorama of the distant ocean. He longed to be back there on summer days and nights. 'My heart would break as the picture came vividly before my eyes,' he said, 'and whenever I thought of Mary back in Castleisland, I felt nostalgic.'

He wrote to Mary as often as he could, reassuring her that he was saving money to enable them to marry in a year or two. She, like his mother, sent him food parcels; he hoped they were not under the delusion that he was starving. Once when Mary enquired if he was putting on weight, he wrote back, 'I can tell you, love, that in these conditions I'll remain a spare, sparse man.' No matter how many pints of ale he drank, he gained no weight; working in the intense heat of the furnaces saw to that.

During the summer of 1952 he found time to go home to Ireland to visit his family in Church Street. In Ballybunion he danced with Mary and repeated his promise of marriage. Although he had missed her company, he felt it was better that she stay in Castleisland and wait for his return.

'You're as thin as a herring,' his father told him anxiously. 'Are you eating enough over there?' When William Keane enquired whether he was still writing poetry, John told him he was writing a novel.

Life had not changed in Church Street. The neighbours welcomed him with typical friendliness; a few talked sadly of relatives who had emigrated to America and England. 'I miss the football,' he told former team-mates, because in Northampton there was no Gaelic football played, though he played some soccer and rugby.

When the time came for him to pack his suitcase for the long journey back to Northampton, he was determined that on his next return he would stay at home for good. Aspects of England, nonetheless, had come to appeal to the liberal in him. Ireland, with its absurd book-censorship laws, had always exasperated him; narrow church and social attitudes angered him. Such repressive attitudes limited a person's vision. 'At times I felt imprisoned in mind,' he said, 'and I think now that it was one of the reasons why I took the boat to England.'

Back in Northampton he returned to the hardening shop and often went home to his digs in Avingdon Avenue too tired to work on his novel. He made English friends and found attractive aspects in the English way of life, believing for a time that he could adapt to it easily enough. In contrast to Ireland, people enjoyed greater freedom; they could read the books they wanted to read, and the shadow of the Church did not fall on them.

With an English friend who played the piano, he went occasionally to an English pub and sang songs. This helped assuage the loneliness, and he experienced no attitudes that made him feel inferior as an Irishman. The ordinary Englishman and woman, in his view, were good company and happy to drink and sing with the Irish.

On Sundays, he heard Mass and, provided he was not working a double shift in the hardening shop, went occasionally to the Northampton Repertory Theatre, where he discovered the plays of Shaw and Wilde. It was here that he saw his first O'Casey play, *Juno and the Paycock*.

He thought that if he and Mary were married they might settle down in Northampton and live a pleasant life, even if his job at British Timken was gruelling. For the first time he had money in his pocket and felt a sense of independence. Among other Irishmen he found loneliness and a wish to return home; some of them spent their earnings on drink and gambling; more than a few men had second wives in England and were struggling to support two homes – one in Ireland, another in Northampton.

He was disappointed when a London publisher rejected his novel, although there were encouraging words in the brief accompanying letter. The *Irish Press* and some Irish magazines published his poems and short stories, and he was confident that in time he would be accepted as a writer.

He bought the Irish papers and, in the *Irish Independent* one day, read an advertisement for a chemist's assistant in the village of Doneraile in County Cork. He wrote an application and, to his surprise, was accepted. The wages were two pounds ten shillings a week and his keep, and he was asked to report for work in two weeks.

He had become popular with many of his workmates: there was a genuine regret among them when he gave notice to British Timken. Beryl and Henry were upset to see him go; they regarded him as different from the others in the house in Avingdon Avenue. He had read his poems to them and they would tell their neighbours, 'We have a poet from Ireland staying with us.'

In the Black Boy pub they celebrated his departure. He sang English and Irish songs to piano accompaniment, and his workmates joined in the choruses. The two years in Northampton had passed quickly, but without Mary he knew he could not settle there. He suspected that many of his fellow Irishmen envied his good fortune in finding a job at home. He was glad to see the back of the furnaces. It was no life, he told himself, for a young Irishman.

5

SNOW IN KNOCKNAGOSHEL

Doneraile was a marked change from Northampton, and John Keane took a little time to become accustomed to a more leisurely way of life. It was early 1954, and he was anxious to make the most of his new job. He lodged in rooms above the chemist's shop in the main street. The building was like a museum, crammed with silver plate and ornaments; his employer, aged ninety-three, was a leading authority on antique silver.

Keane's duties did not overtax his energies. They included manning the antique petrol pumps outside the front door on occasions and, in the pharmacy, making up a pile ointment for Lord Doneraile and packaging a scour powder. This powder was evidently highly effective, because orders for it were received from such far-flung places as New Zealand and Venezuela.

In the evenings, he sat at an oak table in the sitting room writing his second novel. When it was finished he sent it to the publishers, but without success. 'It went the merry rounds and came back to me time and again, rejected,' he said.

For recreation, he played Gaelic football and had the honour of once donning the red jersey of Cork in a challenge match between Waterford and Cork in Lismore. 'I never wore the green and gold of Kerry,' he was to say regretfully, 'and it had been one of my sporting ambitions.'

Playing football with him in Lismore was Batt Crowley, who worked in Doneraile as a state forester. Though he was obsessed with football, Crowley took an interest in Keane's writing and urged him to read contemporary fiction. 'Batt was a tremendous influence on me then,' Keane recalled. 'He had a benign, sobering influence on me, and I learned from him.'

They trained together in Fermoy and played with the town's senior team and ate juicy steaks in a local hotel after their training sessions. On other occasions, he and Crowley drank pints of stout or joined in sing-songs. Whenever he could, Keane went back to Castleisland to see Mary. He wrote to her constantly, enclosing with his letters an occasional short love poem

The atmosphere of Doneraile intrigued him; it was so different from that of Listowel. It seemed to him one of the last bastions of the ascendancy class. He wrote later, 'Most of the local gentry were retired brigadiers, majors, captains, lords, knights and what have you.' He came to love the local townspeople. 'They were people after my own heart, the salt of the earth,' he said.

Although pleased to be home in Ireland, he was earning little money, and marriage on less than three pounds a week seemed inadvisable. Mary had stood by him when he knew she could have met a professional man or a businessman with some money. Whenever he took her to dances they discussed again the possibility of emigrating to America. He had contacted an aunt in America to ask if she would claim him. Two of Mary's brothers were doing well there. But something held the couple back.

Keane's mind was eventually made up for him when his former employer in the chemist shop in Listowel offered him a job with reasonable pay. His decision to leave Doneraile was hastened by the refusal of his elderly employer to pay him holiday money. The employer's excuse was that he never took a holiday himself.

Back in Listowel, Keane decided to propose to Mary. He was now twenty-six and eager to have his own house where he could raise a family and write. He travelled by car to Castleisland one evening to meet Mary, having worked up enough courage to make his proposal.

Mary remembers him asking, 'Will you marry me, love?' It was not the highly romantic proposal she would have expected from her young poet. They were walking hand in hand together down the main street. 'I was accepted at once,' John recalled.

When Mary got back to her lodgings, Julia O'Connor was making tea. Looking up, she asked, 'Well, any news for me, girl?'

'John proposed to me,' Mary told her, unable to conceal her delight.

As she poured the tea, Julia seemed satisfied. 'And the wedding? Any word of that, girl?'

Mary laughed. 'Give us a chance, Julia!'

Keane wondered if his new job in the chemist's shop could ensure any kind of security in marriage. He discussed with Mary the possibility of buying a sweetshop or perhaps opening a hairdressing salon. They ended up agreeing that a public house would be the best buy. John had seen an advertisement in the *Kerryman* and posters around Listowel advertising for sale the Greyhound Bar in William Street. They had just enough money for a deposit if their auction bid was accepted. John's father, now retired from teaching, had given him some money, and Mary had her dowry. Between them they could manage the sum of five hundred pounds.

Mary had some private misgivings. At school, the nuns had warned the girls against marrying a publican: publicans 'don't make good husbands,' they were told. For the sake of John, however, she was ready to ignore the nuns' admonition. John, too, had his reservations. From his experience of drinking in the town, he knew there were 'bucks and blackguards' who went out of their way to make life difficult for pub owners, and for women serving behind the bar. He felt, though, that he could take care of himself and run the pub the way he wanted. 'In those days I was prepared to tackle the roughest and toughest of them with my fists,' he recalled.

At the auction, their bid of £1,800 was accepted, and the Greyhound Bar passed into their ownership. It derived its name from the previous owner's success with greyhounds, and there was some surprise in Listowel when word got around that 'Johneen' Keane was now a publican as well as a poet.

The Greyhound was a small, cosy bar with room at the striking oak counter for just five bar stools. Mary had no experience of bartending, but there was a small grocery shop in the front, and she had some experience of working in her family's grocery business. The security of owning a pub pleased her, though the couple reminded themselves they had a bank loan of £1,300 to repay.

After the excitement of the auction and the purchase of the Greyhound Bar, John and Mary addressed their approaching wedding day, which they fixed for the morning of 5 January 1955, in Knocknagoshel Church.

*

It was to be a white wedding, or so the weather ordained. The morning was bitterly cold, with a blanket of snow covering streets and footpaths. With road conditions treacherous, the cavalcade of wedding cars moved at a funereal pace towards the church, and when the wedding guests alighted, a number of the men hurried into Eddie Walsh's public house across the street to warm themselves with a few quick whiskeys.

By the time Mary and her sister Norrie, who was the bridesmaid, arrived, John Keane and his brother Michael, the best man, were seated soberly in front of the high altar.

'I remember John was nervous,' said Michael. 'In his new suit, he looked very thin; he had still not put on weight after his experience in Northampton.' Mary O'Connor looked pretty in a navy suit trimmed with white.

The ceremony was performed by Father Curtin, who at the time was a member of the board of selectors for the Kerry football team. Since John Keane was the first in his family to be married, it was considered a very special occasion. His parents sat proudly among the Keane clan, remembering their own wedding day in 1923.

The ceremony over, the bridal party and the guests filed out of the church into the snow-covered street. The air was chillingly cold. Before some of the men set out for the wedding breakfast at the International Hotel in Killarney, they again crossed to Walsh's public house for more drink to warm them. It promised to be a lively day.

As best man, Michael was determined to ensure that the first Keane wedding would be talked about for months to come.

But when he stood up to make his speech at the breakfast table, he dried up. 'I don't know what happened to me that morning,' he said later. 'I should have spoken a lot better than I did.'

John made a short, witty speech, and referred to the history he was making that day for the Keanes. Later he was to say, 'I think Mary took an awful gamble in marrying me. She could have married a man infinitely better off than myself.' His sister Peg had passed his room the night before the wedding and had stopped to look at him asleep. He looked so very young that she wanted to cry.

John had tried to analyse why he was so attracted to Mary, and he convinced himself it was their 'sorrow for each other – you can see the wronged part, the hurt, and in recognising this there is an instinctive mantle thrown out from your body to cover the other party for all time. If the love is there in the beginning, it will be there in the end.'

For Mary, it was an occasion to cherish. She was proud of the way John had stood by her, and she was pleased to be joining a talented family. There was confirmation of this as soon as the singing and storytelling began. The first Keane wedding was celebrated in style. It was unusual to see John raising a glass with no alcohol in it for a toast. 'Drink didn't mean a thing to him that day,' recalled his brother Michael. 'He was able to enjoy himself without it.' John had seen other bridegrooms drunk on their wedding day, and he wanted none of that. There followed songs in Irish and English, and with such music, poetry and laughter inside, nobody cared that it was snowing outside.

In the afternoon, John and Mary left by train for Dublin to start their honeymoon. 'It had been an enjoyable wedding, as weddings go,' observed the groom. 'It was a lovely day for me – beautiful, really.'

In Dublin, he introduced his bride to some of his friends. He thought of calling on Brendan Behan, but had no address for him. 'The honeymoon didn't last as long as we would like, but it lasted long enough,' he recalled. 'In our grandparents' time, there was no such thing as a honeymoon. They got married, had the reception in the bride's home, popped into bed in their own home, and that was that.'

Mary put it more pragmatically: 'We decided to go home when we ran out of money.'

*

With Listowel a town of pubs, the newly-weds realised they would have to work hard to make a decent living from the Greyhound Bar. They opened the pub and grocery early in the morning and closed late at night. Sunday nights were best for business, but there was always the risk of being raided by the gardaí, because Sunday-night trading was not permitted. Gradually they built up a regular, well-behaved clientele. Sometimes Keane drank with the customers and treated them to pints or the odd whiskey. Noticing his hospitality, Mary wondered if, after all, he was cut out to make a living. She would caution him, 'Don't forget we have the bank loan to pay back.'

As the months slipped by and they settled into their new life, the couple began to make some money to meet the repayments. Things were looking up, though it meant working long hours for no great profit; at best, it was a living, and competition in the bar trade was tough.

Mary had her own personal worry. On the advice of her local doctor, she consulted a specialist in Cork, who cast doubts on her ability to bear children. When she confided this news to John, he accepted it without apparent upset; he was optimistic, he told her, that in time they would have a family.

He lived a full life, continuing to play football at local level, walking and fishing on the River Feale when he could, and keeping up his reading. From time to time, he and Mary had arguments – and, like most young lovers, got over them. John saw himself as a gentle husband, and so 'making up was always sweet,' as he put it. At night he wrote poems and one-act plays. He began a play for radio, *Barbara Shearing*, and told his wife he was pleased with its progress.

Early in 1958, this play was broadcast by Radio Éireann. It was the moment Mary Keane decided her husband was to be a writer: 'I listened to the play and thought it was well put together,' she said. What pleased her more was the realisation that writing suited her husband's temperament: he was calmer and more relaxed when he wrote. At times he became so involved with his characters that she had to remind him that it was late at night or that he hadn't eaten for hours.

She was fascinated with the ease with which he chatted with the customers who came into the pub. He joked with them, listened to their stories and never took them for granted. To Keane, they were characters. 'I had a certain talent for taking them off, especially the more ponderous people,' he said. 'I could do three or four different voices for the entertainment of my cronies when the pub was shut and we'd be drinking in the back room.' Most of the customers who patronised the Greyhound Bar were elderly and came in from the country areas. At weekends they sang and danced to the music of an accordion or fiddle.

'I could not help seeing some of them as characters for a play,' admitted Keane. 'I encouraged them to sing and recite and tell stories.' They did not know it, but already they were being written into the play he called *Sive*.

6

THE ROAD TO ATHLONE

By the spring of 1959, business in the Greyhound Bar and grocery was improving, and visitors were asking for John B. Keane, the author of the play *Sive*, which had been given its first performance on February 2 in Walsh's Ballroom.

Until then Keane had been known as 'Johneen'; he had been christened plain John but had taken the name Brendan at his Confirmation out of respect for Brendan the Navigator, patron saint of the Kerry diocese. Now he decided to call himself John B. Keane, if only to distinguish him from any other John Keanes in the county.

It was a time of hope and promise. He had become a father when Mary gave birth to a boy they named William, or Billy, after John's father. 'It was a wonderful relief for John and me,' Mary said. 'John wanted children, yet when the consultant in Cork told us that it might be impossible, he showed courage. I admired him for that, for I know how he felt.'

With the annual amateur drama festivals coming up, John B. was looking forward to the performances by the Listowel Drama Group of *Sive*. It was important that the play should be nominated for a place in the All-Ireland Drama Finals in Athlone in April. Both Bill Kearney and Brendan Carroll were confident of *Sive*'s prospects, and this encouraged the playwright.

Interest in the amateur-dramatic movement had never been more marked, and success at Athlone was much sought after. Furthermore, the movement attracted groups from all over Ireland and recognised no borders. Scarriff was chosen for the Listowel group's festival launching pad. The stage props were packed into a van and transported to the Clare venue on the day of the performance. John B. and his friends followed by car and were greeted by Seán O'Beirne and Paddy Vaughan of the Clare Drama Festival, which was known as 'the friendly festival'. The local hall, founded in 1947, had no electricity, and a collection of lights lit by car batteries and oil lamps illuminated the stage and auditorium.

In a pub in the main street, John B. and his friends enjoyed a few drinks before taking their seats in the crowded hall. All the talk was of *Sive* – as though the other competing groups did not count. The playwright was on edge, but as the play progressed he knew he had a receptive audience. When the tinkermen, Pats Bocock, and his son, Carthalawn, entered, the atmosphere became electric. There was total silence as Carthalawn directed his curse at the matchmaker, Thomasheen Seán Rua:

> *May the snails devour his corpse,*
> *And the rain do harm worse;*
> *May the devil sweep the hairy crature soon;*
> *He's as greedy as a sow,*
> *And the crow behind the plough;*
> *That black man from the mountain, Seánín Rua.*

The excitement in the audience was sustained to the final scene. As the curtain fell, people in the seven-hundred-seat hall rose to their feet, cheering and applauding. Scarriff had never seen anything like this.

In his adjudication, Micheál Ó hAodha summed up: '*Sive* is, of course, a new play. I doubt if we have ever seen plays of this nature handled with such surging irony and blistering style. The author has a supreme gift for dialogue.' He described the production as the finest contribution to the amateur movement since M. J. Molloy's *The Paddy Pedlar*.

John B. and his Listowel friends stood up in their seats as their group was announced the winner with ninety-four marks – twenty-one ahead of their nearest rival, the Athenry Players. More importantly, they had won the nomination to Athlone. 'For me,' Keane said afterwards, 'the whole thing was electrifying.'

Nóra Relihan remembered, 'We were thrilled. It was a great

night for the group, and our confidence in the play had been justified.'

The playwright celebrated with his friends. It was the small hours when they arrived home in Listowel.

*

Limerick, a few weeks later, was ill-prepared for the arrival of *Sive*. The tiny Playhouse Theatre, which housed the Féile Luimní productions, was filled to its limit of two hundred seats on St Patrick's night. Keane and his friends had to push their way through the crowds in the narrow laneway to get to the theatre. When the doors were firmly shut at seven thirty, half an hour before curtain up, more than a hundred people were outside, clamouring for admittance.

P. J. (Paddy) Fitzgibbon, a local journalist and playwright, was demanding angrily of a priest to let him through. 'I'm an Abbey playwright,' he protested. 'You must let me in!' Fitzgibbon and his colleagues were eventually admitted to the auditorium through the O'Connell Street entrance but, to their chagrin, were told they must stand in the wings because there were no seats in the auditorium.

Gardaí were called to avert a confrontation in the laneway as hotheads tried to fight their way into the theatre. The growing reputation of *Sive* was creating problems not normally associated with festival occasions. 'We were all caught up in the excitement,' said Keane. 'The Playhouse was simply too small to cater for everybody.' Yet the cramped size of the theatre only added to the atmosphere, ensuring that the audience missed nothing. The terrifying beat of the bodhrán filled every corner and each word was clearly heard. At the final curtain, there was prolonged applause and stamping of feet. Keane stood applauding the cast as the adjudicator, the broadcaster H. L. (Harry) Morrow, appealed for calm.

Morrow told the audience, 'I am still staggering from this prodigious play and its equally prodigious production by Brendan Carroll. There is no question of it being the play and the production of the Féile. I shall be very much surprised if it doesn't prove itself to be the play and the production of the year in drama festivals all over the country, and it will be more than interesting to see how it fares at Athlone, for which I have no hesitation in nominating it.'

Of course, he added, the play had faults of construction. 'But they are the sort of faults that even Shakespeare suffered from, and only time and experience will prevent Mr Keane from repeating them.' For Morrow, the play's great glory lay in the dialogue, 'dialogue that is rich, as gutsy and full-blooded as Synge's.' But how it would have sounded coming from players other than the Listowel Drama Group he did not care to think.

Having paid tribute to the producer and the cast, Morrow remarked, 'I do not salute the management of the Abbey, who, I am told, had the stupidity and impertinence to reject the manuscript of this play without a word of explanation or apology. I despair!'

To seasoned Limerick playgoers, it seemed absurd that *Sive* was being hawked around the amateur circuit before it could gain national recognition; in their opinion, it should have been accepted by the Abbey and so have given the young playwright the spur he badly needed. It was these same playgoers who roundly applauded H. L. Morrow's censure of the Abbey management. Some people wondered whether, in the long run, a festival success would be the best thing for Keane, for it would not help him learn craftsmanship or technique.

Amid the euphoria in the auditorium, Keane could hardly hear Morrow's words. It was to be another night of celebration after the event. The adjudicator gave the premier award to Listowel, Brendan Carroll was adjudged best producer, Bill Kearney best actor and Nóra Relihan best actress.

*

Caught up in this heady atmosphere, John B. and his friends were ill-prepared for the controversy that awaited them in Charleville. When *Sive* failed to win the premier award, they were brought down to earth with a jolt.

The award went instead to Tuam's production of *Thunder*

Rock by Robert Ardrey. The adjudicator who made the decision was Tomás MacAnna, the Abbey Theatre set designer. Keane, seated some rows from the stage, looked dumbfounded, and there were jeers from the Listowel contingent.

'There was bitter disappointment among our group,' recalled Nóra Relihan. 'We felt we had done more than enough to win.' But it was MacAnna's words that angered Keane: 'Tonight's production of *Sive* is a rewritten version and has been rewritten in the way suggested by the Abbey Theatre.'

The Dublin evening newspapers took up the row, though in later years the playwright commented, 'The Abbey Theatre did not suggest any change. I got the play back with a rejection slip and nothing more. Any alterations in the revised version were suggested by Micheál Ó hAodha.'

In view of MacAnna's role in the earlier rejection of *Sive* by the Abbey, there was a distinct possibility that the row might become personalised, and the newspapers treated the story in that manner. For the first time, the playwright's name was becoming known outside Kerry. In fairness to MacAnna, he did say at the outset of his adjudication that he had been thrilled by the ballad-singing in the second and third acts and thought that Keane was on the edge of a new and completely original development in Irish writing – the serious, as distinct from the frivolous, ballad play.

Still, nothing would appease Keane. He thought it disgraceful of MacAnna to relegate *Sive* to second place. 'And so did everyone else who was present in Charleville,' Keane recalled. 'I know the audience was disappointed, even incredulous, when the marks were announced.' For hours afterwards, he and his friends debated the verdict, and Keane concluded that because of the Abbey's rejection of his play, it would have seemed inconsistent if MacAnna had voted it the best play at Charleville.

Father P. V. O'Brien, who produced Tuam's *Thunder Rock* but had not seen *Sive*, remembered Tomás MacAnna 'giving a long adjudication, and a voice from the hall saying, "Get on with it!"' Although he talked to the playwright about drama in later years, Keane 'never mentioned the Charleville controversy.'

MacAnna knew he had done the unpopular thing in the eyes of Listowel. 'I do recall criticising one or two aspects of the production,' he said, 'but what truthfully happened was that, to my mind, *Thunder Rock* was the superior achievement on that particular night. The play was challenging and had not been seen on the amateur-drama circuit. But by placing *Sive* in second place I had no animosity towards John B. Keane and the Listowel players. It was simply the way I felt on the night. Of course, I was aware before I went to Charleville that *Sive* had been rejected by the Abbey. I was one of the readers of the manuscript, and I do admit that I was one of the people who didn't like it all that much.'

In some quarters of the amateur-drama movement, Listowel's reaction was deemed contrary to the spirit of the movement. One evening newspaper asked, 'Is John B. Keane too sensitive to criticism?' Listowel were accused of being 'bad losers', particularly since they had already won their nomination to Athlone. But the group did not see it that way; like the playwright, they believed they had deserved to win at Charleville.

*

Soon, the Kerry Drama Festival would provide another opportunity for *Sive*. There was a prospect of keen competition, notably from Cork's Presentation Theatre Guild, whose production of Ugo Betti's *The Queen of the Rebels* was talked of as a strong contender. Shortly before the opening of the festival, the secretary, Mary Leane, discovered that a black market was operating in tickets for *Sive*. 'We could have packed Killarney Town Hall twice over,' she recalled.

With the acrimony of Charleville behind him, Keane arrived in Killarney two hours before curtain up. Over drinks, he and his friends debated *Sive*'s prospects and wondered what the Dublin adjudicator, Jim Fitzgerald, would think of the production. Fitzgerald, a director with the Dublin Globe Company, had some brilliant productions to his name and was not one to pull his punches as an adjudicator.

As Keane and his party took their seats, the playwright

was, by his own admission, 'in lively mood', and so was the audience. Hundreds who had been unable to buy tickets were turned away from the town hall. From the start, the overreaction of the audience threatened to spoil the performance of the cast. People laughed in the wrong places; others applauded during tense moments, as though unable to control their emotions. As the final curtain came down, it was the cue for the now-customary applause, cheers and stamping of feet.

It was some time before Jim Fitzgerald could quieten the audience in order to make his adjudication. A slight, curly-haired figure, he commented on the play's strong character-isation and three-dimensional writing, believing it was this, rather than the melodramatic plot, that was the play's virtue. He said he thought the author was in the direct tradition of many Abbey dramatists of the previous twenty years.

'Perhaps the tragedy is,' he remarked, 'that none of these writers seems to have found a subject big enough for the immense force and vitality at their disposal. This has been, in my view, the mystery which has rendered Irish writing ineffectual generally, but particularly in the theatre for as long as I'm old enough to remember. MacMahon, Macken, Behan and now Keane. Is it the stranglehold of naturalism of the Abbey? I don't know. Is it a subconscious suppression we all suffer from due to the special conditions in this country? I don't know.'

Some of the audience expressed impatience with his speech. 'Get on with it!' one man called. Fitzgerald continued, 'One feels of artists like Keane that within him is a truth or a need to cry out about something. But release comes only in an almost savage flood of words, violent, coloured, jumbled, but never saying what the artist seems to want to say.'

From the body of the hall, Keane directed some words to the stage. Heads turned, but it wasn't clear what he was saying. Fitzgerald paused and then repeated himself about 'jumbled words', and went on: 'They seem choked, the words emerge as thick, undigested vomit, their power and intensity perhaps the greater for the fact that they are expressing only inarticulateness.'

Keane stood up to protest, offended by the use of the word

'inarticulateness'. When the playwright had resumed his seat, Fitzgerald continued with his adjudication. 'Perhaps it is up to us, the interpreters, to find a path or channel for the flood of words,' he said. 'But how? I believe that we in Ireland stand on the brink of a new renaissance. Everywhere creativity wild, undisciplined, can be found. The fantastic rise of the drama movement itself is a facet of this.'

Listowel took the premier award, but only just. The group had won with a score of eight-nine – only a single mark to spare over Cork's *The Queen of the Rebels*. To the more perceptive playgoers in the hall, Fitzgerald's adjudication provided food for thought; some considered it 'fair-minded and balanced'. Keane felt that Fitzgerald's remarks were aimed specifically at Abbey playwrights, and since he had yet to reach that stature, he saw no reason why he should be considered one of them.

*

Back in Dublin, Jim Fitzgerald contacted Andrew Flynn, the managing director of the publishers Progress House. Flynn was a man of the theatre: he had scripted revues for the tiny Pike Theatre and was a friend of Eamonn Keane's. Fitzgerald told him that there was a play called *Sive* that was beginning to take off; it was very Irish and typical of life in the south-west, Fitzgerald said. Although the play had some faults, the sheer momentum of the writing carried it through these faults as though they did not exist, he reported.

Flynn was friendly with Micheál Ó hAodha, who agreed to arrange a meeting with Keane in Ó hAodha's office in Radio Éireann in Henry Street. The broadcaster knew that the playwright was anxious to have *Sive* published.

'I found John B. of a quiet disposition when we met,' Flynn said. 'I could see how some people could mistake this quietness for shyness, but I detected a certain brusqueness and felt it would take some while to get to know the real man. I told him I had formed a small company to publish plays, preferably by Irish authors, and *Sive* had been recommended by Jim Fitzgerald.'

Keane seemed pleased at this news about Fitzgerald. But

when Flynn suggested an advance of £25 on royalties, the playwright unhesitatingly demanded 'More.'

'OK, I'll make it fifty,' Flynn said.

'That's better,' said Keane.

The two men shook hands, and Ó hAodha remarked, 'Every amateur society in Ireland will want to buy a copy of your play next year.'

To Flynn, the playwright had a different personality than his brother Eamonn, and took time to accept a stranger, but he thought that in time they could become good friends. He believed it was Eamonn who had encouraged John to write: 'I knew the way Eamonn talked about him that he had great faith in his talent.'

7

A Cheque for *Sive*

James N. Healy had lost his accountancy job in Cork when the firm he worked for folded in late 1958. To tide himself over, he took on acting work and joined Irish Actors' Equity. Under his stage name, Nigel Hay, he was already known in musical circles in the city; in 1951 he had founded the Gilbert and Sullivan Society and played leading roles in its productions.

With two friends, Dan Donovan, a teacher and amateur drama producer, and Frank Sanquest, a set designer at the Cork Opera House who worked in the art department of the *Cork Examiner*, Healy set about establishing a new theatrical company specifically to put on plays by Irish dramatists. They planned a six-week season of six plays at the city's Father Mathew Hall in the summer of 1959.

To Dan Donovan it made good sense to have in their ranks a designer, a producer and an actor. He urged his fellow directors to consider *Sive* as their first choice of play and told them of the extraordinary impact it was making at local festivals.

It was now March, and at this time James N. Healy was directing *The Belle of New York* in Tralee, with the comedian Jack Cruise as the star of the show. He decided to drive over to Listowel to find John B. Keane. All he knew, from what he had read in the papers, was that Keane was a publican who had experienced mixed fortunes with his play. He was told by one man in Tralee, when he enquired for information about the playwright, 'Keane, is it? Don't go near that fella – he's mad!' That made him smile: for as long as he could remember, anyone who wrote poetry in Ireland was considered to be at least half-mad.

Healy reached Listowel on a chilly market morning and drove through the winding streets until he found the Greyhound Bar. It had a quaint interior, with beer barrels and a scattering of bottles, and in the grocery area were packets of spices and teas, jars of candied peel and bull's-eyes, bootlaces and bags of sugar. He asked the young woman behind the counter if John B. Keane was at home.

Mary Keane's recollection of that first meeting with Healy was that it was a fair day in the town, with cattle on the streets, and when he came into the grocery area in front of the bar, he could have been a cattle dealer. 'He was wearing an oldish coat and a hat,' she recalled. But after he had introduced himself, she decided he was too well-spoken to be a dealer. Her husband was sleeping late; he had been writing into the early hours, so she asked Healy to come back later.

She went upstairs to tell John B. about the caller, and he showed interest in him. Anything to do with *Sive* made him sit up. 'Maybe he wants to do my play,' he wondered.

When Healy returned, Keane led him into the back bar. 'I've heard of you,' he said cautiously. 'What do you want?'

'I believe you've written a play called *Sive*,' Healy said. 'I'd be interested in doing it.'

He pronounced the title like the word 'sieve', and Keane corrected him.

The playwright was to say that he took to Healy at once; he reckoned the man would not have driven over from Tralee if he was not serious about doing his play. He noticed that, underneath the overcoat, the man sported a bright scarf around his neck and a flowing handkerchief in his top pocket. He looked the theatrical type.

Healy wrote later, 'I discovered within a short time that John B. had a way of taking to you or, figuratively, throwing you out the door.' Keane told him that he liked his face and that Healy could have the play.

Healy had not expected to clinch the deal so easily. He reached into his pocket for his chequebook and made out a cheque for fifty pounds – 'My last fifty pounds', as he put it – for the performing rights of *Sive*. They agreed to sign a contract in Cork within a few weeks. 'John B. couldn't have known it was the last bit of reserve I had,' said Healy.

It was to prove a most significant deal for Keane: he had found a new outlet for his plays. But before he could turn his thoughts to the Southern Theatre Group, he had an important date to keep in Athlone at the All-Ireland Drama Festival.

*

Mary joined him on the train journey to Athlone and they checked into the Hodson Bay Hotel, where they were welcomed by friends in the amateur-drama movement, including Brendan O'Brien, the festival secretary, and P. J. Lenihan. The annual ten-day event in Athlone had assumed a character of its own, and though the play was still the thing, the social aspect of the festival could also be memorable.

The topic of conversation in the town was whether Listowel would win the Esso Trophy. In the foyer of his hotel, John B. was interviewed by a young reporter who asked him about *Sive*'s prospects. 'I know there are sceptics,' the playwright told him; 'non-believers and doubting Thomases who have still to be convinced about my play, but I am confident we will win.'

In P. J. Bannon's pub, opposite the Dean Crowe Hall, where the performances took place, the odds went up on an outdoor noticeboard. *Sive* was quoted at 6 to 4. 'That clinches it,' decided the jovial P. J. Lenihan, father of politicians Brian Lenihan and Mary O'Rourke. 'Bannon is never wrong.'

Early that morning, Maura Bannon, the publican's wife, had been woken by a loud knocking at the front door. She opened it, to be confronted by two young men.

'Any chance of a drink or a bite to ate?' asked one of them in a Kerry accent.

'We're hungry and thirsty, God knows,' added the second man.

'I'm sorry,' answered the still sleepy-eyed Mrs Bannon. 'Come back in an hour or two and I'll be happy to oblige you.'

The pair were members of the advance party of the Listowel followers; they had set out the previous day and hitch-hiked the hundred and twenty miles to Athlone. Such was the loyalty

Keane was now inspiring in his fellow men from Listowel who wanted to see him succeed in Athlone with *Sive*.

The festival adjudicators were John Fernald and Barry Cassin. Fernald was principal of London's Royal Academy of Dramatic Art and had directed *Saint Joan* at the St Martin's Theatre, where he had first met Cassin, a tall, pipe-smoking actor and director, and an experienced adjudicator.

Fernald had read the script of *Sive* and found it 'utterly fascinating'; he was looking forward to seeing it staged. When someone suggested that, as an Englishman, he might not understand its idiomatic form, he retorted, 'If such an assumption were correct, a Russian producer reading French plays would find them incomprehensible.' He told Barry Cassin that he regarded *Sive* as pure theatre. But he was cautious. 'I mustn't be bowled over by the script before I've seen the play on stage,' he said.

By noon on the day of the performance, Athlone was crowded with drama enthusiasts and journalists. Members of Dublin's professional theatres had come to see whether the excitement about *Sive* was justified. Keane had joined in a sing-song in his hotel on the previous night and had been introduced to Ernest Blythe and Gabriel Fallon of the Abbey Theatre. Blythe was polite and seemed surprised when told by the playwright that he had given the performing rights of *Sive* to the new Southern Theatre Group in Cork.

An hour before curtain-up in the Dean Crowe Hall, John B. and Mary joined a party of Listowel friends in P. J. Bannon's public house. Bannon remembered, 'He looked nervous and subdued, not the type of man I had expected to meet. We exchanged a few words and after I wished him luck, he turned to me and said, "The odds are right, P.J."' Behind *Sive* at 6 to 4 came *God's Gentry* at 2 to 1 and *The Wood of the Whispering* at 3 to 1, with the rest at 10 to 1.

Nóra Relihan was nervous before curtain-up. 'We felt we had to justify ourselves, and we were so anxious to succeed that I felt uneasy,' she recalled. 'There was no doubt but we were pent up before we went on.'

As the Keanes took their seats, they sensed the air of expectancy in the hall. John B. hoped the tension would not affect the cast. News came through before the performance that the Abbey Theatre had invited the Listowel group to present *Sive* for one week in Dublin. 'This announcement killed the festival as a competitive event,' complained the producer of another visiting group. 'It was a mistake and should not have been allowed to happen.' But it did not concern the hundreds of people who had failed to get into the hall, some of whom had travelled miles in the hope of seeing *Sive* performed.

*

The cast opened nervously. With the entry of Pats Bocock and Carthalawn, the tempo quickened, and by the final scene few in the audience were untouched by emotion. At the final curtain, John Fernald turned to Barry Cassin and declared, 'Sheer theatrical magic!'

The Listowel contingent greeted the fall of the curtain with their habitual frenzied enthusiasm – which was quite foreign to Athlone festival performances. Keane jumped to his feet like the others to applaud the cast. Once again he had found the performance an emotional experience. 'I did not know what to say and that's unusual for a Kerryman!' he recalled.

In his adjudication speech, John Fernald praised the play's impressive setting and noted that Brendan Carroll had paid great attention to detail. He thought the play had sagged in the second act, but he had found the ending extremely moving. The work for him lacked convincing curtains, and he criticised the lengthy intervals, which were detrimental to the play's impact. The difficulty about *Sive* was that the second act 'hardly existed at all' in terms of plot, he said. If the author could find some way of pushing it forward, it would be a blessing. What he had achieved was the 'bold and brilliant' creation of the tinkers – a piece of theatrical magic – but after the tinkers left the stage, the play did not progress enough.

Fernald praised the simplicity and sincerity of Margaret Dillon's Sive and said that John Flaherty and John Cahill had played the part of the the tinkers beautifully. Almost every member of the cast had acted with realism, and Bill Kearney as the matchmaker had performed with 'great vitality,' Fernald said.

The play was not to have the festival scene entirely to itself, however. The Dean Crowe Hall was packed later in the week for Sligo Drama Circle's production of Donagh MacDonagh's *God's Gentry*. John Fernald described the production as 'very enjoyable', and it was clear that Sligo was strongly in the reckoning for the trophy.

After the performance of *Sive*, John B's stamina showed no sign of waning. In the Hodson Bay Hotel, he led a lively sing-song with his friends Tom Honan, P. J. Lenihan and Brendan O'Brien. 'We sang Irish and Jacobite songs till daybreak,' Keane recalled. 'It was a great drinking session, but there wasn't a drunk to be seen; it was that kind of party.'

He and Mary left Athlone promising to return the following weekend for the final adjudication. Mary resumed her work in the bar and grocery and cared for little Billy, now almost two. In the quiet of an upstairs room, John B. worked on a new play, *Sharon's Grave*. He told very few people about it, preferring to wait until the euphoria surrounding *Sive* had passed.

On the following Sunday, April 26, he and Mary returned to Athlone and were joined by the loyal Listowel contingent to await the festival verdict. The Hodson Bay Hotel buzzed with anticipation. In the foyer, Keane met Gabriel Fallon, who said, 'I've just heard a great line, and I'm going to give it to you.' A man from Westmeath was going upstairs to bed when he met Fallon coming down. 'How are you?' Fallon asked politely. The man, his eyes almost closed with fatigue, replied weakly, 'Sir, the best of us is not well!'

Some Athlone playgoers were convinced that Sligo would win the premier award with *God's Gentry*. 'It was as good a production as I'd seen at the festival,' Brendan O'Brien commented. Yet to the majority of festival-goers, there seemed an inevitability about the final result. And so it proved – to the intense satisfaction of Keane and his friends. Listowel beat Sligo by 87 marks to 80. The Listowel playwright's reaction was enthusiastic. 'I had arrived,' he said later. 'My name was firmly before the people. The amateur-drama movement had rocketed me to fame. I think my play helped rejuvenate the whole movement.'

Brendan Carroll recalled, 'When we received the Esso Trophy, I had a feeling of total satisfaction, because in Listowel we had been trying for years and had failed to carry off the premier award. We were also thrilled with the Abbey's invitation. We would be making history.'

Looking back after thirty years, Barry Cassin noted his impressions at seeing *Sive* for the first time. 'My initial impression was that it was structurally weak – I'm thinking here of the letter scene,' he said. 'But for all that, the play, with its colourful language, was most striking and possessed a vitality that assured it of a place in theatre history. It had a touch of theatrical magic.'

Aileen Coughlan, the *Irish Times* correspondent, expressed reservations about the production. 'It came to Athlone with the tag, "This is the greatest thing in the theatre",' she recalled. 'I was to find the theme slight and banal. I couldn't see it as great. I think John B. Keane has magic for other people, but not for me. I wasn't excited by *Sive*. Keane does not take me with him.'

Keane returned to Listowel a proud man. Although he had yet to be accepted by the professional theatre, he was flattered by the Abbey's decision to stage *Sive*, even if it meant a production by an amateur group. In his home town, the urban district council, on behalf of the people of Listowel, presented scrolls commemorating the group's triumph.

*

On Saturday 23 May, John and Mary joined the cast of *Sive* at Listowel railway station for the journey to Dublin, where the play would open on Monday night for a week's run at the Queen's Theatre, the Abbey's temporary home after their original building burned down. Reporters and photographers waited at Kingsbridge station for the train's arrival. Margaret Dillon obliged the photographers by posing, seated on the company props, with a guitar. Keane was quick to tell reporters that the Abbey had not accepted *Sive* on a professional basis; rather, the management were inviting an amateur group to perform his play. 'I think this is a compromise,' he said, 'because they have been forced into a corner by public opinion and by the newspapers. If the Abbey had accepted the play, I feel sure it would have run for weeks.'

What most annoyed him was the financial aspect of the invitation. The Abbey's decision would mean a loss to him. 'I believe the play would have made, with a good run, well over £1,500 in royalties – perhaps even more,' he said. 'Instead, the Abbey have taken a mean attitude in order to save their own esteem. I will only receive payment for a normal week's run. I think the Abbey just won't admit that they were wrong in the first place.'

In spite of his misgivings, the first night was memorable. Supporters had arrived from Kerry in a cavalcade of cars. His brother Michael and sister Peg greeted him and Mary in the cramped theatre foyer, as did Éamon Kelly and his actress wife, Maura O'Sullivan, both former members of the Listowel group. Kelly thought the Abbey should have accepted the play. It would have been 'a marvellous gesture,' he said, but he could only presume that the directors were being 'cagey', reckoning that *Sive* was merely 'a flash in the pan'.

The Queen's was loud with Kerry voices. Someone had told Keane that it would not be easy to create an atmosphere in this run-down old theatre of melodrama and revue, but as far as he could see there would be no problem that night. The play was enthusiastically received, once more prompting the question: how could the Abbey have rejected it? Later, as John B. and Mary joined the cast in a party in Éamon Kelly's house, such misgivings were forgotten.

The next day, Keane bought the newspapers. The *Irish Times* critic wrote, 'Mr Keane got an ovation last night, and he probably deserved it, since his play curdled my blood as it has not been curdled by an Irish peasant-quality play since I first saw *Autumn Fire* and *Spring*.'

Gerald O'Reilly in the *Evening Herald* wrote, 'The apathetic Abbey directorate that snubbed the country's most promising young playwright since O'Casey made belated amends last night when it gave over the theatre to an amateur group from Listowel for a presentation of *Sive*. This is a work of the quality that could portend greatness for the author. Only in construction do his understandable shortcomings reveal themselves.'

Seán Page in the *Evening Press* was more critical: 'Anyone who goes to the Abbey to see *Sive* expecting to see a flawless presentation of a great new play will be disappointed. Quite apart from isolated flaws, there is an overall unevenness and there are many discords. This general roughness may explain why some of last night's audience (to judge from overheard remarks) felt the play was received more enthusiastically than it deserved.'

Undeterred by such criticism, Keane took telephone messages of congratulation in his hotel. The fact that most of the critics agreed that the Abbey management should have accepted *Sive* in the first place pleased him. Seeing the play for the first time, Éamon Kelly thought it was just a step away from the storyteller. '*Sive* was a tale Kerry storytellers could have related as they sat by their firesides,' he said. 'John B. had brought the story out of the room and onto the stage.'

The production filled the Queen's for the week's run, though Nóra Relihan remarked, 'People came out of a sense of loyalty.' She thought the first-night performance had been almost spoilt by the overreaction of the audience. 'Many people applauded in the wrong places, others went wild over the tinkers,' she said. 'They weren't a help at all. And I think I gave a poor performance that night.'

Ernest Blythe, who sat alone in the stalls on first nights and seldom betrayed any sign of emotion, went backstage to congratulate the cast. It later transpired that he was interested in engaging Nóra Relihan for the Abbey company. She declined for family reasons: 'I was married in Listowel with a young child and I didn't want to come to Dublin.'

*

Home in Listowel, John B. was not allowed to forget *Sive*. 'Every parish priest wanted to build a school out of the proceeds from the play's presentation,' he recalled. Andrew Flynn of Progress House found the first printed copies of the play had been snapped up and decided to issue a second edition within the year.

The phenomenal success of the play brought about a split in the Listowel Drama Group; Keane believed that such a split was inevitable. He said, years later, 'At the time, some of the group wanted to go one way, while other members wanted to go another. You'll find that after a success, a group tends to break up. Because of its wealth of talent, Listowel could accommodate two groups. I found no real animosity among the various parties.'

Nevertheless, according to one member, long-standing friendships among the players were severed. Some believed it was the price that had to be paid for the success of *Sive*. But the split came as a surprise to Brian Brennan, who had played Liam Scuab. 'I never did expect there would be a break-up,' Brian said. 'I was glad to be out of it and off to Dublin, for I was disappointed that attitudes should change so soon after Athlone. I feel now that success went to the heads of these people.'

'It was great to have lived through *Sive*,' recalled Brendan Carroll. 'But I was disappointed with the way things turned out. I thought the group should not have split up.'

Keane managed to hold on to most of the friendships he had forged through *Sive*, and refused to take sides. By the summer of 1959, he was engrossed with his new script, *Sharon's Grave*, which he would send to Ernest Blythe at the Abbey. For relaxation, he sometimes played chess in the back kitchen of the bar in William Street with his friend Tony Guerin. 'He was a good chess player,' said Guerin, 'but when Mary was busy he'd serve in the bar.' To Guerin, the Keanes' marriage seemed solid, and he heard no arguments between the couple. He reckoned that Mary was a steadying influence on her husband, who liked to talk about young Billy and took pleasure in holding him in his arms.

John B. did not drive at this time, so Guerin, whose family ran a car-hire firm, drove him to functions and football matches. Soon the playwright would be off to Cork, where the Southern Theatre Group was to begin rehearsals of *Sive*.

8

The Summer of *Sive*

On the June weekend in 1959 when he arrived at the Imperial Hotel in Cork for his first meeting with the cast of *Sive*, Keane knew he was about to forge a valuable connection. Years later, he would talk about this period in glowing terms, describing it as 'the happiest time of my theatre career.' With the doors of Dublin's theatres apparently closed to him, there was good reason to be grateful to the Southern Theatre Group.

Keane had brought with him a typed copy of *Sive* and one of his own bodhráns. When he walked into the lofty hotel lobby, he was instantly recognisable from his newspaper photographs. He obliged the girl at the reception desk with his autograph before going up the broad staircase to a large room on the first floor, where he was welcomed by James N. Healy, who introduced him to Dan Donovan and other members of the cast, including Michael McAuliffe, Charles Ginnane, Michael Twomey and Kay Healy.

'We are delighted that John B. Keane can attend our rehearsals,' Healy announced. 'I think I can say we are looking forward to working with him.' The lanky playwright shook hands with everybody in the room, and then they sat down to business. A few of the cast thought him shy, but the ice was broken when he joked with them and showed the bodhrán. James N. Healy had already bought a bodhrán for five pounds in Cork, and this would be the instrument that would be used in the production.

To Michael Twomey, it looked like 'the half of a drum'; he had never seen a bodhrán before. 'I didn't know what the hell it was,' said Twomey, who had appeared in a number of plays produced by Dan Donovan, and was cast as Carthalawn. He considered it mainly a singing role, and his musical abilities were never strong. 'I thought I would have to pull out,' he said. But Keane encouraged him. 'Playing the bodhrán is terribly simple,' he assured him. Twomey took up the instrument with one hand and with the back of the fingers of the other hand he beat out a rhythm on the skin that lined the instrument. 'In no time at all,' Twomey said, 'he showed me how to work out a beat, and after that I was able to pick it up fairly rapidly.'

Rehearsals were held in a dusty first-floor room in South Main Street. Two members of the Listowel Drama Group, Nóra Relihan and Margaret Dillon, were invited to play their original roles of Mena and Sive, while Tom Vesey, who had been trained in the Loft, the famous drama school founded by Father O'Flynn, was to play Pats Bocock. Charles Ginnane was asked by James N. Healy to play the part of Seán Dóta; he had previously worked with Healy in Gilbert and Sullivan productions.

As director, Dan Donovan had no hesitation in casting Healy as the matchmaker. He knew him to be a versatile character actor in musicals and saw no reason why he could not be equally effective in straight drama. At the first rehearsals, Healy felt he had not got the accent right, but he acted his scenes with Mena with conviction.

Donovan had seen a performance of *Sive* in Listowel and had come away deeply impressed. The play captured a way of rural life that was fast disappearing; in the reading, 'the play leapt out of the pages at you', as he put it. Having read the script carefully, he found no reason for any appreciable changes, though he introduced some of his own ideas.

In conversation with Keane, Donovan found him open to suggestions. 'He was on my own wavelength,' Donovan recalled. 'He represented something I understood well because I was from a semi-rural background. He was most responsive during rehearsals, willing to change lines or cut a long passage if required. I saw *Sive* as more than the magic of the tinkers; there was the intriguing theme of the old man matched to the young girl, and this raised the question of the "made marriage". I saw Mena as a tragic character, a bitter and frustrated wife, a woman who had married a man she didn't much love. With no children of her own, she had become embittered.'

Inevitably, the question of the authenticity of accents came up. Some members of the group felt they could not capture the idiom of Kerry. Charles Ginnane was to say, 'Both Nora Relihan and Margaret Dillon had a feeling that we weren't quite right, that the play's dialect was best spoken by a south-western company. I suppose our Cork accents were a little too far to the east.'

Healy found Keane's mind teeming with ideas and stories he had heard in his pub in Listowel, and he seemed concerned to get them down on paper. 'I don't think it was ambition that was the spur, nor money; he just wanted to write,' Healy recalled.

Michael Twomey remembered Keane at rehearsals. 'As we said the lines, he would sit and listen,' Twomey noted. 'Then he might think of a line and suddenly say, "Put that in there." At other times, Dan and Jim would be suggesting things. It became a real workshop style of production.'

Twomey became friends with the playwright, who would come to Cork at weekends for rehearsals. One Sunday morning, he invited him on a trip to Robert's Cove. 'My girlfriend, Marie, and I picked him up at the Country Club Hotel by St Luke's, and when we reached Robert's Cove the three of us walked along the cliffs. It was the first time I felt I got to know John B., and I was to regard him as the most outstanding and extraordinary person I had met. During that walk he recited poetry and the thoughts flowed out of him. It was fascinating to hear him talk about life in such a beautiful way.'

*

Frank Sanquest admitted that he needed to bring no great imagination to the design of the set for *Sive*. As he said, 'You couldn't do much, for it was a cottage interior with whitewashed walls with the countryside showing outside. There was no room for experimentation. It was a simple domestic scene.' Keane did not discuss the design for the play with him, and when he saw the set on the stage of the Father Mathew Hall before the opening night, he raised no objection. He remarked only on the fact that the kettle in the kitchen was too large.

Cork's most distinguished theatrical event for many years was scheduled for Monday 29 June. Keane was in confident mood as he and Mary checked into the Imperial. Success was important to him, but it was also important to the new theatre company, which would be judged on its first performance.

Among the first-night audience was the Lord Mayor, Senator Mary Dowdall, and members of the Listowel Drama Group. As with the performances in Athlone and at the Abbey, the reception was highly enthusiastic. At the final curtain, there was thunderous applause. Members of the audience stood in their seats clapping and whistling.

Michael Twomey had felt the response during the performance. 'I had never experienced anything in any play like the impact the tinkers made on the audience,' he recalled. 'We started playing the bodhrán off stage in a corner, and the moment those first notes were heard by the audience, a terrible stillness came over them. It was to be the same at each entrance Tom Vesey and I made, and every time we walked on stage there was applause before even I sang a note or Pats Bocock uttered a word.'

James N. Healy was taken aback by the reception. 'It was the most exciting night I had experienced in the theatre,' he said. 'I hadn't expected the reaction to be so spontaneous, so overwhelming. We had six hundred people in tears.' Dan Donovan knew the play could run for weeks. Even then, he was convinced that it would be the first of many plays by John B., who had a storytelling skill that gripped an audience. Language was Keane's gift, and with more experience, Donovan saw him developing into an important playwright.

The next morning's headline in the *Cork Examiner*, 'SIVE ENTHRALS CORK AUDIENCE', accurately summed up the reception given to the production. The review began, 'Seldom, if ever, has a Cork theatre audience been so moved, so enthralled, so spellbound as it was last night when *Sive* had its first presentation in Cork . . . When the final curtain fell on the final moving scene of the old grandmother crying her sorrow, the audience was stunned into shocked silence.'

Keane had gone backstage to congratulate the cast. 'I think we can do better next time,' James N. Healy told him; he felt the cast had been too pent up before going on stage. It was, however, an auspicious debut by the new Southern Theatre Group, and it now seemed that the directors would have to scrap their plans to stage six plays over six weeks. 'I think we were a little overambitious,' remarked Healy. 'And of course, we had reckoned without the phenomenal popularity of *Sive*.'

*

Keane returned to Listowel extremely pleased. It was an exciting time. Mary was expecting their second child, and John B. was awaiting word from the Abbey Theatre about the new play he had sent them, *Sharon's Grave*. Despite their rejection of *Sive*, he still hoped to become an Abbey playwright, and for that reason he had buried his pride and put his luck to the test for the second time.

At weekends, John's school-age brother, Denis, helped Mary with the running of the bar and grocery. Denis was grateful for the pocket money. 'John always thought of me,' Denis recalled. 'He was very considerate in that way. On his return from Cork or Dublin, he'd usually have a present for me.'

The playwright had little time to himself. Before long, he was preparing for a trip to Dublin for the production of *Sive* at the Olympia Theatre. After the play's six-week run in Cork, which Dan Donovan described as 'the summer of *Sive*', the Southern Theatre Group was to make its first visit to the capital; Donovan admitted that this would be a crucial engagement for them.

Michael Twomey, who was soon to marry, had to drop out of the cast of the Olympia production. During the Cork run, however, he had earned £120, or £20 a week – a figure that was twice the sum that most professional actors earned in Dublin at the time, and enough to ensure an enjoyable honeymoon. John B. Keane believed there was 'a great thirst' in Dublin for *Sive*. The visit was certainly attracting publicity, and profiles and photographs of the author and the cast appeared in the morning and evening newspapers.

On opening night, Dublin directors and actors, as well as Kerry supporters, filled the theatre bars, and photographers waited for Keane's arrival. Columnist Terry O'Sullivan, in the *Evening Press*, wrote the next day, '*Sive* seduced us again from the path of duty, and not for the first time. Into the Olympia last night we went for our customary "Hello-Goodbye", but that kind of formula didn't work last night. Though we had many other appointments, we were held fascinated by the bitter poetry of this play, and the gorgeous sound of the speech, Kerry's answer to O'Casey.'

Generally the reviews were favourable and pleased the author, who made no secret of the fact that he read the critics. In the *Evening Press*, Seán Page paid tribute to the Southern Theatre Group: 'It has a team of good actors who work well together and a producer who can get the best out of them. I expect they will make many forays on the capital in future. It is unlikely that they will be able to adhere very closely to the principle of 'producing plays by Munster playwrights'. Mr Keane's play has come along at a very opportune moment, but the directors can hardly expect to find a Munster playwright behind every stone. At all events, they and Mr Keane have been fortunate to come into the limelight at the same time, because they have got a punchy new play which has caused a stir, and because he has got actors who can make the most of his dialogue. Dan Donovan's production has done a lot for *Sive*. None of the actors has been allowed to wander aimlessly about the stage, and the character actors have been kept firmly in their place.'

In the *Evening Herald*, John Finegan wrote, 'A fine, resolute presentation it turns out to be, acted – by the men especially – with great vigour. The large audience showed their approval in no uncertain terms.'

Siobhán McKenna was an interested observer at the first night and suggested that *Sive* could be successful on Broadway provided a backer could be found. It was the most exciting play she had seen for a long time. The characters, the language and the absolute honesty of it gave a picture of Ireland 'without insulting the country or "*plámásing*" it.' She did not agree with those who said that it was played for comedy. She thought the tinkers 'absolutely wonderful in both performance and conception.' It took a stroke of genius to create them; they were the finest modern variation on the Greek chorus that she had seen.

Keane was disappointed that, because of her stage and film commitments, the celebrated actress would not be able to accept the role of Mena in a future production. Some Dublin theatre people suggested that Cyril Cusack would make an outstanding matchmaker alongside McKenna's Mena.

News of the play was not confined to Ireland; it made the front page of the Sunday arts section of the *New York Times* under the headline: 'BIG HIT CALLED SIVE'. Not since the days of Sean O'Casey's early plays, wrote Hugh G. Smith, had there been such commotion in the theatre. Twenty thousand theatregoers had seen the play in Cork. Dublin had clamoured for it, and it would have filled the Olympia to capacity beyond its two-week run if the theatre could have retained it. It had all been 'rather overwhelming' for the young Kerry 'liquor-saloon owner,' the paper reported. His play had been rejected by the directors of the Abbey Theatre, but 'acclaimed by the people as a work of moment,' it continued.

The *Times* of London also noted the arrival of *Sive* and, under the heading, 'CHANCES THE ABBEY MISSED', its correspondent wrote a lengthy review, in which he commented: 'Beneath the harshness and bitterness born of poverty, Mr Keane has glimpsed a beauty as rare as the subdued harmony of a Millet painting. Besides a novel piece of dramatic invention, he has brought a note of primitive ecstasy into his play which gives it its kinship with Synge's exotic vision of peasant Ireland . . . The acting and the production by the Southern Theatre Group, who are mostly from Cork, was superb . . . And what a pleasure to listen to such beautiful speaking voices. They spoke the melodies of the Kerry accent with bell-like clarity and a real feeling for the beauty of the words.'

*

The Listowel playwright had come a very long way in a comparatively short time. He was advised to exercise caution, however, when some newspapers began to speculate wildly about *Sive*. One report claimed that the play was to be filmed in Ireland – and a crew was already on its way to Kerry – another that a West End production was planned, and a third that there was interest in the play on Broadway.

Keane ignored these stories and instead visited the towns where the Southern Theatre Group had taken their production on tour. Limerick playgoers packed the City Theatre for a run of the play, but in Clonmel in November, the production provoked controversy when Brendan Long of the *Nationalist* reviewed it. Though he conceded that its impact on Clonmel people was undeniable and enthusism for it great, to present it in the year of Brendan Behan's *The Hostage* as something new and exciting was 'utterly preposterous,' Long wrote.

Under the heading 'SO THIS IS SIVE', he wrote, 'Judged as it must be against the background of today, *Sive* almost belongs with *Noreen Bawn* in the travelling tent shows.' Long singled out the playwright's shortcomings:

> From a beginning that buds with promise, we are carried through a deepening unreality to a climax which is so infantile as to be almost embarrassing.
>
> Again, too, the dialogue of this play does little to enhance the saying of what is required to be said. Mr Keane casts his lines in the mould of Synge, Murray and Molloy, but he does not so easily command the colour and the poetic insight which the mould requires. He seems determined, nevertheless, that the most simple everyday statement shall be clothed in a panorama of words, and with what arid land-scapes is our patience sometimes tried!

The reviewer gave credit to Keane for 'some occasional flashes of inspired lyricism and some compelling moments of real conviction.' He suggested that 'there is manifestly in him the seeds of more flowers if he can re-channel his theatrical thinking into the genre of today.' Sensitive to criticism at the best of times, it was not easy for Keane to accept such comments from this unexpected quarter of Tipperary.

In the rival Clonmel paper, the *Munster Tribune*, the editor, Raymond Smith, summed up: 'Not since I saw Seán O'Casey's *The Plough and the Stars* some years ago in the Abbey Theatre have I been so stirred by any play . . . Here is real life in all cold reality. The language is hard and bitter at times as passions rise and characters curse. But is not this the way people speak in the mountainy districts when hate stirs the soul?'

Shaw, he said, had written, 'Drama must present a conflict. The end may be reconciliation or destruction, or as in life itself there may be no end, but the conflict is indispensable.' To Smith, 'It is conflict all the way in *Sive*.'

The debate continued for weeks in the columns of the *Nationalist*, with letter-writers defending the play and the playwright's reputation. Brendan Long stuck to his guns; he stood over what he had written. But though he professed 'little faith in theatregoers', he invited his opponents to 'join me for a pint one of these days.'

9

The Legend of Sharon

Keane suffered a bitter disappointment towards the end of 1959 when the Abbey Theatre returned *Sharon's Grave* without, as he complained, 'a decent explanation'. One source revealed that Ernest Blythe, the Abbey's managing director, had found a few of the characters in the play 'too grotesque for words.' But the playwright suspected that neither Blythe nor his fellow directors had bothered to read his work. 'Before I sent the manuscript to the Abbey, I deliberately glued two pages together, and when I got it back they were still untouched.'

James N. Healy had already asked for his next work after *Sive*, so Keane now had no hesitation in giving *Sharon's Grave* to the Southern Theatre Group. Reading the script, Dan Donovan found the play to be from the same territory as *Sive*; it captured a similar folk atmosphere, though wilder, and the playwright's powerful gift for storytelling stood out. He counted it an honour to be asked to direct the work.

Although he saw only a small part for himself – that of the medical quack Pats Bo Bwee – in the play, James N. Healy agreed with Donovan that with its imagery and mythical beliefs, the play was rooted in the countryside. He recognised in this new work the compelling forces of good and evil in conflict – the pagan as opposed to the Christian way. As in *Sive*, there was the same absorption in the expressionism and fantasy of the Kerry countryside, the same probing through weakness of the body towards the problems of the soul.

Sharon's Grave was set in a Kerry farmhouse in the 1930s. Donal Conlee, an old farmer, is dying, and his daughter, Trassie, is thinking of marriage. The idea of possessing a woman is the ambition of Dinzie Conlee, Trassie's brother, who will go to any lengths to achieve his purpose. Throughout the play, Dinzie is carried pickaback on the shoulders of his burly brother Jack. The plot is woven around the legend of Sharon, a fairy princess who drowned in a cliff-hole.

Dan Donovan decided to cast Eamonn Keane, who had moved to Britain, as Dinzie Conlee. The director contacted him in Edinburgh, where he was finishing a run in O'Casey's *Cock-a-Doodle-Dandy*, and Eamonn agreed to return to play the part. Finding an actor to play Jack was a problem, for he had to be powerful enough to carry Dinzie on his back throughout the action of the play. Michael Twomey, cast as the simple-minded brother Neelus, remembered a big actor named Flor Dullea who might fit the bill: Dullea was a teacher from west Cork who had moved to the city. When he met Dullea, Donovan reckoned the Corkman would be an ideal choice. The young lovers, Trassie Conlee and the thatcher Peadar Minogue, would be played by Maura Hassett and Séamus Moynihan, while Kay Healy would portray the prim schoolteacher.

The play went into rehearsal in late December, with the first night scheduled for Monday 1 February 1960 at the Father Mathew Hall. The arrival of Eamonn Keane for the first rehearsal took the cast by surprise. He had made the long journey from Scotland and by the time he reached Cork he was, in Dan Donovan's words, 'quite high'. 'I think he was also very tired,' said the director, 'and he needed a rest.'

Sharon's Grave survived the actor's 'tired and emotional' entrance, and soon the rehearsals fell into a pattern. Donovan regarded Eamonn Keane as a very instinctive actor, quick to pick up a point at rehearsals. 'He had the sharp Keane intellect,' the director recalled, 'though I considered him less reflective than his brother, John B.'

Eamonn's name was not unknown in Cork. He had made news in the late 1950s when he had been dismissed from the Radio Éireann Repertory Company following remarks he had made at a Donegalmen's dinner in Dublin. The circumstances of the sacking had angered John B., who described the treatment of his brother as 'unfair and unjust.' He thought Eamonn had also been let down by his colleagues in the repertory company, who should have stood by him. The episode rankled with the playwright for years.

John B. attended rehearsals, pleased to see Eamonn taking the role of Dinzie. The workshop approach to his play appealed to him. Sometimes Dan Donovan would say, 'John B., I need something here.' The playwright would scribble a few lines and hand them to the director. 'He wrote some of his best lines in this way,' Donovan recalled. 'He began to understand when gaps in the script needed to be filled and how to find a better curtain-line.'

Flor Dullea remembered that Keane more than once laughed his heart out during the wake scene; at other times he would sit silently, listening to every word. 'I found he had an incisive mind and a sharp wit,' she recalled. 'He got to the core of things and was blessed with a beautiful turn of phrase. I enjoyed his company, and I knew that he enjoyed mine.'

Early in the rehearsals, Dullea suspected that Eamonn Keane had little time for amateur actors, even for the semi-professionals of the Southern Theatre Group. As time passed, however, he became engrossed in the play and seemed more at ease. Once, Dullea refused to continue with his lines until Eamonn had stopped shouting.

Just a week into rehearsals, some of the cast noticed that Eamonn had not only mellowed but was pairing off with Maura Hassett during the breaks. They wondered if the couple were starting a romance. But there was an unpredictability about the actor, and when John B. was told that his brother had fallen in love with the leading lady, he was philosophical about it. Eamonn was a poet and a dreamer and capable of the great love affair, but it had all happened so swiftly. Could it last, or was it one of his brother's fleeting passions?

Kay Healy was among the first to notice the affair. 'I went with Eamonn to a public house after a rehearsal and he was quoting poetry to Maura and acting very romantically,' she recalled. Two weeks later, Maura Hassett confided to her that she was going to marry Eamonn but that her mother had asked her to wait for a while longer.

Like the rest of the cast of *Sharon's Grave*, Kay Healy was taken aback by the speed of the romance. She took a call from Maura's mother, who sounded anxious. Could Kay, she wondered, persuade the couple to delay the wedding? It would give them the chance to get to know one another better. 'What can we do about it?' she asked. Kay Healy was honest and could only echo the question: 'What *can* we do about it?'

Eamonn and Maura were in love and the affair was the talk of Cork; it was also remarked that she was twenty-four – ten years his junior. The newspapers called. 'It was love at first sight for both of us,' Eamonn Keane told a female reporter. 'I don't know what's happened to me. I never believed it possible. It's wonderful.'

John B. was pleased for his brother's sake, only hoping that the now well-publicised affair would not interfere with rehearsals. Flor Dullea recalled that the other members of the cast tried to carry on as though nothing untoward was happening, 'but we could see that the affair was a beautiful, romantic thing.' James N. Healy worried that Maura Hassett's former boyfriend might cause problems; there was a rumour that he was going to turn up at rehearsals.

Between his passion for Maura and his involvement in rehearsals, Eamonn Keane was totally absorbed. Maura was a good influence on him: he drank less and turned up on time for every rehearsal. The affair generated some useful publicity for the play, and before long the Dublin papers carried photographs of Eamonn and Maura with stories of their romance.

The build-up to the first night followed the pattern of the productions of *Sive*. One Dublin columnist's piece was headlined, 'WILL THIS REJECT BE A SUCCESS TOO?' He was not the only journalist to tilt at the Abbey's decision: some twenty critics and journalists were expected to attend the première.

A date was fixed for the wedding of Eamonn and Maura, and it seemed likely that people would be attracted to the Father Mathew Hall just to see for themselves the most talked-about lovers in Cork.

*

Mary Keane would miss the first night; in late January she had given birth to her and John B.'s second son, Conor. But the family would be represented by the playwright and his brothers, Billy and Denis, and there would be the customary loyal Listowel contingent, who rarely missed a Keane theatrical occasion.

On the afternoon of the première, John B. held court in the bar of the Imperial Hotel and talked to visiting journalists. 'I wrote *Sharon's Grave* in three weeks,' he told them. 'As for the critics, *Sive* proved to me that they cannot kill a play. Of course I hope they'll like *Sharon's Grave*, but I'll not give a rattling damn if they decide to hate it.'

He talked with a tinge of sarcasm about the Abbey's rejection of *Sharon's Grave*: 'Ernest Blythe said that you can't have three idiots on the stage at the same time. His opinion was that it would make a good book or a good film, but not a play. As far as the three idiots are concerned, I felt like saying that many of our national institutions seem to be guided by even stranger characters and survive well enough.'

In his neat blue suit, he exuded confidence. It seemed extraordinary that within a year he had become a personality in his own right. He knocked back a couple of whiskeys and chased them with a pint of stout to calm his first-night fears.

There was not an empty seat in the Father Mathew Hall when the curtain rose. An overenthusiastic audience again threatened to spoil the performance, but the experienced cast tried to ignore the football-final atmosphere. At the final curtain, the play was accorded a tremendous reception, 'nostalgically reminiscent of balmier nights,' wrote one reporter. In Michael Twomey's opinion, the duo of Dinzie Conlee and his brother Jack had made the same impact on the audience as the tinkers in *Sive*.

While the *Cork Examiner* acclaimed the play, some critics had their reservations. One summed up the feeling: 'It is a queer, wild play about queer, wild people, and while it has some very poetic passages, many dramatic situations and a few good character studies, yet, on the whole it fails to grip.'

That was a minority view. Most of the critics had found the piece absorbing and reckoned it would enjoy a long run. Tom Hennigan, the *Sunday Press* columnist, seemed overwhelmed. 'Keane will shock you, amuse you and perhaps repel you,' he wrote, 'but he will never bore you. Yawns cannot live in the same theatre with the playwright.' He continued, 'As this poignant story of a malevolent cripple and his Toulouse-Lautrec longings for a wife and hearth moved with Greek inevitability to its Grand Guignol close, we were struck by the sheer operatic quality of the plot and writing. If Verdi were alive today and teamed up with Keane to put *Sharon's Grave* to music, what a final scene we'd get – the baritone of the doomed cripple, the soprano of the terrified, beautiful cousin, and the tenor of her mad brother.'

It seemed unfair that so many playgoers compared the play to *Sive*. Keane was at pains to point out that '*Sharon's Grave* is a different experience. It's futile making comparisons. It's set at a time when a travelling thatcher could knock out a day's pay in rural Ireland and the advance of slates was still a few years off.'

One critic compared the love scene to that between Christy and Pegeen in *The Playboy of the Western World*, and added, '*Sharon's Grave* is an even better play than *Sive*. It may not have the gimmick of the tinkers and the tambourines, but in the double character of Dinzie and his brother Jack – one a mind without a body, the other a body without a mind – Keane has created a memorable and tragic figure.'

Eamonn Keane's performance as Dinzie was lavished with praise, as was Maura Hassett's as Trassie. But the couple had more on their minds than the play, and in a few days they would be married. John B., who was to be best man, loaned his brother some money for the occasion, and Mary Keane decided to make the journey from Listowel for the wedding of the year in Cork.

The Saturday-night performance was cancelled to enable the lovers to marry. The joke among the cast was whether they would return after the weekend to resume their roles in the play. 'I had no fears at all,' said Dan Donovan. 'Eamonn was a real professional when it came to acting.'

Hours before the ceremony was scheduled to take place, hundreds of sightseers gathered outside the Church of the Assumption at Ballyphehane in Cork to catch a glimpse of the bride and groom. Children from the secondary school where Maura Hassett taught were given time off to attend the wedding. A guard of honour outside the church was formed by members of the cast of *Sharon's Grave*, and the bodhráns were played. When Eamonn and Maura, who wore a three-quarter-length white dress with a lace headdress, emerged from the church after the ceremony, they were cheered by the crowds. A hundred guests joined them at the Imperial Hotel, where a poem, written by Sigerson Clifford for the occasion, was read. Children from the bride's school toasted her with songs in three languages and the bodhráns were played again. John B. read a telegram from Brendan Behan wishing Eamonn and Maura luck.

Andrew Flynn had come from Dublin. A close friend of Eamonn's, he had not dared miss the occasion. 'I remember it for a deal of lively speeches in both Irish and English,' Flynn recalled. 'It was the first time I had been at a function where Cork and Kerry got together – and enjoyed it!'

Eamonn had been offered a leading role in Dominic Behan's play *Posterity Be Damned!* and another in a Michael Powell film. But the newly-weds confirmed that they would remain in the cast for the Dublin presentation of *Sharon's Grave* at Easter. When they set off for a brief honeymoon to County Waterford, the party was in full swing. John B. could not recall that he had ever seen his brother so happy. 'I don't mind a bit being upstaged by Eamonn,' he told the other guests. 'Today he deserves centre stage.' On Monday night, when the performances were resumed, James N. Healy read to the audience Sigerson Clifford's wedding poem.

Keane's youngest brother, Denis, who had been an usher at the wedding, returned to Listowel with his mind filled with *Sharon's Grave*. What he had found most stunning was the character of Dinzie Conlee; he would not forget his brother's portrayal. Dinzie reminded him of 'Billeen' Sweeney, who drove his donkey and cart into Listowel and drank at the Greyhound Bar. 'Billeen could be wicked with his tongue. Like Dinzie in the play, he delivered biting remarks that made you laugh despite yourself.' Denis came away from the Father Mathew Hall wanting to be an actor.

*

After a long run in Cork, the cast of *Sharon's Grave* prepared for another visit to the Olympia Theatre in Dublin. Keane and his wife would join them.

'The first night of *Sharon's Grave*,' Fergus Linehan reported in the *Irish Times*, 'reminded me somewhat of Croke Park on all-Ireland day when Kerry are playing.' James N. Healy was unhappy about the more critical reviews and he wondered if the writers understood what Keane was trying to say. None of the reviews dealt in any depth with the complex character of Dinzie Conlee, although John Finegan in the *Evening Herald* came closest to Healy's own understanding of the character. Finegan wrote: 'Dinzie wants a home, he wants a wife – and is prepared to go to any lengths to achieve his purpose. But the author has not divested this Kerry Caliban of all compassion. The scene in which he reveals his secret longing to a girl whom he is bent on tormenting, wins him a certain amount of pity. His end, clinching a legend, is terrible.'

Des Rushe in the *Irish Independent* thought that the big Olympia stage showed up faults in the play and that the production lacked imagination and had too slow a pace. Maxwell Sweeney in the *Sunday Independent* commented on Eamonn Keane's 'brilliant performance' as the vicious cripple and was taken by Maura Hassett's sensitive acting. Seán Page in the *Evening Press* observed, however, that '*Sharon's Grave* is not a patch on *Sive*. It has most of the faults of its forerunner and very few of its virtues, and as soon as the first-night fervour surrounding last night's performance dies down, it will probably retire discreetly from the professional stage and will never be a real competitor to *Sive* in amateur circles. Neither the acting nor the production are up to the standard of the same group in *Sive*, except in some minor roles, where Mr Keane was not striving too hard for effect.'

The critic R. M. Fox, in the *Evening Mail*, was deeply moved by the love scene between the thatcher and Trassie. Fox claimed that no one but John B. Keane could have written that scene: 'It is original and it has, I think, a touch of dramatic genius. It is time, too, that we began to recognise the men of genius in Ireland, for we have not too many.'

Before the end of the Southern Theatre Group's two-week run at the Olympia, both Dan Donovan and James N. Healy were sensing a slight resentment towards them from elements of the Dublin professional stage. 'The fact that we were able to fill a theatre as big as the Olympia created envy, even some jealousy,' Donovan said. Healy advised the cast to take no notice of remarks made by other actors. And Keane argued that if the Olympia management of Stanley Illsley and Leo McCabe wanted the Southern Theatre Group in their theatre, then that was their business. Financially, the playwright had done fairly well in royalties.

Healy sensed that *Sharon's Grave* might never enjoy the same box-office appeal as *Sive*, mainly because of its eccentric characters and morbid theme. Yet, when the group toured the production in the south of Ireland, they filled halls and theatres. Limerick playgoers packed the local City Theatre, in spite of a lukewarm review from P. J. Fitzgibbon in the *Limerick Chronicle*, and the production was considered a success.

Charles Ginnane, who was the stage manager for the tour, recalled that Eamonn Keane would carry a hard-boiled egg in his pocket and on stage hand it to Michael Twomey instead of his watch. In Millstreet in County Cork, Ginnane had told the organisers in the hall that when the stage lights went down and the curtains were closed in the middle of the first act, this did not denote an interval, and they were to ignore it. It was the moment when Ginnane placed a dummy corpse of Donal Conlee in the bed. 'We had gone to great trouble to explain this' Ginnane recalled. 'But they banged on the lights, played a record of *St Teresa of the Roses* and began selling raffle tickets.'

Worse was to follow in Dungarvan in County Waterford. In addition to his job as stage manager, Ginnane also appeared as the dying old man, Donal Conlee, clad in a nightshirt in bed in the first scene. At the end of the scene, he had to leave the bed to place the dummy corpse, with a bow tied under its chin, in his place, and check the props, such as candles and a crucifix, for the next scene, the wake. 'I was still checking the props when I distinctly heard the swish of the curtains opening behind me,' he said. Instead of hurrying into the wings, he made for the door of the set. 'I pulled it *in*, but of course it opened *out*. I nearly pulled the set down. I squeezed out through about six inches of aperture and pulled it shut behind me.'

By now the audience were paralysed with laughter at the sight of the actor in a long white nightshirt struggling with the stage furniture. Michael Twomey as Neelus was the next character to enter; he was to welcome the neighbours to Conlee's wake. According to Ginnane, the door had stuck and people were struggling with it. Twomey recalled that somebody then removed the offending door and placed it against the wall of the set. The audience thought they were watching a farce. When Flor Dullea entered carrying Eamonn Keane on his back, Eamonn saved the situation by looking at the door, then at Neelus, and asking, 'Well, Neelus, you were up to your tricks again, were you?'

*

The playwright had not forgiven Brendan Long of *The Nationalist* for denigrating *Sive*, and he now took the opportunity during the tour by the Southern Theatre Group to go to Clonmel for the presentation of *Sharon's Grave*. At the final curtain, he strode on stage to make a brief speech, at the end of which he invited Long to join him to 'explain the discrepancies' in *Sive*.

'Mr Long is in the house,' the playwright called out, 'and I think he should come up here.' The journalist was, in fact, attending a classical concert at the Savoy in Limerick, but it took some time for Keane to be convinced that Long was not among the audience that night in Clonmel.

The episode illustrated how touchy Keane could be about his work. If he reckoned that a critic was deliberately unfair to him, he took time to forget. Actors and journalists noticed this side to him – his quick temper, his blunt remarks. When tired, he could get edgy, and he did not suffer fools gladly. If, after a few drinks, he suspected someone was mocking him, he reacted swiftly. Yet he made many friends in and out of the theatre. 'Cork is good for me,' he said. 'Working with Jim Healy and Dan Donovan has taught me a lot.'

He was a celebrity, not by any means a polished one, but rather a down-to-earth individual who thrived on hard work and had no pretensions about himself. Although he was now over thirty years old, he still played football in Listowel. He facilitated journalists with interviews when he could, enjoying their company. But if he did not take to them, they quickly got the signals.

When Liam Robinson visited Listowel in 1960 for the *Sunday Express*, Keane told him, 'What success I have had demonstrates that the critics cannot kill a play. But I don't give a damn.' The playwright stepped from behind his bar to jóin Robinson in a drink; then he stepped inside again to pull a pint for a farmer, having introduced him as 'the best poacher in the kingdom'.

Trying to pin down the crinkly-haired playwright was no easy matter. Robinson explained to his readers, 'Some of the difficulty lay with the ever-changing set, some with the man himself. His behaviour alternates between that of a highly strung puppet and a Steinbeck character who lies down outside his shop and soaks in the sun.'

Keane was obviously in the slumped-in-the-sun position when he told his interviewer, 'I have no rules about writing. I work in fits. It takes three to four weeks to knock a play together. But I do try to overcome the Kerry writers' obsession with words. Juggling with them, throwing them up in the air – lovely, grand-sounding, sonorous words which, when they are spun together, mean damn all.'

When the journalists departed, Keane would climb to his room to resume his writing. Mary knew it would be many hours before he entered into the ordinary world again. He had begun a new play.

10

The Risk-Taker

'John,' Phyllis Ryan asked Keane persuasively, 'why don't you write me a play for the Theatre Festival?'

'Sure I will.'

It was the type of instant request that, coming from someone else, the Listowel playwright would probably have ignored. But from his first introduction that afternoon, he had taken to Phyllis Ryan. Years later, he would be only too happy to recall their meeting in the Tower Bar in Dublin.

'Phyllis and I were kindred spirits. Neither of us had much money. We had nothing to lose, and we were prepared to take a gamble on anything.'

He admired her achievements at the tiny Gas Company Theatre in Dún Laoghaire's main street, and he regarded her not only as a risk-taker but also as a genuine woman of the theatre. He had written a play which he had given to Nóra Relihan's drama group in Listowel, but it had failed at amateur drama festivals to gain a nomination to Athlone. It was a play that he felt might be well suited to Phyllis Ryan's Orion Productions, and he counted himself fortunate to have met her in the Tower Bar on that afternoon in March 1960. This would be his initiation into the Dublin Theatre Festival, an international event which had been gaining prestige under the aegis of Brendan Smith; he was well aware that dramatists had come to regard the festival as a shop window for their work.

While Phyllis Ryan concentrated mainly on staging plays by American and Continental playwrights, she had also staged works by Hugh Leonard, Tom Coffey and Patrick Galvin. Most of her life had been devoted to the stage. Her career had begun at the age of twelve in the Abbey School of Acting, and she was given the child role in Denis Johnston's *The Moon in the Yellow River*. At the age of sixteen, she created the part of Brigid, the Canon's maidservant, in Paul Vincent Carroll's *Shadow and Substance*, among a distinguished cast that included Cyril Cusack, Ria Mooney, Arthur Shields and Maureen Delaney. Leaving the Abbey, she freelanced and gradually became interested in theatre management, and in particular how managements discovered new plays. In this respect, she picked up useful tips from Hilton Edwards and Micheál Mac Liammóir and furthered her knowledge with Godfrey Quigley's Globe Company. Eventually she launched her own company.

She first became interested in John B. Keane when she saw *Sive* at the Olympia Theatre. 'I considered the play brilliant and very theatrical,' she said. Now, chatting to the playwright in the Tower Bar, she got the impression that he lacked confidence in himself and didn't fully realise he possessed the gift of play-writing. It would be her job, she felt, to make him believe in himself.

*

A few weeks later, she received in the post a copy of *The Highest House on the Mountain*. Reading the manuscript, she immediately labelled it 'strong meat', especially the character of Julie Bannon, who is accused by her father-in-law, Mikey Bannon, of being a prostitute. Julie is married to his son, Patrick, and the pair have returned from England to visit Mikey in his farmhouse in the south of Ireland.

Phyllis Ryan telephoned Keane to tell him she was accepting his play for production. 'I found great honesty in the writing,' she recalled. 'There was a seam of poetry running through it that reminded me of some of the writing in *Sive*.' She informed the playwright that Barry Cassin would direct the play for the Theatre Festival in September and that he would probably suggest some changes.

Cassin was familiar with *Sive* but had never met the author. He arranged a meeting in Dublin's Wicklow Hotel, and after they had shaken hands, he thought to himself, 'So this is John B. Keane! So this is him!' Keane looked younger than his thirty years and had a soft, unmistakably Kerry accent. He seemed affable and good-humoured. Together they discussed *The Highest House on the Mountain*, and when Cassin asked for cooperation in some rewriting, Keane promised, 'I'll give you all the help I can.' In Cassin's view, some of the speeches were too long and the language was somewhat overcharged. But he was convinced that the play could work; it was a powerful subject with strong characterisation to match.

For weeks he worked on the manuscript, making adjustments and cutting lengthy speeches to sharpen the action. In his experience as a producer, few new scripts arrived in perfect form; usually they had to be worked on, and *The Highest House on the Mountain* was no exception. Andrew Flynn, who was involved with Orion Productions, had confidence in the play from the first time he read it, and told Keane he intended to publish it. Both *Sive* and *Sharon's Grave* had sold exceptionally well.

Flynn joined Phyllis Ryan, Barry Cassin and Keane in the Ormond Hotel in Dublin, where they spent some time discussing the play. Cassin was worried about the time lapses between certain scenes and suggested that a new romantic scene was required immediately.

'We persuaded John B. to retire to his bedroom in the hotel, lock himself in, and come down with the new scene as quickly as he could. I remember he stood up and, before leaving us, said, "I'll do my best."'

Flynn called for a round of drinks. Cassin drew on his pipe. Phyllis Ryan recalled saying a quick prayer. An hour later, Keane rejoined them and handed six handwritten pages to Cassin. The director read them in silence, then handed them to Flynn, who read through them and declared, 'Fine.' Phyllis Ryan was to agree.

Martin Dempsey was cast as Mikey Bannon. He is described in the play as sixtyish, wearing overalls, cap and hobnailed boots. He likes his food. 'There's a great content in me these days,' he remarks in the second act, 'with the good dinners and the regular cooking!' When the actor first read the script, he decided it was far too long, but he preferred it that way because it was easier than working on a play that needed padding. Cuts in overlong speeches were made during rehearsals. Dempsey explained, 'During one particular scene I take a shine to Julie. In the original script I was supposed to have twenty-five lines, but after discussion with Barry we decided to cut the whole thing to a mere two words; they are spoken as Julie begins to climb the stairs. Looking after her, I say to myself wistfully, "'Tis years." This was enough to indicate to an audience that it was years since I'd had the feel of a woman.'

To Dempsey, the theme was not all black. There were amusing lines, as when he remembered a cattle-jobber: 'I tell you he was the biggest man I ever saw. From west Limerick he came. I heard afterwards that he had twenty-seven buttons in the fly of his trousers.' Mikey's preoccupation with food also introduced light relief. He tells his son, 'Imagine a roast goose . . . or chops! There's nothin' in this world or the next as sweet as a chop. Suppose now a fellow came in that door with a fryin' pan full o' chops. I bet you'd jump up and eat a few.'

Dempsey had grown up in west Kerry and accepted Keane's writing as true to the Kerry idiom. 'Every word he writes is accurate in that respect, terrifyingly true, and his observation of people is beyond the normal,' he said. 'There is no more perceptive playwright of the rural scene than John B. Keane. I could listen forever to the poetry in his plays, and he has a flair for injecting comedy at grim moments that often works.'

Gerry Sullivan was cast as Patrick Bannon, Julie's husband. It was his first role in a Keane play, and he appreciated the rhythms of the language. He was playing a strong character, a son in conflict with his father, anxious at the same time to protect his wife. In his view, the play would prove controversial for conservative theatregoers.

Anna Manahan was excited to be cast as Julie Bannon. Watching a performance of *Sive* at the Olympia, she had been impressed by the playwright's dramatic gifts. Having carefully read *The Highest House on the Mountain*, she too felt it would create controversy, but much depended on how Barry Cassin handled certain scenes, such as that in which Mikey makes a pass at his daughter-in-law.

As an actress, she was not unfamiliar with controversy. Three years earlier, in 1957, she had figured in *The Rose Tattoo* case when the Pike Theatre Company director, Alan Simpson, was charged with 'presenting for gain' an 'indecent and profane' performance. Before Simpson's arrest and the play's cancellation, Anna Manahan had received outstanding notices for her performance as Serafina, the Sicilian widow. Tennessee Williams' smouldering drama had received its European première at the 1957 Dublin Theatre Festival.

For the actress, *The Highest House on the Mountain* had powerful echoes of both Williams and Eugene O'Neill. She only hoped that people would not dismiss Keane's new play as sleazy.

*

Keane travelled to Dublin for the opening night. The Gas Company Theatre was not the most glamorous festival venue, although it seemed that most of the newspapers were sending their senior critics to cover the event. The playwright was greeted by Phyllis Ryan and Andrew Flynn, and took his seat in a centre row in the tiny auditorium. Denis Keane was there, and his sister Peg and her husband, John Schuster. Compared to the Dublin first nights of *Sive* and *Sharon's Grave*, this was a tame affair. Perhaps the out-of-town venue was to blame, or the festival's counter-attractions in the bigger city theatres. Still, Keane was undeterred, content to be included in the major theatrical event of the year.

The audience response was warm, vindicating Phyllis Ryan's faith in the play. When the curtain came down, Gerry Sullivan said to Pat Nolan, who was playing Sonny Bannon, 'I think we have a success on our hands.' Anna Manahan felt the audience had been stunned into silence on a number of occasions, particularly at the moment when Connie Bannon accuses her of being a prostitute. Martin Dempsey sensed the same shock among the audience when he spoke the line, ''Tis years.'

Outside the little first-floor theatre that night, Keane thanked his friends for supporting his play. It was something he liked to do, but on this occasion he felt they had come to Dún Laoghaire in spite of bigger theatre attractions elsewhere. He went back to Peg's house for supper; it was now customary for the Schusters to entertain the cast of his plays. He was in exuberant mood, believing that Orion Productions had brought a sophistication to his work, and he was pleased when Phyllis Ryan invited him to write another play for the following year's festival.

The next day, the critics did not disappoint him. John Finegan in the *Evening Herald* saw the play as 'a tragedy steeped in the phrases and accents of Kerry.' He praised the performances of Anna Manahan, Gerry Sullivan and Martin Dempsey. Seán Page in the *Evening Press* was even more enthusiastic: 'Let the word be passed around. A powerful, moving, exciting, well-made play has been given its première. And who, having seen *Sharon's Grave*, would have believed that it was in John B. Keane to write it! But there it is, plain as the nose on your face. Mr Keane has hammered out a brave dramatic language of his own and has escaped from the long shadow of J. M. Synge. That alone would warrant a toast in champagne. But there is more. He has also escaped from the perennial trivialities of that country kitchen in which the talents of so many Irish playwrights have slumped.'

It was Séamus Kelly's review in the *Irish Times* that not only delighted Phyllis Ryan but succeeded in raising Keane's position among Irish dramatists. Kelly observed, 'The more we see of John B. Keane's plays of north Kerry, the more do they take on the aura for Irishmen that Tennessee Williams' plays of the Deep South must have for Americans.' Kelly described *The Highest House on the Mountain* as Keane's best play, but added, 'The main difference between Williams and Keane is that Williams is a major playwright, whereas Keane, as yet, is not.'

The Listowel playwright had the satisfaction of seeing his play enjoy the longest run in the festival. Yet, despite the value of his connection with Orion, he had no intention of abandoning the Southern Theatre Group. He had already assured James N. Healy that he could expect a new work from him. Back in Listowel he decided on the title, *Many Young Men of Twenty*. It would be about emigration, and audiences could look forward to a Keane play with music.

*

The success of *The Highest House on the Mountain* prompted Andrew Flynn of Progress House to hasten its publication. He asked Barry Cassin to supply an introduction. It brought a thoughtful piece from the director of the play, in which he suggested that Keane's place in the theatre was unstable. Praise and blame for his work had been equally extravagant. He had been identified as a sort of Deep South Kerry white hope and dismissed as a Boucicault reactionary. His plays had been described as 'lyrical', 'nasty', 'powerful' and 'melodramatic', yet no one could deny that he was there (very much there) and that he was successful.

Theatrically, John B. Keane was a man from outer space, Cassin added, who had made his name under freak circumstances. *Sive* had caused a sensation entirely through an amateur production, and *Sharon's Grave*, which was also successful, had been launched by amateurs. This was excellent for amateur drama, but he wondered if it was the best thing for Keane.

Cassin went on to make his most potent point: 'The reward of professional proficiency is to make good work better and inferior work good, and even an effective writer like Keane needs direction that amateurs are unlikely to provide.'

The director recalled, 'When I first met him, I was impressed by the fact that he neither pretended nor thought that he knew it all. Any changes suggested for the good of the play were willingly embraced, and tiresome rewriting did not irk him. He was not subdued by the takeover atmosphere of a professional presentation but had the good sense and humility to realise that, by observing the work of professionals, he could improve his own.'

It was a useful assessment at this stage of Keane's career, when it also seemed that he needed a good theatrical agent. Cassin reckoned there were 'years of writing before him' but implied that he should in future rely solely on professionals to point the way. It was the advice of a man of the theatre who, like Phyllis Ryan, had learned the profession the hard way – and at a time when financial rewards were abysmal. Keane, however, was already committed to both professional and semi-professional companies.

11

SIVE IN HAMMERSMITH

It has been the ambition of Irish playwrights from Sean O'Casey to Brian Friel to have their work performed outside Ireland. Keane was no exception. He was disappointed that, despite the publicity he had received, *Sive* had not attracted either British or American interest.

In the early autumn of 1960, however, he was encouraged by a telephone call from London. In the course of a conversation with Judith Coxhead, she enquired about possible film scripts and went on to discuss *Sive* with him. Until recently, she had been personal assistant to the film director Michael Powell, but was now anxious to try her hand at stage production. She had come to know Eamonn Keane after Powell had offered him a role in a film, and it was Eamonn who had suggested she call Listowel.

Never one to let an opportunity slip, Keane gave Judith Coxhead permission to stage *Sive* in London. He was struck by her enthusiasm and persistence, but it was probably his eagerness to have his play staged in London that made him inclined to overlook her lack of theatrical experience. Since he was busy writing *Many Young Men of Twenty*, he was content to let her look after the casting of *Sive*.

Her choice of set designer was Robert Colquhoun, better known as a painter of portraits and landscapes. For casting, she relied for the most part on London-based Irish actors. P. J. Stephens would be Pats Bocock to John Cahill's Carthalawn, the role Cahill had created with the Listowel group. Jacqueline Ryan, Phyllis Ryan's daughter, was to be Sive. Although only sixteen, she had considerable acting experience, having starred in the film *Jacqueline* at the age of twelve, as John Gregson's daughter. Brian Phelan was to be Liam Scuab, her young lover in the play.

When James N. Healy heard about the impending London production, he was both surprised and disappointed. For some time he had been hoping to present the Southern Theatre Group in *Sive* in London, and perhaps other English cities. He stated that Tennents, the London theatrical agents, were prepared to back him, but on learning of the proposed Coxhead production, they dropped out. To Healy, this was an opportunity thrown away by Keane. 'I think he should have consulted us first, before making his decision,' said Healy.

The first night was scheduled for Thursday 25 October, and promised to be a big Irish night in London. The Irish Ambassador, Patrick McCann, accepted an invitation to attend. Long before the curtain rose in the Lyric Theatre in Hammersmith, the foyer was thronged with theatregoers. Andrew Flynn, who had invested money in the show, was confident it would be a success and enjoy a long run. But Phyllis Ryan wondered whether her daughter, Jacqueline, was suitably cast as Sive, and Eamonn Keane worried about the non-Irish players in the cast. Would their accents sound authentic in this most Irish of plays?

As he entered the foyer, John B. Keane looked tense, but those who knew him realised he was invariably nervous on first nights. Danny Hannon, a construction worker from Listowel, who was based in London, noted in the audience scores of former pupils of St Michael's College; he remembered Keane as one of the best-known boys in the college in his day. 'I was very emotional,' he recalled. 'A Kerry writer having a play on in London was a big event, and we all wanted our townsman to do well.'

It was to prove a most unusual night in the theatre. While in the main the audience was enthusiastic and at the final curtain greeted the performance with thunderous applause, discerning theatregoers were less enthusiastic. Andrew Flynn said, 'I was bitterly disappointed. I didn't enjoy the performance. I had thought it impossible to do *Sive* badly, but the Hammersmith company succeeded. Most of the fault lay with the poor acting and the mixture of Irish and English voices on stage. I felt sympathy for John B.'

From the start, it was obvious that Jacqueline Ryan had been miscast as Sive. Her long golden hair and suburban airs were out of character with the play's simple country girl. Eamonn Keane, forthright as always, said the play had failed because the cast had interpreted it in a stage-Irish way and thus reduced its concealed fury. Referring to the accents, he said, 'Such a collection of voices I have never heard before. *Sive* is set in Kerry, yet scarcely a voice bore the slightest resemblance to the speech of that county. To the English members of the audience, whose ears are not attuned to the various Irish dialects, this will mean little or nothing.'

He fired a broadside at the production, describing it as 'ludicrous', and placed the blame squarely with Judith Coxhead. Good drama had been reduced to melodrama. John B. Keane was crestfallen. Thirty years later, looking back on that first night, he was to say, 'The tragedy was that the play didn't come off on the night. My expectations were high, I know. The truth is that the production had faults and people were miscast. For me, it was an unhappy occasion and an opportunity lost.'

The playwright was to gain little solace from the reviews. The most favourable was penned by G. D. Owen in the *Financial Times*, who wrote that, 'despite all the ranting and the sobbing', there was enough genuine charm and humour in the play to satisfy most tastes, and the acting was of the highest quality. He singled out Tony Quinn's 'superb matchmaker' but added that the prize performance of the evening was that of the wandering tinker played 'with telling arrogance' by P. J. Stephens.

Patrick Gibbs in the *Daily Telegraph* told his readers that Keane had come from Ireland with a reputation which this production at least made difficult to understand. It was easier to see why the Abbey should have turned the play down, as indeed it had. He said that hardly a single scene came to theatrical life, and he blamed the acting. He summed up, 'One would have liked to see how the Cork or Listowel companies would have fared at the Lyric Theatre.' As it was, the cast, which could be described as London-Irish, had made little of their material. Only Brian Phelan, as the young lover, had found 'any real truth or feeling.'

In his *Evening Standard* review, Milton Shulman, regarded as one of the most influential critics of the day, observed: 'After seeing Synge's *Playboy of the Western World* only a fortnight ago, one comes down to sodden Irish earth with a distressing thump with John B. Keane's *Sive*. Much of the overheated, quivering melodrama in this play was just the stuff Synge was rebelling against when he wrote the *Playboy*. Indeed, *Sive* could well have been written fifty years before the *Playboy*, instead of fifty years after it.'

Having outlined the play's plot, Shulman summed up: 'Mr Keane, an Irish publican, does not make literary clichés any more appetising by smothering them with Gaelic sauce. "Your old mother watched over ye like a hawk and sheltered ye from the wind and rain" is a sample of his Irish prose style. Nor, surprisingly enough, is Mr Keane very conscious of the proper closing times. His play rambles on, is heavily padded and never leaps over the obvious. The audience, cheering every exit and practically every intake of breath, was even more irritating than the play.'

The *Evening News and Star* critic, Felix Barker, was impressed by the two tinkermen. 'There are moments of genuine tension when they enter,' he wrote. 'The way these voodoo men put curses on people to the accompaniment of song, drum and imperious tapping of a stick brings to the play just that imaginative quality that it otherwise lacks.'

Although Keane would not offer it as an excuse, history has shown that the London theatre had not always been a happy hunting ground for Irish playwrights; later on, this was to be illustrated when plays like *Philadelphia Here I Come!* and *Da* were virtually ignored by London managements despite their outstanding success on Broadway. The theatricality of the tinkers in *Sive* – and the richness of a past still remembered – seemed lost on the majority of London critics. The critics' reluctance to accept the language as anything other than 'lines over-full with similes and metaphor' must have made Keane wonder if they understood what he was writing about.

He returned to Listowel subdued, though not disillusioned. He was never one to be defeated easily. He put the Hammersmith experience behind him and continued with his work. He travelled to Dublin for a meeting of PEN, at which he took the opportunity to tell his listeners that Irish playwrights were struggling against the odds.

There was some astonishment in the faces of his audience at the Shelbourne Hotel when he told them that he had netted £1,100 and £1,200 respectively from the professional and amateur rights to *Sive*. *Sharon's Grave* had fared even worse: only £400 was earned. For *The Highest House on the Mountain*, he had received the paltry sum of £100. This, he pointed out, made a total of £2,800, which, after payment of travelling expenses, left him with £2,000 for three years' work.

He argued forcibly that it was not the Abbey that was preserving theatre in Ireland; rather was it the famished and neglected professional actors and producers who had as much right to subsidies as the Abbey. He made no secret of the fact that without his public house in Listowel he could not continue writing for such inadequate rewards.

His remarks caused a stir in artistic circles and placed in perspective the reality of the world in which Keane and his fellow playwrights were operating. Yet Keane would say, 'If the crunch came, I'd probably write for nothing.' It was his way of explaining what being a writer meant to him.

His zest for life was unquenchable, and he wore not a few hats at this time. He was in constant demand as a speaker at functions. On one occasion, he travelled to Cahir in County Tipperary to talk about *Sive*. 'That the play is melodramatic is certain,' he told a meeting of Macra na Feirme, 'but what exactly is the difference between the drama and melodrama? All the plays of Eugene O'Neill smack of melodrama, because O'Neill saw its relationship to good theatre. To what extent then is melodrama an infant in the theatre family, and why do critics always speak scathingly of it as if it were something to be ashamed of?'

He disagreed that the tinkers in *Sive* were a form of Greek chorus, and explained that he never intended them as such. 'The tinkers are an integral part of the play and form the core of the dramatic surge in it,' he said. 'In the Greek tragedies the chorus is essentially a shadowy comment which summarises what has gone and hints at what is about to happen. The tinkers in *Sive* are in the nature of wandering bards who narrated in verse the happenings of the countryside.'

He surprised some of his audience by his statement: 'I will admit, of course, to *Sive*'s crudities and clumsiness. It is raw, gawky, and gangling. I think, to be fair to it, it must be called amateur and forgiven because it is amateur. It is beyond question a child of the drama movement, the first child of the movement. The remainder of the children will benefit from the mistakes, and I have no doubt that many great plays will spring in time from the movement.'

Keane has never been one to invite discussion or criticism of his works. Like Brian Friel, he has preferred to let his plays speak for themselves and to allow critics to draw their own conclusions. In that context, the Macra na Feirme members at the meeting in Cahir could count themselves fortunate that Keane had opened up to them on such a delicate subject as his first child of the drama movement.

His wife, Mary, worried that he was working too hard. He became irritable when overtired and she mentioned this to his friend, Dr Johnny Walsh. 'I'd prefer to see him write his plays during the day,' the doctor advised. 'He needs more sleep at night.' But Keane had got into the habit of writing late at night; the peace and quiet suited him. Yet he still found time to join friends in his bar for a drink and a sing-song. 'I love to hear him sing,' Mary remarked, 'because then I know he's relaxed.'

*

Three weeks after Milton Shulman had panned *Sive* at the Lyric in Hammersmith, Keane received a letter from the critic that was to mean a great deal to him. Shulman wrote to say that, for all the faults in *Sive*, he still vividly remembered the play. He urged Keane not to lose hope, but instead to keep on writing.

Years later, in interviews, the playwright sometimes referred to Shulman's letter, as though to convince them that he had continued writing as he had been encouraged to do. It was now 1961 and there was pressure on him to deliver plays to James N. Healy and Phyllis Ryan. Some friends believed that this prolificity was damaging his work.

12

A MUSICAL LAMENT

On a July evening in 1961, a few hours before the curtain was due to rise on *Many Young Men of Twenty*, Keane was back at the Imperial Hotel in Cork, where he had first met the members of the Southern Theatre Group for *Sive*. Watching him pace the hotel lounge, a friend likened him to an expectant father waiting for news from the maternity ward. He joked, lit cigarette after cigarette, and kept frowning at his watch.

'Don't mind me,' he said, stabbing the bell for another round of drinks. 'I'm always like this before a première. It was the same with *Sive*, with *Sharon's Grave*, with *The Highest House on the Mountain*.' He was experiencing the same self-doubt and heart-searching with his new play, though his fears were allayed by the realisation that he was returning to the Father Mathew Hall, the scene of his earlier triumphs.

Tonight was a challenge. He was breaking new ground with his first play featuring music. He had written eight songs, including a pop number, 'The Arithmetic Song'. The theme of the play was emigration, a subject close to his heart, and one he felt gave rise to political hypocrisy. Originally, the première of *Many Young Men of Twenty* had been planned for a Dublin theatre, but as Keane explained, negotiations had dragged on until he was left with no option but to have it staged in Cork. 'I have no regrets,' he told the *Cork Examiner*. 'I'd be happy to have all my first nights in Cork.'

James N. Healy made no secret of the fact that when he first read the play in manuscript, he immediately looked for a good part for himself. He had been lucky with *Sive*, less lucky with *Sharon's Grave*, but he was ready to 'jump for joy' when he read the part Keane had written for him in *Many Young*

Men. He would play Danger Mullaly, the vendor of trifles, and would have some of the play's best lines.

Healy thought the theme of emigration very relevant and realised that Keane had drawn on his own experiences in England. He had highlighted the emigrants' homecoming on holidays and their eventual return to places and jobs they hated. Although the play was billed as a comedy, Healy did not see it as such. 'I agree there are comic moments in it, as well as lively songs,' he said, 'but the underlying theme is the emigrants' longing for home and their desire to share their life again with their own Irish people.'

While the producer, Dan Donovan, was again relying on his experienced company, which included Healy, Michael Twomey, Flor Dullea, Kay Healy and Tom Vesey, he welcomed a lively newcomer, Siobhán O'Brien. A twenty-one-year-old teacher from Cobh, dark-haired and vivacious, she possessed a strong, sweet voice that was suited to both cabaret and musical comedy. 'Siobhán has self-assurance and a quite extraordinary personality,' commented a Dublin columnist who had watched her perform in a show in the Metropole Hotel in Cork. 'She belted out her songs with such vigour that the microphone was superfluous.' Keane had written the part of Peg the barmaid for her.

Michael Twomey, who was cast as the teacher, recalled that at rehearsals *Many Young Men* generated the same enthusiasm as *Sive* had done; he felt it would be just as popular with audiences. Flor Dullea, who was to play one of the emigrants, noticed Keane at rehearsals humming some of his songs and obliging Dan Donovan with new dialogue.

Charles Ginnane, who helped with the stage management, realised they would be playing in the Father Mathew Hall, which was a temperance hall, so they would have to fake the alcoholic drinks. 'I remember that some forty different drinks were required, and it was no joke providing fake stout, fake whiskey and fake port. It became a major production, with a large cast, and a lot of stage business.'

Dan Donovan was taken by Keane's talent for songwriting; he particularly liked the hummable title song, which he felt could sell well as a record.

Oh, many young men of twenty said goodbye;
All that long day
From break of dawn until the sun was high,
Many young men of twenty said goodbye.

My boy Jimmy went that day
On the big ship sailed away,
Sailed away and left me here to die;
Many young men of twenty said goodbye.

Saw the tears of every girl and boy,
Many young men of twenty said goodbye.

In the Imperial Hotel, Keane lit another cigarette and looked anxiously at his watch. It was one hour to curtain-up. He had talked with journalists from the Dublin press not only about *Many Young Men of Twenty* but also about many other subjects, ranging from the Abbey Theatre to Method acting, and from his favourite playwrights to the Irish language. He also told them that his play for the Dublin Theatre Festival, *No More in Dust*, was with Phyllis Ryan's Orion Productions. Reporters noticed that he was restive and inclined to knock his drinks back too quickly; but he was good 'copy' and could be as outspoken as Brendan Behan when he wished.

When he walked across to the Father Mathew Hall to take his seat, the theatre was crowded. His wife, Mary, was not with him; she was expecting their third child within weeks. It was a source of regret to her that she could not be in Cork; she had been at most of his first nights. It was soon evident that this night compared well with the premières of *Sive* and *Sharon's Grave*, for as the play progressed, the enthusiasm of the audience grew. By the final curtain, the cast, as well as Keane, knew they had another popular success on their hands.

There were calls for the author, and Keane, to loud applause, joined the cast on stage but kept his speech to a few words. He thanked cast, producer, stage staff and audience, and then hurried back to his seat. It was typical of the man, and no one, least of all the members of the cast, was surprised.

Backstage, James N. Healy described the first night as 'sensational', and Michael Twomey echoed this description. In the foyer, Keane accepted the congratulations of his Cork and Kerry well-wishers.

The next morning, the *Cork Examiner* headlined its review 'MEMORABLE THEATRICAL OCCASION' and went on to laud Keane's versatility in successfully combining drama and song. As the reviewer put it, 'The author has contrived beautifully to use music and melodies in counterpoint to the poetry of the writing. He is also a master of character and has given to James N. Healy a character with which he will be always identified. Danger Mullaly, the bum who carries bags for tourists, is a man, however, who knows Ireland, its exaggerated faults, its over-emphasised blessings, and it is to Danger that Keane accords the poignant line, "The Wild Geese are gone and now the goslings are flying."'

The work was seen as the playwright's 'swipe at emigration'. When it began a two-week run at the Olympia Theatre in Dublin a few weeks later, John Finegan was to observe in the *Evening Herald*, 'Under the guise of a freestyle musical, John B. Keane has written his wisest and most elegant play so far. No one having seen it will readily forget it or, in the future, be unmoved at the thought of the nightly boatloads to Britain. *Many Young Men of Twenty* is worth half a dozen official reports and a hundred political speeches. It should be compulsory viewing for every TD.'

Finegan was captivated by Siobhán O'Brien's performance. 'She plays the barmaid with great warmth and tenderness,' he wrote, 'and her singing is unforgettable for its beauty and sincerity. This is a performance that will linger in the memory.'

Séamus Kelly in the *Irish Times* commented on the pending general election and suggested that *Many Young Men of Twenty* might make profitable viewing for the candidates. A number of critics made reference to Keane's curtain speech at the Olympia, in which he described his play as 'a social comedy on a particular aspect of evil in Ireland – emigration'. They considered emigration to be one of the valid themes remaining for modern Irish dramatists.

Keane was in high spirits. He perceived a noticeable change

in Dublin attitudes towards him. Lunching with the journalist Raymond Smith, he recalled that when he first came to Dublin, he was treated with contempt in some quarters and dismissed as a country boy. But these people now took him more seriously.

'The literati of this city bore me,' he said, 'with their inconsequential and pretentious chatter. I find it heart-warming to return to my hotel to enjoy the genuine friendship and discernment of the porters who have life weighed up so well.' During lunch, he took telephone calls from friends and journalists; everybody seemed to know Keane was in town. Strolling down Grafton Street next morning, the playwright was hailed by a young man from Listowel, whom Keane greeted like a long-lost friend. They talked about home and the football match between Kerry and Down at Croke Park, and before long the young man was invited to see *Many Young Men of Twenty*. It was typical of Keane's warmth and generosity.

Rehearsals had begun for his Theatre Festival play, *No More in Dust*, but he had no plans to watch them. He had, he emphasised, enough trust in Phyllis Ryan and Barry Cassin. The title came from his poem 'Autumn's End':

> *The small monkeys now in Northern zoos*
> *Grumble with unaccustomed 'flu;*
> *Soft salmon redden in the pools*
> *And sleepy squirrels shout 'Down tools!'*
> *Most green leaves rest in rotting rust,*
> *Hot donkeys roll no more in dust.*

For Keane this play was a departure insofar as he had set the action in a Dublin bedsitter, his first theatrical excursion outside the south of Ireland. He considered the change of setting valid because he was dealing with mainly provincial people in Dublin, one of them a football follower who had come to the city for a big match. Phyllis Ryan, whose company was presenting the work, had no doubt that the play would attract audiences.

Controversy came from an unexpected quarter. It was reported in the newspapers that Eamonn Keane had walked out of rehearsals for *No More in Dust*. John B. was contacted at his hotel. 'That's Eamonn's affair, not mine,' he commented. 'As an actor, he has a right to do what he did if his conscience said so.' Privately, he had hoped that his brother would be in the play; he thought the part was right for him. He knew that Eamonn could be unpredictable, however.

Phyllis Ryan was dismayed. Barry Cassin, the director, searched for a replacement. Eamonn Keane challenged the press reports of the 'incident' stating that 'rehearsals were discontinued after he walked out.' He denied that he had left the production at the rehearsal stage. His version was that, having read the script 'late in the day', he had decided to say no to the part.

'I cannot see this as a play,' he said. 'It would be dishonest of me to act in it when I feel this way. I sincerely hope I am wrong. As I see it, the play is mostly about Dublin, and John has got away from the people he knows. You have got to live in Dublin to know the city well. You cannot write about it looking through a side window. The play has nothing to say, and is nothing like *Many Young Men of Twenty*, which is a good play. He says the right things in *Many Young Men* and you can believe in all the people, but it is not so in *No More in Dust*.'

His criticisms appeared to be vindicated by the mixed reviews the play received, although the *Irish Times* described the work as the playwright's best. 'Keane has caught the atmosphere well, and his people, for the most part, are real,' the paper reported. 'The watery Dublin party, with which the play opens, is well observed, even if the bearded bore and his sycophantic sidekick are overwritten. The dramatic action is well maintained, except for a long dull patch in Act One.'

The critic Robert Hogan drew an interesting analogy with *Many Young Men of Twenty*: '*No More in Dust* is also a lament, only this time the modern world is not Camden Town but Dublin. The Edna O'Brienish country girls in their seedy Leeson Street flat bemoan the past that their parents pushed them out of. But in this instance the past is not entirely seen through green-coloured spectacles. The young countryman up from Kerry for the weekend deserts the girl who has fallen in love with him, and is something of a rat. That fact probably confuses the statement of *No More in Dust*.'

As Phyllis Ryan expected, the play, despite its lukewarm reception by the critics, drew full houses and became a talking point. Keane had no regrets about the play's Dublin setting and was irritated by suggestions that in future he should stick to the south for his locations. The play was not published, and today it is difficult to trace a copy of the script. 'I think this is to be regretted,' his brother Denis was to say. 'It could have been successfully revived years later.' During the play's run, the critic John Finegan went back to see it for the second time. He wrote candidly, 'I'm afraid it shows Keane a long way from his native Kerry.'

Nevertheless, it had been a memorable year for Keane, made even more so by the birth of his third son, John. Mary's pregnancy and his own involvement with *Many Young Men of Twenty* and *No More in Dust* meant that he had to miss the off-Broadway production of *Sharon's Grave*, in which the Irish actress Helena Carroll played Trassie Conlee. Despite some poor reviews, Keane was pleased that the American company had thought his play good enough for presentation. After a Dublin paper published some of the critical reviews, a Killarney reader criticised the editor for not using the praiseworthy reviews from the *New York Times* and the *New York Journal American*. 'Fair play is a fine thing,' he wrote, 'but when it comes to John B. Keane, we forget that justice exists.'

At this time, the name of John B. Keane was seldom out of the news. The playwright admitted to having been 'under the weather' when he found himself in trouble at Dublin's Dagg Hall during a performance of *Sive*, at which the Minister for Defence, Gerald Bartley, was present. In a curtain speech, Keane made a reference to religion in Ireland. He was immediately heckled and someone tried to drag him off the stage – without success. The gardaí were called.

The next day, the playwright said he could not recall what he had said, nor indeed whether he had used an obscene word. 'I have not made any apologies simply because I have not been asked for any, and I do not know what to apologise for,' he told the *Evening Herald*.

When he drank whiskey or brandy, some journalists found him temperamental and impulsive and likely to say or do things that he would normally avoid. Kay Healy once made him apologise to a young female journalist in Cork whom he had strongly rebuked at a performance of one of his plays. 'Being a Kerrywoman, I was able to get him to shake hands with the girl and apologise. I took no nonsense from him. But most times John B. showed a heart of gold.'

James N. Healy, who knew of the playwright's admiration for Brendan Behan, sometimes feared he might go Behan's way and allow drink to get a grip on him. Dan Donovan thought otherwise. 'I think John worked too hard to let anything like that happen,' he said. Yet they both knew the extent to which personal acclaim puts a writer at risk.

Part Two

An Abbey Playwright

John B. Keane in the 1960s, as photographed by his friend Danny Hannon

The playwright's parents, William and Hannah Keane

John B. and Mary Keane on their wedding day

William (Billy) Keane pointing to the house on Church Street, Listowel, where his father, John B., was born

John B. and Mary Keane

Mary Keane behind the bar
the pub on William Street

John Keane and his wife, Sandra, whose untimely death deeply touched John B., her father-in-law

Conor Keane, like his brother John, is a journalist

Joanne Keane, the playwright's only daughter, is a teacher

Eamonn Keane showed faith in John B.'s creative talent and inspired him to write

Michael Keane, the playwright's eldest brother, writes short stories for magazines

John B.'s sisters, Anna (Klaben), Peg (Schuster) and Sheila (O'Connor) after the première of *The Field* at the Savoy Cinema in Dublin

The opening night of the revival of *Matchmaker* at the Tivoli Theatre in Dublin. From left: John Schuster, John B. Keane, Mary Keane, the playwright's youngest brother Denis, and Peg Schuster

A typical greeting for the playwright from
poet Brendan Kennelly

Nóra Relihan played the role of
Mena Glevin in *Sive*

John B. wrote *Big Maggie* for
Anna Manahan

13

THE PREMIÈRE OF HUT 42

At thirty-four, Keane had once more set his sights on the Abbey Theatre. He was anxious to join the elite band of Abbey playwrights that included Brian Friel, Hugh Leonard, Brendan Behan and Bryan MacMahon, whose play *The Honey Spike* had been acclaimed the previous year. 'Despite the way I've been treated, I have still great faith in the Abbey,' Keane said. He claimed he needed an Abbey company to be a real success in Dublin.

'John B. will never feel fulfilled until he's an Abbey playwright,' asserted Flor Dullea. 'Success elsewhere is not enough for him.' Dullea enjoyed the playwright's company in Cork and was aware of his uppermost ambition. To the actor, it was understandable.

Keane's dream was to be realised in the spring of 1962, when he received news of the Abbey's acceptance of his latest work, *Hut 42*. It would be staged later in the year. While *Many Young Men of Twenty* showed emigrants taking the mailboat, *Hut 42* told what happened when they got to England, and how they mourned what they had lost. John Finegan was quick to comment, 'After a lapse of four years, John B. Keane and Ernest Blythe have a rapprochement.'

It was later revealed that Keane had first offered his new play to Phyllis Ryan – and not to the Abbey. But she was committed to staging Tom Murphy's *A Whistle in the Dark*, and returned the script to John B. 'with thanks'. He was to be more successful with Blythe. The play was originally called *Warriors of the Skylight*, but in rehearsal the cast was unhappy with the title.

'Since it was set in a builder's hut, we decided to call it *Hut 42*,' recalled Kathleen Barrington, who was to play the

English welfare officer. She had joined the company in 1958 and made her debut with Ray McAnally in a Lennox Robinson play. In her view, much of the criticism levelled at Ernest Blythe was unwarranted. People seemed to forget that the company was operating in a temporary home – the Queen's Theatre – where conditions were inadequate.

She had not seen *Sive*, but the impression in the Abbey was that its author could be temperamental. To her surprise, however, she found him courteous when she was introduced to him before rehearsals, and helpful with the lines. He seemed to have a fine insight into the Irish in England, and while there was abundant humour in the play, there was also compassion.

The central character in the play is Skylight Maginty, an Irish worker whose closest friend is a Welshman named Idris Mortimer. Both men are confirmed gamblers and have been saving their pounds in the hope of setting themselves up as bookies. The plot turns on the death of an Irish worker who has been compelled to emigrate to provide for his large family. Kathleen Barrington felt that Frank Dermody, the director, was in sympathy with the play; he had once been an exile and hoped to pursue a film career.

Designer Tomás MacAnna had read *Hut 42* with more than ordinary interest. He was aware that Ernest Blythe had rejected *A Whistle in the Dark* because it projected a bad image of the Irish in England. The rejection, he thought, was a mistake and a black mark against the Abbey. The Keane work, by contrast, touched on the awfulness of emigration, as well as the loneliness and frustration facing the Paddies, and was sympathetic to them.

During rehearsals, MacAnna met Keane briefly and they exchanged a few words. 'After the *Sive* episode in Charleville, I suspected he was wary of me,' MacAnna recalled. 'I could not help feeling he was still upset over the Abbey's rejection of the play, and this I suppose was understandable.' Nonetheless, he felt he had made the correct decision on that occasion in giving the Tuam group's production of *Thunder Rock* the highest mark. On the other hand, he was sure that Ernest Blythe had accepted *Hut 42* to mollify Keane.

The playwright was to say later that he was of the same opinion, but he did not discuss it with Blythe. For his own part, he felt a revival of *Sive* at this time would probably have been a better proposition for the Abbey. 'I think Dublin audiences were crying out for *Sive*,' he says today. Nevertheless, he had worked hard to improve *Hut 42*, and on one occasion stayed for a weekend in Dublin to write a new scene.

He was to be bitterly disappointed by the news that Philip O'Flynn, one of the company's stalwarts, had withdrawn from the cast because of illness. Michael Hennessy replaced him at short notice in the leading role of Skylight Maginty. The opening night was scheduled for Monday 12 November, and when John B. and Mary Keane arrived at the theatre, they could have been forgiven for assuming that 'half of Kerry' was there before them. The occasion did not lack atmosphere, recalled Denis Keane. The play's theme appealed to him.

John B. has unhappy memories of the first night. 'The whole thing was a bit of a disaster,' he recalled. 'Nothing really pleased me about the production, and of course Philip O'Flynn's absence was a great loss.' Nonetheless, *Irish Times* critic Séamus Kelly did find some merit in the production. '"Isn't it a great thing t'have England, though sure only for that, we'd have nothing." That line, in the mouth of an aged Irish emigrant builder's labourer with weak kidneys, is one of the key-setters to John B. Keane's latest play, *Hut 42*,' Kelly wrote. 'Act One has another searching line, something about "When did ye ever hear the clergy preach sermons against political pull?" Act One indeed made me hope that the angriest of our anti-McCann school of playwrights was at last coming into his true force. For it's a fine angry act with a great ring of truth in it. In that first act, Keane sets a theme that might make homework for every Irish parliamentarian. He states the case for our emigrants of the past twenty-five years with irony, humour and righteous anger.'

Kelly was to express disappointment with Acts Two and Three, however, believing that they 'dropped into a sort of sentimentality that will no doubt be cheered in country halls but has little to do with the bite promised in Act One.' But he noted that an echo of the bite had returned before the final curtain, when Skylight says, 'We'll come back when England doesn't want us any more, and then let them all look out in Ireland.'

Hut 42 ran for three weeks and did brisk box-office business. Tomás MacAnna thought it was a good, workmanlike play. He felt Keane's real forte was his gift for creating character, as well as his racy dialogue. Ironically, when the Southern Theatre Group staged the play at the Cork Opera House, the playwright enthused about the production. In every way, he said, it was superior to that of the Abbey. The critic of the *Cork Examiner* commented: 'Not having seen the Abbey production, I cannot say why the work did not please then as it did last night. I suspect, however, that the lightness of direction evident last night might have been lacking in Dublin and that the rich humour of the work might have been lost in an attempt to paint the social problems on which the play is loosely founded. Which would be a mistake with this work. Keane is an entertainer, not that he does not have many pertinent comments to make; he has, and he writes his messages but does not trespass in the realm of the Department of Posts and Telegraphs. He is an entertainer, not a purveyor of messages.'

Despite its mixed reception by the critics, *Hut 42* had opened a door for Keane. His pulling power at the box office pleased Ernest Blythe, and with the Abbey actors fighting for more pay, it was essential to promote a playwright who could fill the theatre.

By now, Keane's play *The Man from Clare* had been successfully premièred by the Southern Theatre Group in Cork. Passing the Abbey Theatre one day with his friend Tony Guerin, Keane wondered whether he should go inside to see Blythe. In his pocket he had a copy of *The Man from Clare*. 'Go in and talk to him,' urged Guerin. 'You have nothing to lose.'

They had both agreed it was an Abbey-type play. Keane proceeded to climb the shabby stairway to the first floor, where he was shown the managing director's office. He knocked on the door and it was opened by Blythe, who was surprised to find John B. standing before him. 'Come in,' he said, 'and sit down.' They shook hands and began to speak in Irish. Blythe accepted a copy of *The Man from Clare* and promised to read it without delay. By the time he left the office, Keane was convinced the Abbey would do the play. This was confirmed a few weeks later. He received a cheque for £250 in advance of royalties.

As has been mentioned, it had always been an ambition of John B.'s to wear the green and gold jersey of Kerry on the football field, and that the honour eluded him was a cause of regret to him. Maybe he hadn't tried hard enough, he told himself, or simply hadn't the talent. Yet he knew he needed football, particularly as he began to write poetry and plays.

'For the sake of my masculinity, I needed to play the game,' he said. 'A man requires a rugged side to his character to meet the world. Football gave me courage and bravery.'

He had not to look far for the theme of *The Man from Clare*. It was woven round an annual game played between Shannon Rangers, the north Kerry team, and a side in County Clare. Keane was twenty when he first embarked on the voyage. The day was always an adventure. He remembered that a twenty-foot motor launch was used to transport the Shannon Rangers team, for which he played, from Saleen Pier, north of Ballylongford, to Cappa on the Clare coast. From there, local transport, generally horse-drawn, would be waiting to convey them to the venue of the game. The remainder of the team and a handful of supporters boarded a clinker-built, eighteen-foot rowing boat which was towed by the launch across the wide mouth of the Shannon, past Scattery Island to the Clare coast. The return that night was dependent on the engines, tides, weather, even booze, but nobody minded when it was announced that the team and supporters would be spending the night in Clare. It was an opportunity for merriment and dance, and it was customary for the local girls to dress up and meet their heroes. Although the game earlier would have been fiercely fought, the rivalry was soon forgotten over pints of stout and music-making.

In the play, set in County Kerry, the teams are Cuas and Bealabawn, both drawn from tiny communities; each community viewed the annual game as a great sporting and social occasion. Keane wrote a song for the Claremen of Cuas:

Glory to the men of Cuas
The pride of County Clare;
In the ruck or in the loose
The Cuas boys will be there.

The hero in *The Man from Clare* is Padraic O'Dea, a veteran footballer who had become so obsessed with the game that he tended to exclude everything else, even the thought of love and marriage. At the première in Cork, one Dublin critic wrote, 'It's John B. Keane's most mature play to date.' James N. Healy thought the play 'just missed greatness.' He feared that people with little interest in football might ignore it, in spite of the fact that the play's hero could be anyone who devoted everything to an ideal. Keane had based the hero on footballer Batt Crowley, his friend in Doneraile years before.

For the Abbey production, the playwright wanted Tom Honan to play Padraic O'Dea. He had been so impressed by Honan's performance at the All-Ireland Drama Festival in Athlone that he asked Ernest Blythe to 'bend an Abbey rule' to let Honan play the role. 'These things don't work,' replied Blythe. 'You can't put an amateur into a professional production. We tried it once with a Sligo girl and it was disastrous.' Today, Tom Honan wonders if he should have packed up teaching and taken a gamble with the Abbey.

*

The play opened at the Abbey Theatre on Monday 5 August 1963, with Pat Layde playing the part of Padraic O'Dea. If Keane had been disappointed with the company's production of *Hut 42*, he had no complaints on this occasion. The packed Queen's Theatre audience gave it an enthusiastic reception. 'The cast has done a splendid job,' remarked Keane.

In conversation with the playwright, Patrick Laffan remembers him praising Vincent Dowling's performance. 'He is a very clever actor, very inventive,' Keane said. Laffan and Dowling were the two tearaways in the play. 'We knew it was a funny play,' Laffan says, 'even if the hero is a bit sentimental.' To Kathleen Barrington, the play had tremendous life and vigour, and was an improvement on *Hut 42*.

The critic for the *Irish Times* sounded a warning. 'I found myself wondering at the Abbey last night if Keane's very commendable industry in writing play after play isn't perhaps an enemy of sorts to his development as a dramatist,' he wrote. 'That is not to say that the dramatist's talent is not there in abundance.'

He assured his readers, however, that the Abbey audience responded warmly to the playwright's picaresque characters. But he regretted that the play's serious theme was obscured by too many belly laughs. 'The trouble is that the whine of self-pity destroys the validity of the laughter, and the concluding ten minutes of the last act are embarrassingly mawkish.'

Tomás MacAnna is convinced that it was the success of *The Man from Clare* that cemented the relationship between Keane and the Abbey, and inspired a mutual trust. The play's theme was original and it was the first time that a football character had been paraded on the Abbey stage. Keane was doing what the Abbey had been founded to do – bring the reality of life in Ireland onto the stage.

During the run, Keane returned again to see the production. At the time, the Guinness taken by actors in certain scenes was purchased at a public house in nearby Pearse Street. After the final curtain, the playwright joined some of the cast in the pub, where they chatted cordially about the play. After closing time, they continued to talk in the street outside. Kathleen Barrington saw, however, that Keane suddenly took exception to a remark made by actress Máire Ní Dhomhnaill. 'I had heard Máire praise the play,' Barrington recalled, 'but as she proceeded to point out a technical fault, John B. lost his temper. He took off his glasses and stamped on them. I did not know what to think.'

Keane was the first to admit that he had a short fuse and could be easily provoked. He called it 'turbulence of mind'. He says it has always been present in him, although it had never affected his writing. Others were inclined to lay the blame for it on alcohol. Mary Keane did not worry unduly, for she knew that her husband got over it quickly. But his temperamental nature could occasionally be embarrassing for strangers.

On his return to Listowel, John B. found that his father was gravely ill. It was a cruel blow; they had always been close. John B. had had the satisfaction years before of writing a poem which his father said he liked:

> I am terribly proud of my father
> Bitterly, faithfully proud;
> Let none say a word to my father
> Or mention his name out loud.
>
> I adored his munificent blather
> Since I was as catch as catch can;
> Let none say a word of my father
> For he was a lovable man.

William Keane's death on 8 August 1963 was mourned not only by his family but by many of his past pupils in town and countryside. Hannah, his widow, bore her sorrow silently. It was a consolation to John B. that his father had lived to see his success. Reminiscences flooded back: 'I remember his waistcoat, a tobacco-perfumed parallelogram of pennied pockets. That's what I remember about him, his waistcoat and then the delight in watching him shaving with the open razor, an exercise in which the whole household participated, getting ready his water and his mug and everything else. He was an impractical man in many ways, financially speaking, but he was a lovable man.'

There was, too, his singing. As John B. recalled, 'I can see him now with a glass in his hand above at Olive Sheehy's, and his head back and he singing away at his heart's content. No one sang "The Old Rustic Bridge" like my father. A beautiful song.'

14

Tomorrow's Children

Keane was by now a regular guest on RTÉ's *Late Late Show*, hosted by Gay Byrne, who found Keane's sharp wit and storytelling irresistible. In the words of senior researcher Pan Collins, the *Late Late* had opened windows that had been shut for years in Ireland. For the first time on air, subjects such as sexuality, contraception, divorce and abortion could be debated openly.

The Listowel playwright was capable of provoking anger as well as laughter among the studio audience. 'He had the ability to put his finger precisely on the kernel of a subject,' recalled producer Adrian Cronin. 'John B. never tried to evade an issue and I think he talked a lot of common sense. A comopolitan audience was seeing him for the first time and he came across as a quick-witted Kerryman, a genuine character.'

To Cronin, he made a splendid *Late Late* guest or panellist, whose humour could be mischievous. He knew he was one of Gay Byrne's favourite people. At the time, the guests were paid between £7 and £10, so the producer knew that none of them came on the show for the sake of the money. Among the other guests to impress him were Ulick O'Connor, Bryan MacMahon, Denis Franks and Veronica Mullan, who was the voice of the younger generation. Cronin experienced no great problem in getting them to appear.

Keane pulled no punches. On the issue of divorce, he was liable to say, 'I condone divorce because I feel everybody deserves a second chance. Mistakes can be made; some people rush into marriage, or are rushed by parents or in-laws, with sometimes disastrous results. I would never condone abortion.'

He could be no less outspoken about the Church. 'Sometimes it seems to me to be at odds with Christ's teaching in the gospels,' he said, 'and the Church's attitude in the past to sexuality could be partly blamed for many unhappy marriages. Mention of the word "sex" has tended to drive self-righteous people out of their minds.' His views on alcohol were interesting. 'Drink requires discipline,' he said. 'Everyone can drink and I believe everyone should drink, but it's a matter of training yourself. I sometimes go on a skite myself, say at a wedding or a wake, but I can stop. Alcohol can ruin families if you don't learn to respect it.'

Already his opinions on the Irish language had begun to make enemies for him and, more than once, on the *Late Late Show* he was taken to task by the studio audience. No one could say his view wasn't consistent. 'I speak the language fluently and have written poetry in it,' he said, 'but a lot of nonsense and humbug surrounds it today. What good is Irish to a young man going to England? And the majority of young men nowadays have got to go to England or elsewhere if they want to survive.'

There were times when Denis Keane wondered whether his brother's outspoken views were putting his popularity at risk, for people who liked his plays might be turned off by the image he sometimes presented on-screen. Mary Keane wasn't worried; she saw his performance as entertainment and felt that her husband was being himself. His friends in Kerry would doubtless have enjoyed more of John B. telling stories of Dan Paddy Andy and other legendary matchmakers.

'He was simply a good performer,' asserted Pan Collins. 'You could depend on him. John B. never let you down on the show. We didn't invite him on as a comic, but as a writer who had interesting things to say on various subjects. He was direct, but he bore no malice. As a guest, he achieved success by the unique way he said things; he could be a very humorous man.'

He surprised Pan the first time he arrived as a guest. Before he went into the studio at Montrose, he handed her a box of chocolates. It wouldn't be the last time. As she later said, 'John B. was always bringing small gifts to us. He could be a most generous man. I knew that Gay was fond of him; he usually liked guests who weren't pretentious and had something to say.'

Looking back after thirty years, the playwright had happy

memories of the show. 'I revelled in it. Once, I remember I went on with a share of drink on me and I proceeded to see Gay through blurred vision, but I carried on regardless and no one seemed to notice. If I were to do that today, I'd be eaten by the other guests, and perhaps the studio audience. In those days, the *Late Late* was fun.'

He says he was never conscious of the cameras on him, nor did he ever try to be self-important. He was grateful for the opportunity Gay Byrne provided for him and others to express themselves frankly and maybe become well-known personalities. The show, he felt, made a useful platform for debating issues that had been considered taboo on air for so long. In that way, it served a valuable purpose.

On one occasion, he was asked by Gay Byrne if he had ever considered taking up a career in politics. John B. was quick to reply. 'The Fine Gael party in my own north Kerry constituency approached me to stand for a Dáil seat,' he said, 'but I explained I could never hope to find the time to devote to the job. Not that I'm not politically minded – I am. I haven't missed an election count in Tralee in years, and I've canvassed for Fine Gael candidates in my own area. In fact, you could say I've friends in all the political camps.'

Mary Keane would confirm he was speaking the truth, for over the years she realised there was pressure on him to stand as an election candidate. In her determination to put him off, she entered into a pact with his father, and together they put every possible obstacle in his way. She had been influenced in her decision by what she had observed. 'There was a TD living near us and the poor man had no life at all,' she recalled. 'He had callers every hour of the day; these were people looking for favours or jobs, and I saw John in a similar position if he took up politics. Like his father, I wanted him to stick to writing, the thing he did best.'

If he succeeded in avoiding direct involvement in politics, Keane nevertheless found other ways of getting his views across to the public. The *Irish Times* described him as an angry young dramatist for his swipes at emigration and other social issues. By the autumn of 1963, he was regarded outside the theatre as a crusader, and he strongly advocated changes in aspects of traditional Irish life so as to ensure a more enlightened Ireland for tomorrow's children.

There was a danger, however, of his being misunderstood, for the very institutions he criticised happened, in most cases, to be among those he cherished. He was, after all, a regular churchgoer, a successful Abbey playwright, a Gaelic-football fan and an Irish-language speaker. Keane would argue that his appeals were made with the best intentions.

*

In Limerick to attend a performance of his play *The Man from Clare*, he ran into controversy at the City Theatre. At the final curtain, he climbed on stage and proceeded to address the audience about the Irish language and what he saw as 'the hypocrisy of some of the people behind it.' These people, he said, seemed to maintain that anyone who didn't speak the language was not a true Irishman. He was left with the impression that a form of Freemasonry was being introduced by some of those who professed to be behind the language movement.

A voice from the stalls was heard to exclaim that it was not fair that Mr Keane should give his views to a silent audience. 'I didn't come here,' the man said, 'to take part in a discussion with you. I came here to see and enjoy your play, which I have done.' Others voiced the same views, and the curtain was rung down.

The playwright rose and walked down the aisle and through the foyer into the street, where he was soon joined by about two hundred people. He said he was determined to exercise the right of free speech. A number of onlookers applauded him. Having spoken to them about the language, he thanked them for waiting to hear him.

Next day, the *Limerick Chronicle* devoted an entire editorial to the episode, headlining it 'TILTING AT WINDMILLS'. The leader observed: 'As well as being a playwright of marked ability, Mr J. B. Keane of Listowel also appears to be something of a crusader; and if he is at the moment mixing his theatrical proclivities with a dislike for those behind the Irish-language movement, what matter if the result be stimulating and even bizarre. It must be said that the volatile Mr Keane has a good many friends in his generalised attack on those behind the language movement. Obviously he is one of the many who are not antagonistic to Irish as such, but only to the people whose endeavours to promote it do not always appear to be imbued with altruistic ideals. Quite obviously the subject is going to be a bone of contention for a long time to come, especially if there are people of the calibre of John B. Keane knocking around.'

When he was invited by the *Sunday Independent* to contribute an article to its colour magazine, the playwright's piece was headlined: 'CONFESSIONS OF A SECOND-CLASS CITIZEN'; its opening paragraph set the piece's controversial tone: 'I am a second-class citizen because I do not believe in compulsory Irish. I also believe the ban on foreign games should be lifted, that it should not be permitted to exist within the frame of Europe's most outstanding democracy. I believe that those who play soccer and rugby are as good Irishmen as those who play Gaelic football and hurling. These are terrible admissions, aren't they, and they certainly serve to confirm that I am, indeed, a second-class citizen. My problem is – what should I do to become a first-class citizen?'

He said he was reared and educated to believe that there was room for every type of decent opinion in the country of his birth – that the country was big enough to embrace the opinions, likes and dislikes of all its people. 'My father was a schoolmaster,' he added, 'and he never imposed. I see now how very lucky I was to be born under the broad influences of this penniless but far-reaching instructor.'

Letters to the paper praised his courage and honesty, and a few people, including a Cork reader, Eamonn MacMurchadha, voiced strong disapproval. He advised the playwright, 'Stick to drama, John B., and continue to entertain us with that deep insight and other delightful attributes which are the glorious heritage secured to you and other gifted artists by the grim tenacity and stubborn loyalty of our forefathers.'

Brendan Behan, meanwhile, between his sporadic writings and pub crawls, found time to deliver a broadside at Keane through the letters page in the *Irish Times*. He attacked the playwright over his attitude to compulsory Irish. It was a scathing letter, Keane recalled, and he replied to it as best he could. He had frequently spoken in Irish with Behan and intimated to him his dislike of compulsory Irish.

The matter was to rest there. It was now March 1964, and Brendan Behan was seriously ill. 'My laughing boy', as his wife, Beatrice, liked to call him, died on March 19 in Dublin's Meath Hospital. John B. heard the news with a profound sense of regret. His first reaction was that the country had lost a gifted writer, whose play *The Quare Fella* would endure as a powerfully eloquent plea against capital punishment; likewise his finest book, *Borstal Boy*, for its perceptive insights into Borstal life in England.

During periodic visits to Dublin for productions of his plays, Keane drank with Behan in pubs around Duke Street, listened to his yarns, and agreed with John Ryan, of the Bailey, that 'Brendan has faults but intellectual dishonesty isn't one of them.' Once, in the defence of melodrama, Keane cited *The Hostage* as the perfect example of how this dramatic form can bestow immortality on its author. Behan telephoned him, and joyously blurted, 'Johnny, me darlin', that was great reading in the *Times* this morning.'

'What was great?'

'Ah, don't be so shaggin' modest,' Behan roared into the phone. 'I mean, what you said in the *Irish Times*, of course.'

John B. could scarcely get a word in as Behan expounded on the theme of melodrama. 'The line sizzled when he opened up,' Keane recalled.

'Are you stewed?' John B. asked.

Behan laughed. 'Not a drop, Johnny, as God is my judge.'

Keane reminded him of his earlier attack on him in the *Irish Times* in respect of compulsory Irish. 'You're too shaggin' thin-skinned,' Behan exploded. 'Sure if I took notice of my critics, I'd be in Grangegorman long ago.'

Shortly afterwards, they were both invited to take part in a debate on the Irish theatre in the Shelbourne Hotel Ballroom, where the actor Ray McAnally represented the Abbey Theatre as its spokesman. When he stated at one point that the Abbey paid its dramatists 10 per cent royalties for capacity houses, Keane interrupted to remind him that all he got for *Sive* was 7.5 per cent. McAnally remarked, 'It must have played to half-empty houses.'

Keane reminded him that people were turned away every night. Suddenly, a woman jumped from her seat and berated the Listowel playwright for interrupting while somebody else was speaking. She said she was a Kerrywoman and was ashamed that any person from Kerry should behave in such a fashion.

'The oul' bitch,' Behan muttered under his breath. 'She doesn't like the bloody truth!' She stood in the aisle and would not be silenced. When Keane invited her to come on stage, she refused.

'Well then,' he asked her, 'what *do* you want?'

Behan leaned over and, in a loud whisper, said, 'I'll tell you exactly . . . she badly wants a good screw, that's what she wants.'

'Brendan and myself saw eye to eye on most things,' Keane recalled. 'I remember also that night there was a little short of £300 taken at the box office. This went to a Dublin charity, and Brendan, in typical fashion, added substantially to this sum from his own pocket.'

They were later heckled by a group of students as they left the hotel ballroom. Brendan turned round to them and said, 'It's getting harder and harder to distinguish between Teddy boys and students.'

There was another occasion which Keane thought revealed the typical Behan. Radio Éireann was recording *Sive* in its Henry Street studios and, later in the day, he met Brendan in the Tower Bar. Keane began, in an almost conspiratorial voice, to explain how to combine eating with drinking. 'Brendan's idea was to buy a pound of brawn and put it in his pocket, and when hungry, take out a slice and eat it, washed down, of course, with Guinness. He was serious about it. In those days, people like Brendan thought lunching impinged on their drinking. It was the advice of a lovable man.'

The last time Keane saw Behan alive was in the foyer of the Ormond Hotel in Ormond Quay. It was on the Sunday morning of a big football match between Dublin and Kerry.

Keane was shocked by his appearance. 'Brendan looked terrible and was almost drunk when he arrived,' he recalled. 'My son Billy was with me and our company also included Johnny Walsh and John Joe Sheehy, who, between them, had nearly a dozen all-Ireland senior football medals.'

'I thought you were in hospital, Brendan,' Keane remarked. Behan chuckled. 'I was, but I escaped.'

He sat with young Billy on his lap. To Keane, he had a genuine fondness for children. When Keane called for a drink, Brendan demanded a glass of gin. It was no use remonstrating. John B. thought that, if they had a drink and a chat, he might get Brendan to go back to his bed. Behan drank the double gin and called for another. He threw that back neat and beckoned the waiter for another.

By this time, a number of Kerry supporters had gathered round to listen to the conversation. Keane objected to his having another gin, but Brendan, tieless and with vacant eyes, abused him. He put his hand in his waistcoat pocket and gave Billy Keane a pound note. There were several children in the hotel lounge and he called them and presented them with the contents of his pockets. 'I never had any money when I was a child,' he said wistfully.

Seeing his condition, John B. began to grow anxious. His anxiety soon changed to anger as some of Behan's admirers pressed double gins on him. He pleaded with them to desist. When he went to the toilet a few minutes later, one of the men told him to mind his own business, that they were taking Behan with them on a pub-crawl. One man challenged him to a fight. It was the kind of thing that usually made Keane fume. 'I turned round and hit the man and left him there. He didn't show up again. When I returned upstairs to the lounge, Brendan was maudlin and incoherent, but he still sat with my son Billy on his knee.

'Don't drink any more,' young Billy said.

'Whatever you say, Billy,' muttered Behan, 'but I'll have one more just to wash down the last one!'

A large crowd was by now gathered in the lounge. Brendan insulted most of them, but John B. was relieved when he saw him speak kindly to the old Kerry footballer who sat at his table. At that moment, a boisterous young man pushed his way through the crowd and shook Brendan's hand – much to his annoyance.

'We were in the same brigade in the IRA,' the man boasted.

Behan miraculously sobered up and, taking a hard look at the other, snapped, 'Go 'long, you bowsie! The only brigade you ever saw was the fire brigade!'

John B. saw there was no answer to that, for it was the kind of remark that had made Brendan famous as a wag and a wit. Drunk or sober, the wit flowed, some of it sarcastic and biting, more of it funny. In a curious way, he felt indebted to him. Years before, Behan had accepted him as a young Kerry poet and afterwards in Dublin pubs read out his poems, punctuating them with expressions like, 'Now there's a grand shaggin' line!' or 'Bejasus now, that's nicely put!' Brendan's parents, Stephen and Kathleen Behan, had attended Keane's plays at the Olympia Theatre, and James N. Healy would say that on one occasion Stephen had shouted from the balcony during a performance of *Many Young Men of Twenty*, 'Come on Danger! Come on Danger!'

'Humanity was something ingrained in the Keanes from childhood,' says Peg Schuster, John B's sister, 'and I think both of my brothers, John and Eamonn, recognised this virtue in the Behans.'

Beatrice Behan remembered Eamonn Keane staying for Christmas with them in their house in Anglesea Road in Dublin. 'Brendan used to tell me he found the Keanes great company. I think he admired their imaginations and wit. He tried to visit County Kerry as often as he could and liked the people.'

It came as no surprise to Brendan's drinking buddies that he welcomed John B. and Eamonn Keane into his company. Like himself, they were devoid of hypocrisy and humbug. To Behan, the brothers shared his love of plays, poetry and booze. Eamonn Keane saw genius in Behan, but a touch of the 'rogue elephant' as well. John B. regarded him as very talented and a born writer, and hated to watch the self-destructive forces taking over.

After the match at Croke Park, John B. and his son Billy, and other Kerry supporters, returned to the Ormond Hotel to slake their thirst before the long journey home. He was shocked to be told by a hotel porter that some men had beaten up Behan that afternoon. Apparently, they had approached Brendan for money and he had refused them. The porter described it as a severe beating. Keane felt that in Brendan's condition, any kind of beating would be dangerous.

Days later, Keane learned that Behan was being treated in the Meath Hospital for 'drink complaints' and was at death's door. When death came, John B. made up his mind that on no account must he miss the funeral. And on a mild March day, he joined the cortège that crossed over the Liffey to Glasnevin Cemetery. The sun shone as thousands of onlookers lined the streets. Most of them were scarcely prepared for Brendan's death, for Dubliners had listened for too long to reports of his illnesses. At the grave, Keane stood between Dominic Behan and Beatrice Behan, whose head was covered with a black mantilla.

Years later, Beatrice would write, 'One almost expected Brendan to step out of a taxi, shouting, "What's all this about? I'm not dead!" But he was in some heavenly bar, drinking with Shakespeare and Jonson and Marlowe. The mourners dispersed, disappointed that Brendan, like his young hero in The Hostage, hadn't jumped from the grave to sing 'The Bells of Hell'.'

Likewise, remembering that remarkable day, Keane would write, 'The IRA, like characters out of his plays, marched at either side of the coffin. Two nuns, from his kindergarten days, followed close behind. The gurriers, the bowsies, the ould wans and the chisellers were all there. Respected publicans, wealthy businessmen, lawmen and wanted men, all walked side by side in that last trip to Glasnevin. The Dublin pubs did a roaring trade. Television cameras whirred and a Frenchman spoke over his grave. He would have enjoyed it all but he would have preferred if the ould wans with the shawls and the down-and-outs with the caps on the sides of their heads were up in front where they belonged, because the Dublin poor were closest to his heart and he never forgot that he was one of them. 'Never were so many characters gathered together in one place. It was a scene that only Brendan Behan could create.'

*

As the weeks went by, John B. was determined to secure Mary's position. It was by now no secret that Beatrice Behan had been left a poor widow, with an avalanche of debts facing her. When the revenue commissioners asked her for enormous sums – tax arrears Brendan had incurred over the years – all she could say was, 'Where are the snows of yesteryear?'

Although he did not want to sound alarmist, Keane succeeded in persuading Mary to accompany him to their solicitor in Listowel to arrange for the public house in William Street to be signed over to her. At first, she was surprised by his persistence, but after he had stressed the advantages of the change, she put her name to the document. As she said, 'If John wanted it that way, I was willing to go along with him. Never before had I seen him as serious about anything. Beatrice Behan's plight had touched him deeply.'

She herself had been in Brendan's company on two occasions, once when he came into the kitchen of their home in Listowel and rebuked her for painting the chairs a certain colour. To Mary Keane, he was good-natured and cheerful. 'Brendan and myself went on a skite that day,' John B. recalled.

Behan's passing, however, reminded him sadly that, as the years rolled on, he would lose other good friends. In that same year, 1964, he was saddened by the death of his friend, Maurice Walsh, and his funeral, like that of Brendan Behan, attracted a big crowd, which included President de Valera. Maurice was buried in his famous tweed suit in Esker cemetery in Lucan. Asked for a tribute to the popular novelist, Keane said simply, 'Maurice Walsh is loved here in Listowel. Yes, loved.'

John B. and Mary remembered him in the pub in the old days, cheerfully reminiscing over a glass of whiskey. Keane knew Walsh had often spoken well about his own potential as a writer, and it was something he never forgot. He was aware, too, that he was a friend of both Behan and Kavanagh, and his description of Brendan was typical of Walsh: 'He is a decent stick of a fellow, a rough diamond who is not as rough as he looks or acts.'

To Keane, the novelist epitomised all that is best in Kerrymen and Kerry writers. He was a good friend and a man of integrity. And, as a writer, he was master of his craft; a sense of place was very important to him, and his characters were firmly and colourfully drawn. There was also a tangible rhythm to his dialogue. Like the 'Pope' O'Mahony, Maurice Walsh was recognised everywhere he went, and treated with affection. Yet in his travels he always found time to visit his native north Kerry.

Keane could see why Behan and Kavanagh thought so highly of him as a writer, and, as a man, treasured his company. To everyone's amazement at the time, the novelist never received an honorary degree from an Irish university.

15

Censorship Charge

Keane was conducting his life at a punishing pace, but his appetite for work was remarkable. He succeeded in meeting regular magazine and newspaper deadlines, he found time for lectures and radio broadcasts, and by now the Southern Theatre Group had accepted his latest play, *The Year of the Hiker*. Brisk walks near Listowel kept him fit, and he even managed the odd game of Gaelic football. Despite all this activity, he had organised his life admirably to embrace family, friends, producers and editors.

For relaxation, he still chatted over pints of stout with the characters in his pub, and it didn't take much persuasion to get him to sing an Irish ballad. With his unusual stamina, he thought nothing of making the long journey to Dublin twice, or even three times, a week, and it certainly wasn't for the money, as radio and television paid only nominal fees. Obviously the glamour of television attracted him.

He agreed to be a panellist on *Pick of the Post*, a weekly programme which invited viewers to supply letters for discussion by the panel. 'It was a kind of television agony column,' said producer Adrian Cronin, 'and although I never regarded it as an ideal TV format, the show was proving very popular with viewers, and the feedback was good. We received letters on anything from animal pets to romance in Lisdoonvarna.'

Among the regular panellists were poet and novelist Patrick Kavanagh, actor Joe Lynch, model Betty Whelan and John B. Keane. The presenter was Joe Linnane, who had come to the forefront through radio and was considered 'a mild and amusing man'. Sometimes Cronin had difficulty in getting Kavanagh to the studio for the recording of the show. Some days he had to fetch him from McDaid's pub, off Grafton Street.

The producer reckoned he had got a good 'mix' on the panel. Kavanagh, with his wide knowledge, could be brilliant; Keane was never bland and was liable to make controversial comments that attracted to him a certain notoriety; Joe Lynch could be humorous and possessed the gift of the gab; and Betty Whelan brought a modern woman's mind to the show, being particularly good on subjects relating to women. Sometimes sparks flew when Kavanagh let loose his 'harsh Monaghan vocabulary', as John Ryan of the Bailey had described it. But he could also be very witty.

Keane drank with the poet in McDaid's or Neary's and found him priceless company. 'I loved his wry sense of humour,' Keane said, 'though he could be sarcastic to those who ignored him in a bar. He was chronically short of money, but in the literary circles in which he moved, that was not uncommon. My brother Eamonn was closer to Patrick, and he used to take off his Monaghan accent to perfection. They were drinking buddies.'

Kavanagh, he felt, was not truly appreciated in Dublin: there were those who resented him, despite his achievements. He could be a gentle soul and even dismissive of his own ability as a writer. This was something he had found among other talented writers and poets. It was Kavanagh's epic poem, *The Great Hunger*, that first drew Keane to him. The playwright could recall a time when this poem was 'semi-banned' in Listowel, and he remembered his father once throwing a copy of the poem on the table with the words, 'There's a great poem for you.' Later, John B. himself acted in a stage adaptation of the poet's *Tarry Flynn*.

To Keane, it was Kavanagh's accent that made him stand out. It was a wonderful Monaghan accent and, in a show like *Pick of the Post*, was ideal for making wry comment. Keane noticed that Kavanagh tended to think for a moment before he commented on the contents of a viewer's letter. Depending on his mood, Kavanagh could be sarcastic or amiable, but he was never dull.

On one occasion, a woman wrote in to say that her son

was a pupil of Terenure College and very academically minded. Since he was not robust, he had decided to skip rugby in the college, but to his astonishment, he was being forced to play the game. She thought this very unfair and wanted to know the views of the panellists.

Adrian Cronin remembers that Keane was pragmatic about the matter, and suggested the woman write to the college head and explain her own and her son's position. 'I think John B. was anxious that the boy be given freedom of choice in the games he wanted, or didn't want, to play,' Cronin said later.

Joe Lynch recalled that, growing up in the south of Ireland, sport played an important role and it was natural for most boys to play some game or other. He appreciated the boy's position in this case, however, and believed he should not be forced to play a game he didn't want to play.

Betty Whelan said she found it an interesting case and was inclined to sympathise with the boy's mother. She hoped a solution could be arrived at for the boy's sake.

For his part, Patrick Kavanagh expressed outrage at the mother's attitude and saw no justification for it. He argued strongly that sport was important to young men and helped to develop their characters. He advised the woman to persuade her son to play rugby.

As his temper rose, he suddenly used the word 'effin' – or so it sounded to Adrian Cronin, although it could have been the full Anglo-Saxon expletive. Presenter Joe Linnane looked askance at the poet but was powerless to stop him 'in full flow'. Subsequently, RTÉ programmes chief Jack White decided that the offending word must be edited out. When Keane saw the show at his home in Listowel, he was amazed it was censored. 'I could not believe such a thing could happen,' he said.

When he returned to Montrose the following week, Keane tackled Adrian Cronin and accused RTÉ of censorship. As he finger-wagged the producer, Joe Lynch stepped between them and asked John B. to forget about the matter. The producer could scarcely believe the playwright could get so worked up. 'Joe Lynch was trying to tell him that I had a job to do,' he said later.

As far as Cronin can recall, Kavanagh made no complaints.

'I suspect he never saw the show,' Cronin commented, 'although I'm sure someone in McDaid's would have mentioned the row to him.' The ironic thing was that Keane never used the four-letter expletive in any of his plays and saw no need to do so. His views on the censorship issue were well known at the time, however, and he deplored the censorship of writers like Kate O'Brien, Seán O'Faolain and Frank O'Connor. Even in later life, he contended that Kavanagh, because of the censorship laws prevailing at the time, lacked total freedom to write what he wanted to write. But he remained a panellist on *Pick of the Post* and worked amicably with Adrian Cronin.

*

In between his trips to Dublin, the playwright attended rehearsals of *The Year of the Hiker* in Cork. He could scarcely disguise his enthusiasm for the play. It is the story of 'the Hiker Lacey', who leaves his wife Kate and three children and stays away for twenty years. Wanderlust is partly a reason for his going. 'Everyone contemplates it,' says Keane. 'Every man worth his salt contemplates this excursion off into the wilderness.'

From his experience, he had heard of at least two score men in North Kerry who had left home, not necessarily because of other women, which was rare, but due to wanderlust. Many of them returned, though some stayed away for good. He confessed that occasionally the thought occurred to him, too. 'Every time I see a fine day I'm mad to be off,' he said. 'If I see a blue sky in the heavens I find a compelling urge to be away.'

When James N. Healy first got the script, he was reminded of his own feckless father, who had left home for a time, though he would later return. The intense pain of his leaving had stayed with Healy and it was the main reason why he was strongly attracted to the role of the Hiker. If *Sive* was an essentially Irish situation, he regarded the theme of *The Year of the Hiker* as universal. Keane, he accepted, was good at probing family relationships, and in the play it could be argued that the Hiker left home because of the presence there of his sister-in-law. Not surprisingly, the production was accorded an enthusiastic reception at its first night in the Father Mathew Hall, Cork.

The critic of the *Cork Examiner* praised not only the Southern Theatre Group's performance but also Keane's development as a playwright. 'His days of apprenticeship are over,' the critic wrote. 'The play is a new departure for him. Gone are the gimmicks, the shocks and the tendency to startle.'

On reflection, Flor Dullea, who was cast as Joe Lacey, the son who shows some compassion towards the dying Hiker, said, 'I never saw John B. as happy as on that first night. He was beaming and eager to shake all our hands. I have no doubt the play meant a lot to him.' He remembered, too, seeing James N. Healy, as the Hiker, shedding real tears on stage, particularly in the last act.

For his part, Healy admits that on opening night he overplayed the role and was carried away by the memory of his father. As he said, 'The first four nights were very difficult for me, but I was not helped by the audience. I think they expected the Hiker to be another humorous Danger Mullaly, which of course he is not. I got it right eventually and tried to avoid the sentimental urge.'

Séamus Kelly of the *Irish Times*, who made the journey to Cork for the première, commented that Keane had moved into T. C. Murray's country. (Murray had written a dozen plays – some premièred – with a strong rural backdrop, like the *Hiker*.) Kelly added, 'For all its extravagance of writing, however, Keane has put a compelling sincerity into his essentially simple story. James N. Healy could probably have done better if Keane had put a bit more blood in the Hiker Lacey. As it is, he registers as a spent Don Juan who never really heard the chimes, and as such is a bit unconvincing.'

There was a surprise in store for Keane when the Southern Theatre Group toured the production. Brendan Long, the critic of the Clonmel *Nationalist*, who had panned *Sive* and angered the playwright, now urged his readers to see *The Year of the Hiker* at the local theatre. 'It is not just a good play,' he stated, 'it is a great play, a deeply Christian drama, a work in which the writer has shed the chains of an early and easy success and has at least imposed upon his ideas and his pen the discipline which reveals his true and considerable genius.'

Although Long admitted that it wasn't a perfectly made play, he said he became emotionally involved in it. 'What the play is essentially about is the slow but sure flowering of charity in a garden of hatred,' he wrote. 'And because one is involved, it isn't an entertainment in the crass sense of the word – it is an ennobling experience.'

In spite of its poignant theme, *The Year of the Hiker* was proving a popular success. Michael Twomey, cast as Simey, the son who taunts his father, recalled how intensely moved audiences became by the fate of the Hiker. 'I think anyone would have to be very insensitive not to be affected,' he said. Yet some critics remarked that audiences sometimes 'guffawed when they should have wept', as though confused by the mood of the play. 'Much of the play is over-wordy,' complained a critic in Limerick.

*

On his return to Listowel, Keane gave much thought to *The Year of the Hiker*. He wasn't entirely happy with the manuscript and felt it could be improved upon. Remembering how successfully he and Barry Cassin had worked together on revising *The Highest House on the Mountain*, he decided to ask Phyllis Ryan if she would be interested in presenting the play in Dublin.

By now she had formed a new company, Gemini Productions, one of whose directors was the noted actor Norman Rodway. After reading the script, she felt it could be tightened up. She asked the playwright if he was agreeable to changes, and, to her relief, he said he had no objection. Among the changes envisaged was the dropping of the song 'Red Sails in the Sunset' at the rise and fall of the curtain. It was, she thought, too sentimental.

Barry Cassin approached the script in his typically methodical manner. As director, he felt that the theme could be more clearly pointed up, and Keane agreed. In no way, he said, was the script changed for the sake of it. What was at first only a line altered here and there developed into a complete breakdown of the script and a terse, forceful rebuilding.

Martin Dempsey, who a few years before had created the role of Mikey Bannon in *The Highest House on the Mountain*, was attracted to Hiker Lacey because he was, in a way, a loner like himself. He appreciated the Hiker's domestic dilemma, caught as he is between his wife and his sister-in-law. Two women in the house with one man is a problem anyway. He had seen it before; some men could take it, whereas others simply could not – and left. Wanderlust also came into it, for as the Hiker says, 'There's men like me that gets the urge for wandering and there's no power on earth or heaven that will pull us back once the callin' cries from beyond the fields and rivers.'

At rehearsals, Gerry Sullivan, who was cast as the eldest son Joe, who shows some sympathy for his father's plight, thought the play was beautifully written. The language was racy and authentic and the characterisation convincing. Anna Manahan, cast as Freda, the sister-in-law, reckoned there was more to the play than a man leaving home and family because he wants to see what is on the other side of the hill. She felt that Hiker Lacey would have returned home regularly if his sister-in-law wasn't in the house.

Only at the end of the play does one realise there are faults on both sides. There is also perhaps a sense of forgiveness, which, in Ms Manahan's opinion was 'a lovely part of John B. himself.' She regarded him as a very human writer in his understanding of people; this humanity comes through in the scenes between the Hiker and his son Joe.

*

On Monday 16 November 1964, the Eblana Theatre was full for the opening performance. Among the audience were John B. and Mary Keane. John B.'s confidence in Phyllis Ryan and Barry Cassin was such that he had avoided rehearsals, satisfied they had put everything into his work. The cast, he felt, could not be bettered; it included the brilliant young Dublin actor Jim Norton in the part of Simey Lacey.

The production was accorded a tremendous reception by the audience, and at the final curtain the playwright went on stage to deliver a few words of thanks to the cast. 'We're sure of a long run,' remarked Phyllis Ryan later. She thought Martin Dempsey's performance had been a remarkable one. It was devoid of self-pity; here was a man who had made a lot of mistakes in his life and now he simply wanted to die in peace at home among his family.

In conversation with Keane, Ryan described this as his Russian period, and she remembers he was amused. There was, she felt, a Chekhovian mood in parts of the play. At least one critic agreed: 'The work has a great deal of Russian brooding about it,' he wrote. Phyllis Ryan was inclined to see Hiker Lacey as a natural wanderer, and although his sister-in-law admits to having had a crush on him, this aspect was deliberately avoided in the production.

To Martin Dempsey, acting in the play was a profoundly moving experience. 'I found there was one line that overwhelmed me, and it is when my son asks me what I used to think about, sitting by the campfire,' he recalled. 'My answer is, "the dogs". The old man, you see, is terrified of dogs. I could hardly say the words; they tore the heart and soul out of me. You got this picture of the poor man sitting there alone at night. Once, Barry Cassin attacked me over the scene. I remember him saying, "Be careful, Martin, I saw tears in your eyes tonight." Barry believes no actor should cry. I don't subscribe to that; I'm crying half the time in plays I do!'

Gerry Sullivan is convinced that Dempsey's deliberate underplaying of the Hiker invested the role with real depth. The critics were impressed by what they called 'the compressed writing in the play'. John Finegan in the *Herald* stated that the dialogue pulsed with life and was stripped down to a new Keane style. He felt, however, that the climax was too long delayed and that more might have been made of the last-act encounter between the Hiker and his hardbitten sister-in-law Freda. He thought that Barry Cassin's direction had got every ounce out of the work and that Robert Heade's farm-kitchen setting was something about which to cheer.

Stephen Walsh in the *Irish Independent* said that Keane had created an intensely moving work, rich in human feeling, and that there was an exquisite tenderness in the yearning of this weak, pathetic man for the forgiveness of the family he has grievously wronged by his desertion. There was infinite sadness in the great longing in his heart, in particular for the love of his two sons, now grown up, each of whom sees his father with different eyes. He saw it as a play of immense appeal.

Predictably, it transferred to the Gate Theatre, where it was to enjoy an even bigger success. On the first night, Keane joined a celebratory party afterwards in actress Ruth Durley's apartment, where, in the course of the evening, he was asked by Anna Manahan if he would write a play for her. 'I will then, girl,' he said, giving her a quick hug. He was, in Phyllis Ryan's words, 'over the moon' with the success of his play. He made no secret of the fact that he considered it the best production to date of any of his works.

The Gate run coincided with a visit to the Olympia Theatre of the Southern Theatre Group with *The Highest House on the Mountain*, which from opening night attracted almost full houses. One evening newspaper carried a story headlined, 'TWO KEANE PLAYS VIE FOR PATRONS'. It wasn't true, for both productions were making the box office tick over. A note of acrimony was introduced, however, when someone suggested that the Cork group had deliberately come to Dublin to 'challenge Gemini Productions'.

On hearing the rumours, James N. Healy called a press conference and told journalists, 'We have not come here to challenge anybody or to prove that we are better or worse than anybody else. It is not a deliberate clash of dates. This is our seventh visit to Dublin, on our usual date, and we come because the Dublin theatrical public have always shown by their great support on our previous visits that they are anxious to see us.'

Healy, like Dan Donovan, the director of *The Highest House on the Mountain*, admitted that a note of rivalry had been introduced between his company and Dublin companies – and perhaps a note of envy, too, because Healy's company was prepared to take a gamble by bringing productions to the biggest theatres. But he was anxious to play down any such rivalry. As he said, 'There's room in Dublin for us all.' Keane kept out of the controversy; he was happy enough to see two of his plays filling theatres. Nor did Phyllis Ryan comment on Healy's remarks.

Keane left Dublin by train without giving any hint about the new play he had written. 'I dared not say a word about it,' he would say later. 'I had not decided what to do with it, even if I wanted to see it staged.' All he knew was that his wife, Mary, would likely have a say about its eventual destination.

16

Maurice Moore's Murder

Three years after an unsolved murder in Reamore, a townland seven miles from Tralee, Keane began work on a play which he decided to call *The Field by the River*. It wasn't a decision he arrived at easily; basing his play on an actual murder could be risky, and for that reason alone, Mary Keane did not share her husband's enthusiasm for the subject.

The murder of Maurice (Mossie) Moore had become one of the biggest talking points in County Kerry, with the finger of suspicion pointing strongly at Moore's neighbour Dan Foley. Moore's body was found in a drain on 15 November 1958; the drain ran between his home and Foley's. It later transpired that Moore had been strangled. He had been missing for ten days.

The removal of the body on the following day, Sunday, was attended by hundreds of people from the locality, and that night a wake was held in the house of the deceased – without the body, which had been removed to a Tralee hospital. The wake was in the traditional Kerry style, with people free to roam through the entire house. When detectives arrived on the Monday to dust the house for fingerprints, a local wag remarked, 'The whole place could have been found guilty.'

Moore, a bachelor farmer of forty-five years, had spent some time in Australia as a sheep farmer and returned home to settle in Reamore. He was reputed to be fairly well off. Could robbery then have been the motive? A few people thought it possible, for Mossie Moore, as he was affectionately known, was said to have cash in the house, and a tinkerman had been seen in the area. The general consensus, however, was that Dan Foley had committed the crime; the gardaí were of the same view.

Photographer Pádraig Kennelly claims today that Dan Foley was an innocent man and that the person who Kennelly says was the 'real culprit' was not arrested because of a botched police investigation. Accompanied by a local man, Kennelly had visited Foley's house shortly after the discovery of Mossie Moore's body in the drain.

'On that occasion, we spent two hours in the house, passing a cordon of gardaí, who stood silently outside it,' Kennelly recalled. 'It was the first of many months of daily visits, as I was assigned to the case by various media clients, who all paid me to be there when Dan Foley would be taken out in handcuffs. I became convinced of his innocence and was satisfied that his reaction – "Let them go into court and swear their perjury" – was what many independent-minded Kerrymen would have said in the circumstances. In my belief, the gardaí were too quick in accepting the boundary dispute as the cause of the murder.'

Keane read the reports of the murder in the *Kerryman*. Not long after the discovery of Maurice Moore's body, he drove to the scene, accompanied by Michael Wale, a *Daily Express* journalist based in Dublin. 'There were hundreds of sightseers and a strong garda presence,' Keane remembered. 'I put myself in the shoes of the accused in that bleak landscape, which had never hosted so many people before. Dan Foley had become notorious, and Reamore had become a household name.'

In his estimation, it was no different from any other murder over land, water-rights or passage, except that the people of the area themselves were gentle and neighbourly. As far as he could ascertain, everybody in the locality subscribed to the view that Foley was the man. It could not have been anybody else. There was bad blood, and Foley had an uncontrollable temper. Keane came away from Reamore convinced that Foley had committed the crime.

Furthermore, in his opinion, no outsider could have hidden the body where it was found. He says that the murderer was never brought to justice not because of flawed police work but because the gardaí in question were outsiders, and little information was forthcoming from the people. Pádraig

Kennelly, who today runs the weekly paper *Kerry's Eye*, recalled that the people of Reamore were cooperative with the gardaí and at the time some of them 'sang like canaries' to the police, the press and the public. According to Keane, Pádraig Kennelly 'is entitled to his view, but nobody else shares it.'

A year later, in 1959, the Bishop of Kerry, Dr Moynihan, appealed for information to solve the murder. The bishop proceeded to make certain crimes connected with disputes about land reserved sins in the parishes of Ballymacelliot and Tralee. Only the bishop or his vicar-general could give absolution for these crimes.

'This was a frightening development,' said Tim Danaher, the broadcaster from Listowel. 'It was the kind of extreme action that struck fear into the people of these parishes.'

For Keane, it heightened the drama. As he said later, 'The drama was there for a stage play and I wanted to avail of it.' In spite of Mary's misgivings, he went ahead, but in this case he kept the idea to himself.

In theatrical terms, he saw the theme as bigger than the Maurice Moore murder, though *The Field by the River* would be based largely on it. On another level, it was a man's obsession with land and the ruthless lengths to which he will go in order to retain that land. Its central character would be the Bull McCabe; Keane had no doubt that, at least in County Kerry, he would be identified with Dan Foley.

From time to time, he left aside the writing of the play so as to complete his other work; however, by 1962 the play was completed. He had a habit of showing play scripts to his brother Denis, whose opinions he respected, but on this occasion he did not do so. Meanwhile, the very mention of the Bull McCabe appeared to strike dread into his wife, Mary.

'I was still very apprehensive about the play,' Mary admitted. 'I asked John to put the script away for a year – and he did. I think I was afraid of threats and reprisals. Running a business like ours left us vulnerable, and of course we had a young family to consider.'

John B. was not assailed by the same fears. He was determined that one day *The Field by the River* would be staged.

As he said, 'I knew I had written two great characters in the Bull and the Bird O'Donnell, and the theme itself never left my mind. I reckoned it was the most powerful theme I had tackled.'

Foley continued to protest his innocence as local people talked, sometimes in hushed tones, about the 'Reamore murder'. He had become an isolated and lonely figure until his death in the early 1960s. 'Privately,' said one Kerry farmer, 'I think he suffered terribly.'

In early 1965, Keane took the script out of his desk and posted it to James N. Healy. It seemed the kind of racy drama that was tailor-made for the Southern Theatre Group. Healy thought that it still needed a lot of reshaping, but he agreed with his directors to have a reading of the work. Flor Dullea remembered the occasion. 'I was cast as Tadhg, the Bull's son,' he said, 'and James N. Healy read the Bull's part. It was a subdued reading and later we were told the play would not be going into rehearsal. Candidly, I was surprised, for I considered the plot strong and the dialogue as good as anything John B. had written. We had been accustomed to getting scripts from him that needed a lot of revision and rewriting, so I suspected that James N. had returned *The Field by the River* for rewrites.'

Healy confirmed that he sent back the play to Keane for revision. 'I told him we were still interested in staging it at perhaps a later time of the year,' he recalled, 'but I never heard any more from him about it.' When he was contacted by a *Cork Examiner* reporter as to why the Southern Theatre Group had turned down Keane's play, he said it needed 'a lot of rewriting'. There was surprise in theatrical circles, for the company had staged Keane plays for six consecutive years and the theatregoing Cork public were expecting another première in the summer of 1965.

The *Examiner* described the decision as 'curious' and a 'severe rebuff' for the Listowel playwright. Keane made no comment, though he was surprised by the lukewarm response to what he felt was a good play. He put it back in his desk and carried on with his other work. One day when Fr Kieran O'Shea visited the house, however, he gave him the play to read. The priest said he could see no reason why it shouldn't be staged. It was, in his opinion, theatrically exciting, and he was fascinated by the character of the Bull.

Brendan Kennelly, the young poet from Ballylongford, usually called at the Keane public house on his way home from Dublin, and he and John B. liked to chat over drinks. It was customary for him to enquire about the playwright's current work, and it was during one of these conversations that Keane mentioned *The Field by the River*, and that he had finished writing it. 'I'll read it,' Kennelly said. As he read it, he became totally absorbed. 'You have a great play there, John,' he enthused afterwards. He had known John B. had been writing it, but it was his first time to read the manuscript.

*

Back in Dublin, Kennelly reflected on the play's theme and the character of Bull McCabe. He had made up his mind that he would try to interest some theatre company in it. One afternoon, as he stood outside Trinity College, where he was professor of English, he met Phyllis Ryan and almost immediately broached with her the subject of *The Field by the River*. He must have sounded enthusiastic, for she wanted to hear more. 'Get John B. to give you the Bull,' was how he put it.

'I knew that Brendan was a great friend of John B.'s,' said Phyllis, 'and I sensed he was very serious about the play. He seemed aware of some kind of buried treasure down in Listowel among John B's discarded scripts. I assured him I would go to Listowel.'

She travelled with her close friend, journalist Liam Mac Gabhann, and they were greeted in the Greyhound Bar by the playwright and his wife, Mary. 'We're come to look at the Bull!' said Ryan. John B. laughed. 'He's in the field, but he's not for sale!' he replied.

Over drinks, they discussed the play, and before Ryan left the public house, Keane had promised to post her the manuscript. Eventually, when she had read it, she would say that the power and beauty of the play blazed from the pages. She recognised it as a great piece of writing. It was frightening, too, in its truth, since John B. had told her the full story of the murder of Maurice Moore. She appreciated the risks involved in staging a work that, to a large degree, depicted a murder where the killer was known to almost everyone but was seemingly safe from the law, because if murder was a crime in Kerry, informing was a worse one.

She began to share Mary Keane's apprehensions about staging the play, but John B.'s determination was such that she was left with no option but to go ahead. Casting Bull McCabe was her main problem. She agreed with Barry Cassin that the Bull was a towering, multi-dimensional character. He must not be portrayed as merely an ignorant and brutal individual; he was both of these things, but he was also a man who understood that the earth and the grass of the fields were necessary for his survival and that of his descendants. The more she thought about the part, the more convinced she became that Ray McAnally was the actor she wanted.

McAnally had recently returned from London, where he had been starring in a West End production of *Who's Afraid of Virginia Woolf?* He confided in her that he had had a bad time and had discovered he didn't want to drink any more. 'I want to rest from everything,' he said. Ray's wife, Ronnie Masterson, admitted that he was going through a serious situation in his personal life: he had been drinking again, he hated long runs in the theatre, and he was unhappy. He loved home and had missed it greatly while he was in London.

Phyllis Ryan knew that Ronnie Masterson had a habit of passing along scripts to Ray, and this was the hunch she played to try to get him. Having read her own part, Maimie Flanagan, which she was attracted to because Maimie is the only woman in the play capable of standing up to the Bull, she gave the script to Ray. Not long afterwards, he began to enthuse about it, especially the part of the Bull. The next day, he telephoned Phyllis Ryan. 'I'll play the Bull,' he told her. He could not disguise his enthusiasm. She told him that she had no one else in mind, and the part was his.

Barry Cassin regarded Ray McAnally as the perfect choice for the part. He was by now a major actor and had achieved international acclaim. 'I was a personal friend of Ray's,' Cassin said, 'and when things went smoothly, there was no one easier to work with. But when he had problems, either with himself or the script, it could be difficult. It is the same in my experience with anyone who has a major talent.'

Cassin drove to McAnally's home to talk to him about the play. He admitted that he went there with some trepidation. What if the great man didn't see the play entirely his way? He himself saw Bull McCabe as a man of immense power, a menacing figure capable of inflicting injury, yet in the play he doesn't intend to kill the stranger who wants the field in question, and this is seen in his words, 'The grass won't be green over his grave when he'll be forgot by all . . . forgot by all except me!'

After a brief discussion, Cassin and McAnally found themselves in full agreement about their approach to the character of the Bull. The actor accepted the director's point that the Bull has sensibilities and that what Keane was really trying to get across was the man's fight for survival on a four-acre field by the river. This is made clear in the play in Bull's reaction when he is told that after the field is sold, it will be covered in concrete blocks:

Bull	What about the grass? What about my lovely heifers?
Tadhg	No more meadows nor hay?
Bull	No foreign cock with hair-oil and a tiepin is goin' to do me out of my rights. I've had the field for five years. It's my only passage of water. You're tackling a crowd now that could do for you, man. Watch out for yourself.

Keane was especially pleased that his brother Eamonn was playing the Bird O'Donnell, a local schemer who has an ear for gossip and a taste for whiskey. The playwright had no intention of attending rehearsals, having decided to let Barry Cassin get on with them. The director changed the title to *The Field* and cast himself as the bishop who appeals from the pulpit to the congregation to break their silence and cooperate with the gardaí in the murder investigation. In this scene, he was directed by Ray McAnally. 'Ray was a first-rate director,' Cassin recalled. 'He probed every facet of the character.'

Phyllis Ryan attended a few rehearsals and could not help noticing how McAnally developed the part of the Bull McCabe. 'Every time I saw him rehearse, he had grown in stature,' she recalled. 'He had this amazing ability to get inside a part and eventually live it. Even at this stage, it looked a towering performance.'

Gerry Sullivan, cast as Sergeant Leahy, thought that Barry Cassin had a real feeling for the play but allowed the actors enough leeway to develop their own parts. Robert Carlile, as the Bull's son, Tadhg, found that McAnally could get annoyed if he suspected he was being upstaged. Once, McAnally accused Carlile of upstaging him in Act I and did not speak to him for days. Eamonn Keane was amused. He had experienced much the same thing when he played Christy Mahon in *The Playboy of the Western World*: Siobhán McKenna had sent him 'little notes' warning him not to upstage her. Eamonn swore that he never did.

*

It promised to be a memorable first night on 1 November 1965. Hannah Keane, the playwright's mother, was in Dublin for her son Denis's graduation from University College Dublin and decided to attend the première at the Olympia Theatre. The Schusters, John and Peg, joined the large Keane party, though John B. did not leave his hotel until 7.30 PM.

Denis Keane remembers that there was a tremendous build-up and a buzz in the theatre long before curtain-up. On first nights, he tended to avoid John B. until the play was over. He reckoned his brother would be more pent up than usual on this night, for there had been talk of apprehension among the cast because the play was depicting an actual murder.

Ronnie Masterson confirmed that there was a vague fear of a possible backlash, and she remembered someone in the cast asking, 'D'you think there's going to be trouble?' In conversation with Keane a few weeks before, she had argued that anyone involved in that particular murder in Kerry would not come to the theatre, for fear of being recognised.

The playwright later admitted that he, like his wife Mary, was apprehensive. 'I got a phone call a few days before, when a male voice asked if I had heard about a recent bomb incident in Tralee, and if I was aware of what a bomb could do to my public house,' he recalled. 'There was a second call, but the caller hung up after making a threat to my family. I remember Mary was terrified. I think Phyllis Ryan was also concerned for fear of anything upsetting the opening night in Dublin. But she shared my determination to go ahead.'

He realised it was probably the biggest night of his theatrical career. With the excitement around him, coupled with the drinks he had taken to fortify his nerves, he wondered if he would really enjoy the occasion. He could not wait for the curtain-up. From the moment of McAnally's entrance, accompanied by his son, Tadhg, the performance caught fire. Wearing hobnailed boots, a heavy, belted overcoat over shabby brown trousers, and an angled hat on his head, he was every inch the Bull. He brought his stick so fiercely down on the bar counter that the Bird O'Donnell trembled before him – and again when he asks, 'How's the Bull?' and the Bull snapped. 'Who gave you the right to call me Bull, you pratey-snappin' son of a bitch?'

Barry Cassin watched Act I from a seat in the back of the stalls and could see that the audience was totally enthralled. 'There was this sense of excitement you don't always get in the theatre,' he recalled. He hurried backstage to get ready for his own scene: the bishop's pulpit speech. John B. joined Mary and some friends in the bar and listened to their words of praise. He preferred, however, to wait until the final curtain before expressing himself.

Eventually, when the curtain fell on Act II, the audience applauded rapturously and cries of 'Author! Author!' echoed through the auditorium. Not since the first night some years before of Brian Friel's *Philadelphia Here I Come* at the Gaiety Theatre had a new play received such an ecstatic reception from a Dublin audience. Looking somewhat tired from all the excitement, John B. accepted the congratulations and handshakes, but privately made up his mind to see the production again on a more normal night.

Later he would remark, 'Ray McAnally brought the cow-dung to the part of the Bull, and he looked like a man who smelt of dung.' He could not disguise his admiration for Eamonn Keane's performance. Phyllis Ryan thought the impact of the play on the audience was enormous.

In the foyer of the Olympia, Brendan Kennelly had told her, 'I'll never forget this night in the theatre.' She gave much of the credit for the success of the production to Barry Cassin's direction. As she said, 'Barry has a kind of magic with Keane.' Denis Keane was overwhelmed by the performance but refused to single out individual actors. He preferred to say, 'The whole cast was great.' Mary Keane did not entirely enjoy the evening; the very look of the Bull McCabe filled her with dismay. Hannah Keane hugged John B. and looked immensely proud of her son. But as always, it was Eamonn she noted most of all on stage. 'My mother could not keep her eyes off Eamonn,' said Denis Keane. 'She always called him the actor in the Keane family. In fairness to him, he gave a wonderful performance as the Bird O'Donnell.'

Ronnie Masterson described the excitement of the occasion as 'unbelievable'. She saw what success as the Bull McCabe meant to Ray, although in a funny way he was an actor who almost preferred rehearsals to first nights. He tended to say to himself, 'That's it. I've done it now.' Gerry Sullivan contended that *The Field* was an important breakthrough for Keane. He had arrived and had created in the Bull McCabe a theatrical giant. In Barry Cassin's view, McAnally had got a part worthy of his talent.

The Schusters hosted the first-night party in their home. It continued until the small hours. Later John B. would read the newspaper critics. It was one occasion when he was not to be disappointed. The cast, including Ray McAnally, came in for lavish praise.

Contrary to their earlier fears, when they returned to Listowel, the Keanes experienced no trouble about the production. In Cork, James N. Healy made no secret of his regret about not having accepted the play when it was first offered to the Southern Theatre Group. 'It was a mistake,' he said.

17

A Walk in the Country

When he first met Captain Seán Feehan of the Mercier Press, it was, on Keane's admission, a case of instant friendship. They had negotiated a deal in Cork whereby Mercier would publish his plays and books.

Keane was conscious of a new influence in his life, and although opposed politically, the two men shared at the time a disillusionment with Irish politics that came close to cynicism. They had other things in common, like a love of the countryside, lively conversation and good wine; and more important, a sense of humour that bordered on the ribald.

'I regarded Seán Feehan as a true Tipperary man, though I saw him as half a Corkman, and in essence a Kerryman,' Keane said whimsically. 'We hit it off from the start. We were kindred spirits – gamblers, you might say, in the literary sense, men who wanted to live life to the utmost.'

Feehan, who was born in County Tipperary in 1916, was a strong and vital person. He had started the Mercier Press at the age of twenty-eight with one book and capital of £90. In 1950, he left the Irish army, in which he had been an officer, to devote himself full-time to the job. Deep in his heart he felt that army life was not the one destined for him. Working from one small room and with miserable finances, he quickly developed Mercier into a leading Irish publishing company. The first book he published, *The Music of Life*, was to become a best-seller.

He was particularly interested in the relationship between the publisher and the author and accepted it could be a delicate one, though he saw no reason why it should be antagonistic. He believed it should be based on friendship and respect. Feehan practised what he preached. His authors, including

Keane, found him friendly, inspiring and down-to-earth. 'I loved the man,' said James N. Healy. 'He was knowledgeable and a great character and knew what readers wanted.'

When Mercier set up a recording company, Feehan asked Healy to be the producer. It was planned to make an LP of Keane's *Self-Portrait*, with the author doing the reading. Keane was enthusiastic, and travelled to Cork. Together with Feehan and Healy, he went to a small recording studio in the South Terrace, where he proceeded to read from the pages of his book. The LP would be marketed in Ireland and America. John B. found the publisher full of ideas for books and LPs; he was eager to encourage his authors and to discover new talent.

'Seán was a constant inspiration to me,' Keane recalled years later. 'He had a lot to teach me, and was a great mentor. At the time, he had studied a good deal about publishing, which he said he hoped to put into a book. He was very nationalistic; I was the opposite, as I believed that nationalism can be divisive instead of a healing process. He was also strongly republican; I was sort of left of Fine Gael. But as a raconteur he had few equals, and in spite of business pressures was the eternal optimist.'

One day, over a meal in a County Kerry hotel, Feehan, he remembered, waxed enthusiastic about a series of books which he wanted based on letters to parish priests, farmers, politicians and bachelors. Both of them accepted that the letter was the simplest and most permanent form of communication, but it was also fraught with risks, and men had incriminated themselves by committing their views to paper in the form of a letter. Feehan saw the selling potential of such a series of books, and before they rose from the table, he had convinced John B. to think the matter over.

It was soon agreed that the first book should be called *Letters of a Successful TD*. The idea appealed to Keane. He had grown up in an atmosphere where people sought jobs and other favours from their local TD. It was even conceded that a good Leaving Certificate was of little use without some extra push from your TD. It was the 'done thing'. For his part, Feehan visualised an endless flow of books of letters, in spite of the fact that Keane was a very busy playwright.

Eventually, Keane based the book on a TD called Tull MacAdoo who spends much of his time writing to his student son, Mick, who never ceases to remind his father that 'he is up to his eyes in study but needs £10 by return of post for new textbooks.' When he got started, Keane began to enjoy writing the pages of fictional letters.

'Mick MacAdoo is a stock university student who wants money for booze and fornication,' he explained. 'But he happened to fulfil his father's wishes by going to the university. I knew a few such students in my day.' From time to time, he had friendly arguments with his publisher about the bawdiness of some of the letters.

'We weren't above exchanging abuse on the matter, yet we remained total friends,' Keane recalled. 'He let me get on with the writing.' On another occasion, Feehan suggested a book of letters to a Reverend Mother; he reckoned it could be a very funny book and probably a little irreverent. Keane was inclined to agree, since he was aware of the important place such a nun held in the community. She was expected not only to run her convent but to find jobs for girls as well.

When he broached the subject with his sister, Kathleen, who was a Reverend Mother in a Presentation Convent in County Kerry, she was appalled. 'If you persist with that idea, I'll leave the convent,' she warned him. He realised that his sister meant every word. Feehan, as usual, was disappointed; he never liked any of his 'good ideas' to go to waste. He even hinted that maybe in the future the subject could be tackled. Instead, he suggested a book of *Letters of a Love-Hungry Farmer*.

Keane knew this had originated from another of Feehan's ideas for a book entitled *Sexual Instruction for Small Farmers*. 'I told him I found the idea ribald and amusing but could not understand why he wanted to confine the sexual instruction to small farmers,' Keane recalled. 'Didn't big farmers also need such instruction? At times, Seán had this unusual imagination. He wanted this particular book to have a lurid cover and nothing but empty pages inside. As an overworked writer, I told him I was all for it!'

After a drive or a walk in the country, they would adjourn for a meal to convivial surroundings, where the publisher would proceed to peruse the wine list. To Keane, these were pleasant interludes, as were the sing-songs that sometimes followed around the piano in the lounge. 'Seán was a great man to buttress a drunken sing-song. I can see him now, standing in the lounge, a gin and tonic in his hand as he crushes the ice in his mouth, and then raising his glass, as though to toast all and sundry, exclaiming at the same time, "Is anybody going to fill this for me?"'

Together they retraced the paths of the Munster poets, recited poetry, or talked endlessly about ideas for more avant-garde books. He regarded Feehan as great company and felt that their friendship sprang from the fact that both of their fathers were schoolteachers. Feehan introduced him to other Mercier Press authors, invited him to literary dinners and talked of the paperback as perhaps the most popular book of the future.

'Seán never lost sight of publishing,' Keane recalled. 'On one occasion, he suggested I write a book containing letters to a prime minister. I think he was disappointed when I explained I had no knowledge of how a prime minister lived and worked. I suggested instead we confine it to the letters of an Irish minister of state. He nodded his agreement.'

Feehan treated his authors well, and at a time when other Irish publishers were reluctant to pay advance royalties, he was prepared to do so. 'He was a generous man,' John B. reflected. 'He paid up when money was due, and he was not above asking about one's wife and children. It was proving a fruitful friendship, although I was too caught up with plays to write the novels Seán wanted me to write.'

In Listowel, Keane continued to divide his time between writing, serving the odd pint and watching his sons grow up. He wondered which of them would play football for Kerry. 'John is the athletic one,' he'd remark, as he carried him shoulder-high into the bar. Having written a poem, he sometimes passed it over to Mary without a word. Usually she told him candidly what she thought of it. 'They were happy times,' he would say later, and Mary would add, 'The happiest times were when the children were growing up.'

After a particularly intense spell of writing, he might drop a line to the Honans – Tom and his wife Carmel in Arklow –

and tell them he was on the way up for a day or two. They were close friends; the Honans were producing his plays successfully at amateur festivals. Carmel remembers the playwright going off on walks through the countryside. Later, all three of them would saunter into the Royal Hotel in Arklow for refreshments.

On his way home, John B. would arrange a meeting in Dublin with Phyllis Ryan or another theatrical friend. Phyllis enquired how his play for Anna Manahan was coming along. 'Fine, girl,' was his reply. But at the time, he was more concerned about his new musical.

*

In April of that year, 1966, when he was expected to be in Dublin for the presentation of his new musical, *The Roses of Tralee*, Keane had stayed at home. John B., the actor, was playing the barman in a local production of Sean O'Casey's *The Plough and the Stars*, directed by his friend Danny Hannon, who ran his own building firm. Hannon recalled that the playwright was a diligent actor and played the part in a convincing Dublin accent. He had no trouble with lines or stage directions. He would later direct him in Arthur Miller's *The Crucible*, where he changed to an American accent to portray the judge in the play.

'I enjoyed the occasional chance to act,' said Keane. 'I found it a change from the writing. I was always anxious to help out the locals where drama was concerned.' Danny Hannon considered him 'a respectable amateur actor', and his name on a local bill always attracted people to the theatre.

It would be one of the rare occasions when Keane would miss out a first night in Dublin of one of his plays. He had already attended the opening night in Cork, however, where he was pleased by the enthusiastic response. He liked it to be known that he had written the musical as a kind of light relief; he admitted that working on *The Field* had made heavy demands on him. For the musical, he teamed up with Cork-born musician Michael Casey, who was attached to the music department at RTÉ.

'John B. came to my house in Dublin to work on the score,' Casey recalled. 'It was a new experience for me and I found him very cooperative.' James N. Healy also assisted with the musical arrangements and thought that some of the music written for the show by Michael Casey was both catchy and tuneful. The whole thing was envisaged as a humorous send-up of the Rose of Tralee Festival.

For Keane, it was nevertheless an exciting new departure. After the success of *Many Young Men of Twenty*, which he was always careful to describe as a play with music, he had always wanted to get around to a full-scale musical. He liked to call himself a songwriter by instinct. Apart from the old ballad 'The Rose of Tralee', there were twenty-one original tunes, among the funniest being 'Won't You Come Under Me Shawl!'

On the opening night in the Opera House, Cork, there were a number of exceptional performances, such as Siobhán O'Brien as Anna Cascara, the Rose of Russia, and the trio of 'Shawlies', Peg O'Connell, Kay Healy and Maeve Delaney. Anne Brennan was given one of the most delightful songs in the show, 'One Night in Sweet Tralee'. As the festival organiser, James N. Healy was playing a part that in terms of acting was only a pale shadow of his Danger Mullaly in *Many Young Men of Twenty*.

Keane agreed that, because of the large cast the show required, there was little likelihood of *The Roses* being a commercial success on tour; he was satisfied with presentations in Cork, Dublin and Tralee. For its short run at the Gaiety Theatre, bookings were brisk. Manager Joe Kearns subscribed to the view that Keane's name on any theatre bill almost guaranteed a box-office success. Dublin newspapermen, more especially hard-pressed evening-paper columnists, were disappointed to learn that Keane would not be attending opening night. They considered him always good for a witty quote or a lively interview.

The *Irish Times* regarded the occasion as auspicious enough for them to dispatch their senior music critic, Charles Acton, to the Gaiety, where he said he found 'a light-hearted romance without any heavy-handedness. Many of the laughs were telegraphed well ahead yet made one laugh enjoyably when they came.' In his view, however, the real pleasure derived from the perfect diction. No word of any song or dialogue was lost – and that was a joy in itself. He advised 'a little cutting' in the second act, which was paced too slowly.

'A critic', Acton continued, 'approaches a performance hoping to enjoy himself. Experience has taught him to keep his fingers crossed before new musicals. It is all the more pleasurable to find one like this. It is unlikely to achieve lasting fame, but I would gladly pay to hear it.'

Des Rushe in the *Irish Independent* was more critical. 'A promising formula, but despite the promise it is disappointing and extremely lightweight work,' he wrote. 'There are some catchy tunes, mainly fitted to unexciting lyrics, but the greatest deficiency is in the writing. While there are some amusing patches of comedy, too often the humour is too forced and artificial. Rarely has it subtlety or bite. The piece does not get the zestful treatment it so obviously needs.'

Keane must have been highly amused by the *Evening Press*, which, because of a misunderstanding, dispatched two critics to the Gaiety; unsurprisingly the reviews varied. One was headlined, 'A REALLY PROFESSIONAL SHOW', the other, 'A PLATE OF NATIVE DRISHEEN?' In his review, Desmond MacAvock stated that Keane obviously had the talent to write a native *Oklahoma* if he only had patience over details. 'All these qualities and defects were to be seen last night in *The Roses of Tralee*,' MacAvock added. 'The slender scaffolding of plot is basically Cinderella at the Festival of the Roses in Tralee. Perhaps it is native "corn" – or should I say "drisheen" – no better and no worse than the imported variety so eagerly swallowed every day in cinema and TV and radio.'

On the same page in the *Evening Press*, Fanny Feehan stated in the course of her review, 'John B. Keane is essentially a kind-hearted man – too kind to be a really biting satirist. This show poked gentle fun at the Rose of Tralee Beauty Contest and at other targets. The audiences at times were not too quick at picking up his jibes; in fact, a good many gags went unnoticed – rather unusual for a Dublin audience, who have so many times ruined good plays by their untimely guffaws.'

She had made a valid point, and so it seemed did the *Herald* critic. 'One feels that the show's full potential has not been exploited,' he noted. 'Some of the lively full-company musical numbers could take more uninhibited zest and exuberance, and the third act, with the colourful Rose of Tralee background, could be a more eye-catching spectacular, with imaginative staging and decor. Quite a number of the songs have a hit potential, and one would have liked to hear some of them again.'

The show was again presented at the Opera House in Cork, and having played to some packed houses, it was hit by a heatwave. 'Business fell away,' recalled Dan Donovan, 'and the show was just too big to bring on tour.' But the group had the consolation of receiving a signal honour from the new owners of the Gaiety Theatre when they were asked to revive *Many Young Men of Twenty* for a week's run. Manager Joe Kearns was astounded. 'We turned people away every night,' he recalled. When he met Keane in the Gaiety bar, he told him his only regret was that he hadn't three more weeks of the show.

*

By now, John B. had become accustomed to Mary being in control of the pub. 'I have to pay for my own drinks at the bar,' he would joke to the characters sitting around. Mary was quick to quip, 'That's the price of his generosity with the cash!' At other times she would assert that if he had been a full-time barman, he'd be a millionaire, for the place was always full when he was there. As she said, 'He attracted writers and every kind of musician and songster, and matchmakers too. Everybody wanted him to sing and chat and be himself.'

The public house was regarded as cosy and homely. There was no lounge, and Mary Keane emphasised that her customers didn't want one. 'The local lads didn't want television either,' she said. 'Our regular customers voted unanimously against having a TV set installed. I suppose they wanted nothing to interfere with their conversation.'

Keane was inclined to say that he would never make a businessman. When the mood took him, he'd treat his drinking cronies in the bar to a round. After long hours of writing alone, he found that a chat and a drink relaxed him. He still wrote from midnight onwards, sitting by the fireside in the back kitchen of the bar, his imagination fired by a pint or two. Sometimes, he'd rise and go for a walk through the dark streets, returning later to complete his work.

From time to time, visiting journalists, poets and novelists dropped in to meet him, and he rarely refused to see any of them. 'I never go to Listowel without calling on John B.,' Pan Collins said. Others wanted to visit the birthplace of *Sive*. In spite of his busy writing schedule, the playwright walked a few miles every day to keep fit, he rarely missed a football game, and he even fitted in some fishing. In the back of his mind, though, was the play he had promised to write for Anna Manahan. It was, however, only one of his priorities.

18

THE LANGUAGE FRACAS

Anyone who knew him expressed no great surprise when Keane got involved with the Language Freedom Movement early in 1966. For years, he had spoken out on the language issue as part of his one-man crusade for a new Ireland where free choice would be paramount.

Yet he was to admit that to become involved in this movement was 'in a way suicidal'. He was up against the opposition of his friends. 'Being a Gaelic footballer and a speaker of Irish, some people could not understand why I should join the movement. They failed to understand that my motives were good and that I had nothing to gain from my involvement.'

His motive in joining, he explained, was to 'make a better Ireland for children'; the 'brutality and hostility' he was to encounter proved him right: 'These people were not even prepared to discuss the question. Anyway, I loved the language.'

To Danny Hannon, who was aware of Keane's feelings about the GAA ban on foreign games, divorce, book censorship and the Catholic Church, it seemed perfectly understandable that the playwright would be attracted to the Language Freedom Movement. As he said, 'John would now be speaking from a position of strength because he was a fluent speaker of Irish.'

The new organization, which was started by Christopher Morris, a Dublin architect, and supported by people like Paddy Browne, Frank Crummy, Maura Clarke, Richard Clear and Anne Morris, aimed to replace compulsory Irish classes in school with freedom of choice. In retrospect, Keane was to say, 'I probably went into the movement against my will. I went along with the LFM, not 100 per cent, but it was as near as I could get to my ideal.'

His ideal was a language that would flourish for its own sake, spoken by those who loved the language, not because 'they have been bribed to speak it, or because they see it as an advantage . . . People felt at the time that compulsory Irish was killing the language. I decided to join the movement because of my love for the language and because I thought that compulsory Irish was not fair.'

He studied the leaflets sent him by Christopher Morris, and the membership forms, though he was to admit that establishing a branch of the movement in Listowel was 'like introducing sheep into Texas cattle country'. Nonetheless, he was convinced that he could muster a majority of the townspeople behind the movement and could beat off the organised opposition. 'If anyone labels us *shoneen* or traitor, we'll take immediate legal action on our own initiative.'

Keane took the train to Dublin to meet Morris and found him to be 'a man of integrity and character'. The meeting spurred the playwright to arrange the first branch meeting in Listowel a few weeks later; he had already enlisted two more local solicitors, a doctor, two vets and two teachers. Listowel, he told Morris, would be 'a branch on which you can depend'.

Morris travelled to Listowel to address the meeting, after which 'a strong and representative committee' was elected. The LFM man said that Keane had made 'a powerful impression', and this may have helped the election of a committee which included a niece of Michael Collins and the nephew of a man who was executed by the Black and Tans. Danny Hannon was elected chairman, with Stewart Stack as treasurer and Keane as honorary secretary. 'We will hardly be called unpatriotic,' declared Keane. 'Not in Listowel, anyway.'

Hannon felt that the leadership qualities which the playwright possessed would be a useful asset in his new role. 'I think he was the driving force at this early stage,' Hannon recalled. But it was not to be plain sailing for the opponents of compulsory education in the Irish language. An inkling of the dangers ahead occurred one afternoon in August of that year when Keane was entertaining Christy Brown, the author of My Left Foot, in his bar.

A man sporting a gold *fáinne* entered the bar, accompanied by his wife and two Americans. At first he conversed with Keane in Irish, then finally, reverting to English, asked him if he was a member of the LFM.

'Yes,' replied Keane, 'and proud of it.'

'Then,' said the man with the *fáinne*, 'you should be ashamed of yourself.'

Amid murmurs of protest, Keane retorted, 'You have a neck to come into my house and tell me I should be ashamed of myself.'

The minority, Keane found, had grown 'quite vicious'.

'Some would like physical satisfaction if we gave them the slightest chance,' he wrote to Christopher Morris. But the LFM in Dublin had its own problems. Although the presence of Keane's name and that of Donegal writer Séamus Ó Grianna, known as 'Máire', among the membership of LFM had come as a shock to the movement's opponents, a meeting held in Jury's Hotel was broken up by Máirtín Ó Cadhain and Seán Ó hÉigeartaigh, whom Morris described as 'very aggressive, very unpleasant'. The meeting was abandoned. Morris called the opposition group, Misneach, 'a sort of commando operation'.

'We were prepared to discuss the role of the language in a free democracy, but our opponents were not,' says Martin Reynolds, an architect like Christopher Morris, who was in at the establishment of the LFM. The members had been branded anti-patriotic and anti-Irish in a national rather than a linguistic sense. With a fellow member, he represented the movement at a public meeting in Clonmel Town Hall.

'We were opposed down there by Labhras Ó Murchú and Dónall Ó Móráin,' Keane recalled, 'and it was another hectic, frantic meeting, with demonstrators, including senior boys from the Christian Brothers School, packed into the hall to shout us down. The boys had been told to go there without their uniforms.'

*

A public meeting was arranged for the Mansion House in Dublin towards the end of September. Keane promised to come to the meeting, and he did, with a number of friends and supporters from Listowel, including Ray McAuliffe and Damian Stack. Mary Keane wanted to travel with them, although she was expecting their fourth child, but John B. dissuaded her. Fearing trouble, his sister Peg got in touch with Tony Guerin, who was a friend and member of the Garda Síochána, and asked him to keep an eye on her brother.

Irish-language supporters and opponents of the Language Freedom Movement had mobilised their opposition, so that they outnumbered the LFM supporters by almost three to one. Dónall Ó Móráin, then chairman of Gael Linn, recalled, 'We thought we had rights to attend an open meeting and consequently a few of us decided we would ask our friends to attend. It was a meeting to which everyone was invited; it was not a closed meeting.'

Ó Móráin regarded himself and An tAthair Tomás Ó Fiaich as 'rather prominent' in the language movement at the time, along with An tAthair Colmán Ó Huallacháin, Seán Ó hÉigeartaigh and Risteárd Ó Glaisne. As far as Ó Móráin was concerned, the LFM's claim that it was not opposed to the Irish language was 'just a charade' and their very title was 'an emotive term to disestablish the language'. To him, the LFM was 'intent on removing the whole foundation of the policy of promoting the Irish language'. It was as simple as that. 'We knew that this was what they were up to,' said Ó Móráin, 'and we dealt with them accordingly.'

The method of the LFM opponents was 'to blow down the telephone line and tell people this was taking place and would they attend?' Ó Móráin reckons he did not make more than ten phone calls. But then those ten people might have made ten calls each, and so did certain other people, including Tomás Ó Fiaich. The network went into action very quickly once they realised the implications of what was happening.

The effect was that of a chain letter. Ó Móráin reckoned

some 1,200 people turned up at the Mansion House, about two-thirds of whom 'did not agree with the overall purpose of the meeting,' he recalled. But he would not have known even 5 per cent of them.

Another language supporter, Proinsias MacAonghusa, thought the LFM supporters were 'very small in number' but 'very noisy'. 'When it came to counting heads there weren't many of them,' he commented later.

Keane, who had become used to hugs and handshakes on big theatre nights, found a different atmosphere outside the Mansion House. As he entered the building with his friends, he was taunted and jeered. 'They were spitting and trying to aim blows at me,' he recalled. 'It was shameful. We came through the hall to boos and jeers, but we managed to get on the stage.'

Tony Guerin stood near the back of the hall. He could see that Keane was not going to be intimidated. He knew him to be fearless when principles were at stake, and tonight he looked more determined than usual. All around him, he sensed a threatening atmosphere. He had no doubt there was trouble brewing, and he felt anxious for Keane and the other LFM members on the platform.

Being a committee member, and an LFM speaker that evening, Martin Reynolds had arrived early at the Mansion House and was astonished to find such a large crowd milling outside the building. He hadn't been expecting anything spectacular, although they had received prior warning that 'a crowd called Misneach' intended to cause trouble. They had a reputation for being militant. At the time, the LFM had been receiving threats, and the committee members suspected that Misneach was to blame. They didn't know the people behind the organisation, and were only able to identify one person, but he had left more because of the organisation's methods than because of its ideology.

It was decided at this point to close the iron gate in front of the Mansion House in order to keep out the more hostile members of the crowd, as well as gatecrashers, but this action led to shouts of abuse from the crowd, who began to storm the gate; others tried to scale it. Reynolds could see that among those clamouring to get in were two clerics, An tAthair Colmán Ó Huallacháin and An tAthair Tomás Ó Fiaich. By now there was a large force of gardaí trying to control the crowd. 'We decided to reopen the gate to let in some more people,' says Reynolds, 'and they surged in; then the gate was closed again.'

In the Mansion House, meanwhile, the barrage of noise was such that the LFM people on the platform could not be heard. 'They refused to let us speak,' said Keane, who was the guest speaker. When he tried to speak, a man jumped on the stage and seized the tricolour, shouting that it should not be displayed at such a meeting. Showers of paper were flung on the stage, and a stink-bomb was set off in the hall. Keane recalled blows being exchanged and 'some fellow either drew a knife or a baton on me.'

Martin Reynolds had by now taken his seat beside the LFM members on the platform. He remembers small Union Jacks landing around him, and one of the speakers being shouted down. 'It was bedlam,' he said later. 'Words like "Judas!" and "Blueshirts!" were flung around and no attempt was made to have a dialogue between us and the people who opposed us. They seemed determined to suppress the meeting and not allow it to take place. The meeting was becoming violent and people were hit by objects thrown at the stage.'

At this point, Dónall Ó Móráin climbed onto the stage and pleaded repeatedly for silence. 'We must have a discussion here with all points of view represented,' he said. 'I don't care how anti-Irish any speaker on the platform is, I will defend his right to speak as long as other spokesmen for those who represent my viewpoint are allowed to express an opinion.'

Ó Móráin said later that he wanted all points of view to be heard, 'and I ensured that it happened.' He appealed for order and announced that he would call on certain people in the hall to speak. Christopher Morris took the microphone and told the meeting that as the LFM had organised and paid for the meeting, Ó Móráin should reassure LFM members that his, or other, organisations would provide a reciprocal programme for LFM speakers in the future.

Ó Móráin agreed with a handshake. The crowd applauded

loudly. Proinsias MacAonghusa, who was with An tAthair Tomás Ó Fiaich of Maynooth in the audience, recalled Ó Fiaich being 'cheered by his supporters' when he called for speakers who would support the language. Ó Fiaich, like Ó Móráin, went onto the platform. MacAonghusa recalled 'a great deal of shouting and heckling.'

An *Irish Times* report stated that An tAthair Ó Fiaich stood up from his seat in the auditorium and 'stretched his hand forward imploringly, supporting the demand, but could not be heard in the din.' Christopher Morris remembers only 'Ó Fiaich waving his hands.'

John B. Keane attempted a speech. 'Since the newcomers are so anxious to speak,' he said, 'I'll wait until they are finished.' But the booing intensified with derisive shouts of 'Speak Irish!', 'The Irish Red Guards are here!' and 'Blueshirts!' A large Union Jack was raised, as if at a given signal, and smaller Union Jacks waved 'in a confusing profusion,' Keane recalled.

After a word from the chairman, Keane went to the rostrum. Amidst the din, he looked composed. 'It is an unfortunate but accepted fact,' he said, 'that English is the spoken language of a majority of the people of this country. I suppose we should say that it is a deplorable fact.' Both jeers and boos punctuated his words as he said that, despite the evils of English rule imposed on Ireland, the English language had been an advantage to Irish emigrants. Although Irish had been the tongue of his ancestors, English was the spoken language of the present generation, its parents and grandparents. Then he apologised in Irish for his Kerry accent. It was due, he explained, 'to years of inferior teaching in two languages.'

In remarking on discrimination, he drew the attention of his listeners to a leaflet he had seen relating to the Sign of the Cross. It granted an indulgence of three hundred days in the English version, but in the Irish-language version it gave an indulgence of three years.

The opposition speakers took the rostrum. Seán Ó hÉigeartaigh said, 'If the motives of the Language Freedom Movement are pure, they have failed to make them clear,' adding, 'We are no petty people. We are no transient tribe. It is our duty and our privilege to preserve and hand on to the next generation the heritage of the Irish language. If the Irish language is lost today, it is lost forever. If the language is lost, the nation is lost.'

Christopher Morris tried to make himself heard above the din. The *Irish Times* reported, 'The planned and unplanned events which had turned it into an hour of volatile and, at times, turbulent cross-talk and barracking had left people prepared for almost anything.' The paper referred to the fact that the organisers of the meeting were 'hopelessly outnumbered'. An tAthair Ó Fiaich expressed the conviction from the rostrum that the founding of the LFM was the best thing that had happened to the Irish-language movement for a long time. He compared it to Edward Carson's action in arming the Ulster Volunteers, which had spurred the idea of Irish nationalism. The small, brown-clad figure of An tAthair Ó Huallacháin expressed the view that, 'Considering the emotions and the tensions, this has been a model meeting.' The two groups should pass a vote of thanks to each other, he said.

Martin Reynolds, who had acted as one of the LFM stewards, would certainly not have described it as 'a model meeting'. He remembered the occasion as 'frightening'. At one time, he said, there were fifty of their opponents on stage and it was the LFM stewards who decided to disconnect the amplification system. 'We were not prepared to let them take over the mike completely from us, so it was the only course left open to us,' he said. 'As far as I was concerned, it was confrontation on their part and at no stage were these people prepared to let the meeting continue.'

To Reynolds, it was sheer turmoil, and he was appalled to see LFM leaflets torn up on stage. He assumed they were all fanatics in the language-revival movement and, worse still, they were convinced that only they could be called patriots. 'I think they felt threatened, and saw the primary-school system in danger from teaching through English, and inevitably this brought out the fighter in them to defend their corners. For the revivalists, it was a turning point, for we had questioned the whole concept of nationality. We were denying that an ability to speak Irish was equivalent to being a patriot.'

By the time that the defenders of the Irish-language policy were making their contribution, Keane had left the platform amid the continuing hubbub. He recalled being 'brutally assaulted' when leaving the hall as he and Tony Guerin made their way from the stage through the back of the Mansion House.

'At least five fellows came at me and I got a terrible clout on the ear – an ear which has been affected ever since,' Keane recalled. 'I could see in the distance the guards and the garda superintendents. Blows were being exchanged fairly fast. At one point Tony was standing over me; at another stage I was standing over Tony. Our loyal friends were also being attacked, but we managed to get away. There were mobs going around the streets looking for our blood. I could have taken any of them single-handed – no bother. But I was a fearless man until I saw the power of a mob. Without Tony Guerin's assistance, I don't think I would have come out alive.'

They crossed the Liffey towards the Ormond Hotel and took refuge in a fish-and-chip shop. The couple who ran the shop allowed them to make their way to the back of the shop. In the confusion, Keane had lost sight of some of his friends; he wondered how they were faring.

Dónall Ó Móráin insisted that Keane had not been threatened within the confines of the Mansion House. 'We had no ambitions to be involved in skirmishings of any kind whatsoever,' he recalled, 'and certainly not at the back of the Mansion House. I totally reject any suggestion that he was threatened within the hall. What happened at the back door I don't know anything about. I was trying to ensure that Seán Ó hÉigeartaigh and a couple more people would be allowed to speak. Physically, I got support for that, and he may have felt he was threatened. If I were in his position, I must say I would have stood my ground firmly. I would have had no compromise naturally if I had been in his shoes, because the whole meeting would have been against me.'

Keane saw it differently. 'It was a terrible night, as well as a terrifying night,' he said later. 'The mob had gone berserk. They were being spurred on. I couldn't believe that so-called civilised men could react like this, or that such behaviour could be countenanced.' He saw them as men who were trying to make enemies where enemies did not exist. 'They were the men who had missed the real revolutions,' he said, 'and they are the worst enemies of Ireland.'

Gay Byrne called Keane to invite him on to *The Late Late Show* that Saturday night, but the playwright could not return to Dublin. In the interests of fair play, Keane recalled, 'Byrne chaired another meeting of the LFM in the Olympia Theatre. Several hundred of our people were there to act as stewards, but the other side never showed up. The gardaí were ready for trouble that night, and so were we.'

A meeting arranged for the City Hall in Cork was circumvented by the actions of Proinsias MacAonghusa. 'I checked with Dublin Castle and discovered that they hadn't registered the name of the Language Freedom Movement,' he recalled. 'So I registered the name with another chap. Then I wrote to Seán Casey, who was then the Lord Mayor of Cork, and told him, "These people are using our name." So no meeting was held in Cork.' Keane claimed the meeting was called off because of a bomb scare.

Those who had outnumbered the LFM supporters at the Mansion House meeting did so, according to Dónall Ó Móráin, 'not by any urging at all from the likes of myself. They decided they would vent their spleen, or emotions – call it what you will – at a public meeting to which they were invited.' For him, 'The battle was fought and won on 22 September 1966.'

He believed that the LFM organisers lacked educational substance and that 'the likes of John B. Keane were dragged in for emotional reasons.' But 'they had no educational base and hence, I think, they collapsed.'

Christopher Morris, who claimed he did not 'want to milk' either John B. Keane or Gay Byrne, saw it differently. 'LFM was the first of the liberal movements in Ireland,' he said. 'It started to melt the ice.' He also believed that some of the *Gaeilgeoirí* were aware that Sinn Féin was organising opposition that night at the Mansion House. 'They didn't want to be associated with Sinn Féin and I was asked by one *Gaeilgeoir* to hold the meeting,' he recalled.

Looking back, Keane expressed his astonishment at his fellow Irishmen for their 'appalling behaviour. It was cruel, it was cowardly, it was totally intolerant.' In his view, the LFM achieved its purpose by drawing the attention of the country to an injustice. 'We also felt that the Irish language was in the wrong hands,' he said.

He was to face intimidation in his pub because of his involvement. 'Parties of four or five fellows would come into the pub looking for trouble,' he recalled. 'But I always faced up to them by stepping outside the counter and telling them, "Anything you have come here for, I'm prepared to give it to you!"'

The Fine Gael coalition was to change the policy towards the Irish language, giving the language equal treatment with English. The LFM lasted for three years. But in the end, in Christopher Morris's contention, the movement won out. Dónall Ó Móráin accepted that 'they got a lot of publicity at the time, and it suited certain political parties.'

For Keane, however, the memory was to linger. 'That night in the Mansion House I encountered a particular brand of Irish cowardice I never want to see again,' he noted. Nevertheless, he had no regrets. 'I would do it again,' he said.

19

Big Maggie Polpin

For the Keanes, it was to be an eventful opening to 1967. On January 28, Mary Keane gave birth to a baby girl who would be christened Joanne. After three boys in a row, both John B. and his wife were elated. The latest arrival made the playwright ever more conscious of his family commitments, and in spite of the success of *The Field*, he would still have to rely on the public house in William Street to subsidise his writings and the children's education.

The next eighteen months would see him complete a new play, *The Rain at the End of the Summer*, for the Southern Theatre Group and start work on *Big Maggie* in order to fulfil his promise to Anna Manahan. By now, John B. felt comfortable writing about women. 'There'll be a bit of my mother in Maggie,' he revealed, 'and a bit of Mary, too – the nice little bits. Mary has developed a nice jaundiced sense of humour working in the bar, and you'll find this in Maggie Polpin.'

Eventually, Denis Keane read the script and said he was captivated. Maggie reminded him of a woman in Listowel who treated her children in the same unyielding manner. As a mother, she was overprotective and perhaps even puritanical. To John B., Maggie was as real as any woman walking the street – a mixture of many Irish women who grew up in hard times. They were great women and he had been influenced by them. Phyllis Ryan felt privileged to be given the play to stage and saw immediately that Keane had written his finest female character, a woman in the Mena Glavin mould.

Big Maggie opens in a cemetery, where Maggie, accompanied by her children, has come to bury her husband. 'The opening scene has to be hard,' Keane said, 'because Maggie is

189

looking back on a tough existence with a useless husband, and she is now left to rear her children. In the second act, there is some light relief, and I think this balances the play.'

Barry Cassin, who would direct the work for Gemini Productions, was impressed by the bigness of Maggie's character, yet he thought she must be attractive to look at if she was to be convincing in the seduction scene with the commercial traveller.

Keane had written the play for Anna Manahan and naturally was disappointed when he learned she was unable to join the cast. At the time, the actress was appearing on Broadway in Brian Friel's *Lovers* and, in the hope that she would be free, Phyllis Ryan had delayed the première. Eventually the part went to Marie Kean, the experienced Abbey actress.

Rehearsals were not long in progress when it became abundantly clear that she was ideal for the role. 'Marie was getting right inside the character,' recalled Phyllis Ryan. 'I was spellbound by her opening scene in the graveyard.'

Gerry Sullivan was cast as the commercial traveller, and says when he first read the play he got 'loads of laughs', but that when he conveyed this to Barry Cassin, he was told the play wasn't supposed to be funny. Shortly after rehearsals had begun, he told the director there were scenes he couldn't play because they lacked credibility, or were naive, and in his view would confuse an audience. The script was 'worked on' and the problems solved. The idea of the commercial traveller chasing Maggie's daughter, while at the same time getting a pass from Maggie herself, had, he agreed, a comic fascination for an audience.

The play would open on 28 January 1969 at the Opera House in Cork. 'It was my idea,' says Phyllis Ryan. 'I thought it was about time we had a first night outside of Dublin.' Keane arrived in Cork in exuberant mood and in the late afternoon enjoyed a few drinks to steady his nerves, as he said. On his own admission, the play meant a great deal to him, and he was satisfied with the cast, which included not only Marie Kean, but Archie Sullivan, Brenda Fricker and Dearbhla Molloy.

It was to prove to be one of Cork's most successful theatrical nights. The audience acclaimed the cast and were not satisfied until Keane made a curtain speech. As ever, this speech was brief and to the point: he thanked the cast and Gemini Productions for 'giving everything' to the play. In later years he would say, 'It was one of my most memorable first nights.'

Gerry Sullivan felt that the playwright might have slightly misjudged the mood of the play. 'I got the impression that John B. regarded it as a serious commentary on aspects of Irish life, especially marriage,' Sullivan recalled. 'But the Cork audience loved the pathos in the play as well as the comic bits. I was inclined to see it as a tragicomedy with moral undertones.'

Afterwards, Keane invited the cast to a friend's public house, where a party atmosphere soon developed. Gerry Sullivan was amused by the playwright's friends from Listowel. 'I'd be talking to one fellow and he'd tell me he drove John B. to Cork that day. A few minutes later another man would tell me the same thing. Everyone in the bar seemed to have been his chauffeur.' Keane did not drive at the time and usually hired taxis. 'He was spending a small fortune on them,' says Mary Keane. 'I used to tell him that it had to stop. "You'll have to take driving lessons," I told him.'

She made no secret of her love for *The Year of the Hiker* but she found it hard to warm to *Big Maggie*. 'I suppose I saw something of myself in her, as I can be determined and overprotective towards my children, so I didn't like to see it paraded on stage. I know that Maggie has to be hard because she has been left with children to rear, yet I found the hardness difficult to accept.'

Phyllis Ryan regarded the first night as tremendously exciting and the Cork audience's response as overwhelming. She tried to analyse the play's success and put it down to the fact that almost every member of the audience had a Big Maggie, either as a mother, or as an aunt or cousin, so they identified with her, and the character struck a chord.

The critic from the *Cork Examiner* commented: 'Big Maggie is a character which one will admire and hate. And make no mistake about it, the situations which are presented, and the words which are used, are strong. But it must be said that

Keane has with tremendous honesty enquired into how an older generation and a younger can hope to live on a limited holding and even how we can expect to discard some of our most revered shibboleths and replace them with pragmatic valuations.'

Following two highly successful weeks at the Opera House, the production moved to Limerick, where it again packed the City Theatre. 'We did phenomenal business,' recalls Phyllis Ryan, 'and by the time we opened at the Olympia Theatre, word had preceded us, so the advance booking was tremendous. We were scheduled to play five weeks, but Marie Kean could only do four. We got Joan O'Hara for the fifth week, and she played the role in a different manner to Marie and was outstanding. For the Belfast première, we had Doreen Hepburn, and though small, she enjoyed real success in the part.'

Eventually, Ronnie Masterson played the role in Dublin. She saw Big Maggie as a very caring mother with lots of humanity in her character. Ronnie thought this was a facet of Maggie that hadn't been highlighted enough, and the truth emerges when one of her children says to her, 'You're hard', to which Maggie replies, 'It's the hardness of concern.'

'I love the role,' Masterson said, 'and I think I achieved a certain understanding with the audience because I emphasised the compassionate side of the woman. When she makes a pass at the commercial traveller, it is only done as a means of protecting her daughter, whom he fancies. I think the audience sympathises with her over-concern and, at the same time, appreciates her problem, as she has been left to bring up a family.'

When Anna Manahan stepped into the part, the Dublin theatre critics treated the occasion as a first night. Anna reckoned it was going to be hard to make an impact after the success of others in the part. She need not have worried. The Olympia audience gave her and the cast a standing ovation and, before the final curtain was rung down, Keane joined them on stage. After he had paid a brief tribute to the other Big Maggies, he looked across at Manahan and said, 'This *is* it.'

Afterwards, backstage, Anna remarked to Mary Keane,

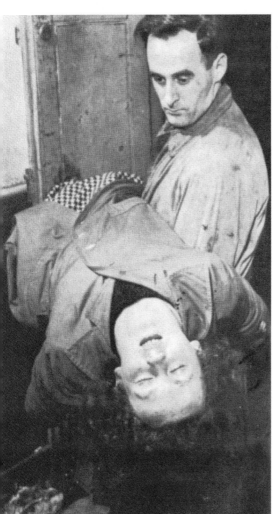

Brian Brennan and Margaret Dillon in the tragic final scene of *Sive* in a production by the Listowel Drama Group

Barry Cassin directed several of Keane's plays, including *The Field*

Ray McAnally as the Bull McCabe in *The Field*

A scene from Gemini's production of *The Year of the Hiker*, with (top) Jim Norton, Gerry Sullivan and (on floor) Martin Dempsey, who played the Hiker

James N. Healy, as the Hiker, and Michael Twomey as his son Simey in the Southern Theatre production of *The Year of the Hiker*

Richard Harris as the Bull McCabe in the screen version of *The Field*.
He was nominated for an Oscar for his powerful performance.

Phyllis Ryan significantly
advanced Keane's career
as a playwright

Brenda Fricker's portrayal of Maggie Polpin
made a profound impact at the Abbey

Ben Barnes directed Keane's
plays at the Abbey and
the Gate Theatres

John B. Keane died in Listowel in May 2002;
his funeral drew many mourners
(© Photo by Don MacMonagle)

Crowds follow the hearse for the burial

(© Photo by Don MacMonagle)

John B.'s widow, Mary, flanked by her son Billy
and daughter Joanne
(© Photo by Don MacMonagle)

The cortège passes the Keanes' pub in Listowel
(© Photo by Don MacMonagle)

'John didn't make a speech about me; all he said was, "This is it." What did he mean?'

Mary's reply was, 'Anna, this *is* it, isn't it? I mean, John wrote Maggie for you. I remember him seated in the back kitchen saying how he could hear you recite the lines he had written. I can tell you, as far as John is concerned, this *is* it.'

To the actress, the part was special for another reason. She saw in Maggie Polpin an indomitable quality that reminded her of Scarlett O'Hara. She visualised the scene in *Gone with the Wind* when Scarlett comes back to Tara, finds the mansion burned to the ground and proceeds to pick up the root of a vegetable from nearby. At that moment, she swears she will never be hungry again, if she has to beg, borrow or steal.

There was, she felt, the same element in Maggie's defiance when she seems to be saying to herself, 'That's it, I'm going to take over the running of the house.' And Maggie has the quality that defies life, that even stands up in a sense to the Almighty, and utters, "I'm me." It is a fantastic example of courage against all adversity, although Maggie is hard in the end as she says, ''Twill all be theirs one day. And maybe they'll thank me then.'

In the *Irish Times*, critic David Nowlan commented: 'John B. Keane, it is said, wrote *Big Maggie* with Anna Manahan in mind for the part. Last night, in the Olympia Theatre, she took the part for the first time. For one who saw none of her predecessors, it is difficult to assess the performance relative to what others have already seen. But on last night's showing, the author seems to have chosen his actress well. A low mountain of invective and concern, Ms Manahan strutted through the evening with a powerful cumulative effect – mostly in cold control, but blazing into dominance at the drop of a bit of backchat. She was ably supported by Cecil Sheehan's gravestone mason and Robert Carlile's hen-pecked, worm-turning son of the house. Liz Davis and Dearbhla Molloy were fine as the precocious and demure daughters, while Gerry Sullivan was probably quite right to play the commercial traveller with more than an occasional broad wink to the delighted audience.'

Des Rushe, in the *Irish Independent*, stated that *Big Maggie* wasn't one of his favourite plays and that he found it quite impossible to share the popular enthusiasm for it. As he wrote, 'It is only grave cause, coupled with a stern sense of duty, which has taken me back to the Olympia Theatre to see it for the third time.' After commending Anna Manahan's sensitive portrayal of Maggie Polpin, he said that her best efforts could not, however, make Maggie an acceptably credible character, because Mr Keane's waywardness in characterisation and plot development kept getting in the way.

It seemed incomprehensible to Phyllis Ryan that some critics were finding Big Maggie an unreal character, when in fact she was full of truth, and dramatically strong. In her view, John B. Keane wrote convincingly about women, and this was illustrated in the graveyard scene, when Maggie shows a chilling detachment from her husband's memory.

Barry Cassin felt that Keane was a better writer of women's parts than most other Irish dramatists. He wrote with understanding and sympathy – qualities that previously hadn't been shown by other dramatists in Ireland. He detected also a strong morality in Keane's works, perhaps an older morality, as for instance when Maggie smacks her daughter on the face for having spent the night with a man in a hotel. He had a way of making one aware of the moral points he was making.

'Maggie Polpin is by no means an outrageous character,' said Cassin. 'Ultimately she is fighting for her family, even if she adopts tough methods. I have no doubt audiences identified with her, although some urbanites might not accept her old-fashioned approach. I remember they didn't understand why Bull McCabe and his wife haven't spoken for years. The silence between the couple didn't make sense to the urban mind; it was a rural phenomenon, and I could accept their puzzlement.'

As time progressed, Big Maggie was to prove itself a hugely popular play. Barry Cassin began to see it as the most successful Irish play ever. It kept coming back. On one occasion, when he believed the public had seen enough of Maggie, the Olympia management had a few blank weeks and decided to revive the play. 'This play is run out, it's dead,' he told them. He had to eat his words later and admit he was wrong; Big

Maggie filled the house for the two weeks and broke more box-office records. At this time, he found it hard to understand the Abbey Theatre's attitude, for having presented *Hut 42* and *The Man from Clare*, the directors simply deserted Keane, as though they were unsure of his ability.

'I speak as an outsider,' Cassin explained, 'but that is the picture I was getting. In their eyes, he was not good enough. It puzzled me, as well as the theatre world. For the playwright, it must have been discouraging to be the biggest box-office draw and still be unacceptable within the doors of the Abbey. I am quite sure that John B. Keane was hurt.'

Phyllis Ryan had thought a good deal about *Big Maggie*, and wrote at a later date: 'No play I can remember in a life spent in theatre made such a powerful impact on the Irish playgoer. In terms of business, any previous records were broken all over the country. In terms of emotional response from audiences, it seemed they could not get enough of this play, and large numbers of people from every walk of life went four or five times to see it.' There was, it appeared, a Maggie Polpin in every household.

*

Meanwhile, in Listowel, John B. was as indefatigable as ever. He was proving himself a prolific playwright – in some people's view, too prolific for his own good. The Southern Theatre Group had already premièred his play *The Rain at the End of the Summer*. Set in Cork, the theme explores the minds of the O'Brien family and the new morality that is beginning to exert itself in the country. In writing the play, James N. Healy felt that John B. was making a concession to the Dublin critics who had been pressuring him for years to provide more sophisticated drama, and their criticism had provoked him.

Healy had had reservations about the Gaiety Theatre for the première. Gaiety audiences, he felt, weren't attuned to Keane's plays in the same way as those at the Olympia Theatre were. The cast looked impressive, with Healy playing the central role of Joss O'Brien, and Jim Norton and Dermot Crowley as his sons. The occasion lacked sparkle, however, and would not be recalled by the playwright's admirers as in any way memorable; compared with *The Year of the Hiker* and *The Field*, it paled badly.

The veteran *Irish Times* critic Séamus Kelly told his readers: 'J. B. Keane is the most exasperating playwright in the country today. He has the triple gifts of good characterisation, humour and lively – and on the whole, credible – dialogue, but he superimposes these worthy techniques on melodramatic plots that would have made even Ted Slaughter blush.'

Des Rushe's review in the *Irish Independent* was headlined 'STILL WAITING FOR KEANE OPUS' and began: 'The long wait for the major dramatic work which many people believe John B. Keane has in him is not yet over. Indeed, on the evidence of his latest work, *The Rain at the End of the Summer*, the day of greatness is more remote than ever. For compared with *The Field* and several earlier and lesser Keane plays, this is extremely weak stuff.' The theme of conflicting moral attitudes, ending in the disintegration of the smug O'Brien family, did not, he said, involve him, nor was he affected by their dilemma.

Maureen O'Farrell in the *Evening Press* summed up: 'J. B. Keane has floundered in this, his first foray into modern Ireland. He fails to catch the attitudes and petty snobberies of the class which he has chosen to portray and concentrates instead on the "girl in trouble" theme. This is a commonplace plight in drama, as in life, and does not generate sufficient excitement to sustain the play. The result is slight, repetitious and rather trivial domestic tragicomedy.'

Máirín Morrish, who had been singled out for her performance as Kate O'Brien, had earlier played in *The Year of the Hiker*, and felt Keane was more at home in north Kerry than in Cork. However, despite the lack of enthusiasm for the play in Dublin, the people of Cork packed the Opera House for weeks. Furthermore, the production provoked a lively theatrical debate, with *Evening Echo* critic Robert O'Donoghue being taken to task by the well-known Cork solicitor Gerald Y. Goldberg for describing the theme as 'sensational'.

While Goldberg emphasised that he respected the critic, he disagreed with his review. 'I saw the play and came away moved,' Goldberg said. And he added: 'I am not a follower of

John B. Keane, but I recognise the rich vein of genius which underlines his writing, his understanding of people and events, his brilliant use of language, his powerful and at times very subtle evocation of plot, and his ability to point character in contrasting and disparate tone. If the paint used is stronger than what Mr O'Donoghue prefers, why should the artist be characterised as "coarse"? This play was not meant to be a "torrid suburban melodrama", nor was it ever turned into "an evening of entirely fanciful farce".'

Looking back, Jim Norton felt that the play in rehearsal would have benefited from a workshop approach, with Keane himself on hand. Although the cast had worked hard on the script, it was not ready for staging. Being a domestic play, it would perhaps have made an impact in a more intimate theatre than the Gaiety.

Unlike *The Year of the Hiker*, which he still described as one of the author's best plays, Norton thought that *The Rain at the End of the Summer* was poorly structured. He believed that Keane seemed uncertain in an urban setting and that this affected the characterisation. Yet his admiration for the playwright remained undiminished: Keane's natural theatricality and racy language stood out like a beacon, and he was able to communicate emotion in a way that appealed tremendously to audiences.

He felt one of the secrets of Keane's popular success was that he wrote about subjects that people up to then had only talked about privately. In this respect, his plays had a therapeutic value for those who saw them. 'I think these people felt less desperate after seeing them, and this opened up discussion. They encouraged people to talk through their problems.' In this regard, John B. broke new ground, and plays like *The Hiker* and *Sive* would in his view endure.

PART THREE

HIGHS AND LOWS

20

Maurice Walsh's Advice

In a Chelsea restaurant, John B. Keane and Danny Hannon sat down to steak-and-kidney pie. 'A good old English dish,' quipped Hannon. They were in London for a week of relaxation. Keane was anxious to keep abreast of what was new in the theatre and also to meet his English agent.

To Hannon, the playwright had been tense as usual starting out on the journey from Listowel, but after a day or two he knew 'he would be himself'. They booked into a West End hotel and decided to dine out. On the first evening, they purchased tickets for *The Contractor*, the David Storey play, and afterwards went backstage to meet T. P. McKenna, one of the stars of the show. To Keane's delight, the actor – a former member of the Abbey Theatre Company – was familiar with his stage successes, especially *The Field*.

Next evening they saw the thriller *Sleuth*, which appealed to Keane because of its tense and subtle ending. The play starred another leading Irish actor in London, Dónal Donnelly. In the middle of the week, they took in *A Winter's Tale* and also managed to fit in a late-night cabaret.

Keane was by now in his element. He enjoyed the atmosphere of London, which he invariably regarded as friendly and devoid of alienation. He drank in the pubs around Piccadilly and the Strand and never failed to be amused by the cockney wit. 'John B. had a good capacity for drink,' Danny Hannon remembered, 'but he was able to control his drinking, and so he enjoyed it. He was great company to be with, if sometimes embarrassing when he was overgenerous and wanted to pick up the tab in every restaurant we visited.'

If Keane happened to see a bookshop, he went inside and leafed through the pages of a dozen books and plays. 'He was an education to be with on a holiday,' says Hannon. 'His stamina was endless.' On another occasion when they dined in a West End restaurant, Keane decided the pretty young waitress serving them was Irish, and said to Hannon, 'I'd bet that girl knows of me.' But when he good-humouredly asked her, 'Have you heard of John B. Keane?' she looked at him in surprise and said, 'Who?'

Hannon chuckled. He knew that John B. liked to be recognised, and in Ireland at least, this was the case. As they walked through London together, Keane gave him the impression that while he loved the city for a visit, he would never live there. As he remarked, 'I'd get a feeling of claustrophobia in the summertime.' This was no surprise to Hannon, who always counted John B. an open-air person. Before the week was out, the playwright was already thinking about home.

To Hannon, John B. had not changed. Neither fame nor money had affected his personality. Whenever he and his wife, Eileen, accompanied him to the theatre in Cork, they were made feel a part of his close circle of friends. 'John B. went out of his way to ensure you were one of his party, and you were not allowed to forget that,' Hannon recalled.

By now he was getting scripts from the playwright to read. But he quickly realised that this did not mean he could be critical. As he said, 'John B. did not invite criticism of his work, but if he did ask me what I thought of a script, I'd give him an honest answer.'

Keane had turned forty. He was still lean and fit, and his mind was as alert as ever. If Hannon found little change in him, others would say the same. Andrew Flynn, his first publisher, still enjoyed his company when they met. 'Time didn't matter,' said Flynn. 'If we met in a hotel foyer, the old friendship was instantly rekindled.'

According to Barry Cassin, the Listowel playwright had wanted fame and success very much – and why not, Cassin asked. Keane was now enjoying fame in the same way as Hugh Leonard and Brian Friel. Denis Keane felt that his brother had grown in confidence and was more secure in himself. To Peg Schuster, John B. remained her favourite brother, with his ready wit and generosity of spirit. Nonetheless, she refused to regard him as a saint. Michael Keane, who had always acknowledged his brother's talent, found him unchanged by fame. 'From our young days we were close, and that friendship has never wavered,' Michael said. 'I don't think as a family we'll ever change.'

Something else about the playwright remained constant. He was still volatile, or as a Listowel friend described him, 'John B. is a simmering volcano when provoked.' James N. Healy recalled a late-night incident in a theatre club in Cork when a burly individual insulted the playwright, then walked off the premises. A few minutes later, Healy and John B. walked down the stairs into the street, and out of the corner of his eye Healy spotted the man standing near the doorway. Before he realised what had happened, Keane had dropped the man on the footpath with a swift blow of his fist – and without uttering a single word. 'After that,' Healy decided, 'I knew he could take care of himself.'

Keane admitted the old turbulence had not left him, and it could be exacerbated by whiskey. Occasionally he lost control, and once landed in court in Listowel following an incident involving a local senator, D. J. Moloney. The case aroused a good deal of interest and newspapers dispatched reporters to cover it.

The playwright was defended by the barrister Dermot Kinlan, who told the court that at one time Senator Moloney had had a disagreement with Keane over his play *Sive*, as a result of a statement made by the senator during the debate on the estimates for the Abbey Theatre.

Sive had been sent to the Abbey in the late 1950s by Keane, and was rejected. During the debate in the Oireachtas, Senator Moloney stated that *Sive* had been accepted.

On the night of the incident, Keane congratulated Moloney on his election to the Seanad but went on to complain about what the senator had said in the Oireachtas, and proceeded to grasp his coat. He did not strike him. Mr Keane was extremely sorry, said Kinlan, and apologised for the 'unfortunate incident', as Keane described it.

Earlier in the hearing, a garda superintendent told District

Justice Feran that Keane and Moloney had not been on speaking terms for some years. It was one o'clock in the morning and Keane was accompanied by his wife when he stopped in the street in Listowel and had some words with the senator. The defendant was being taken home by his friends but resisted, and during his arrest he struck Garda Lorden. The Justice bound over the playwright to be of good behaviour for two years, and fined him twenty-five pounds for assaulting the guard.

Throughout the hearing, Father Kieran O'Shea sat beside the playwright. 'I went along to give John some moral support,' the priest said. 'Or in case the district justice wanted character references.' John B. sat passively through the hearing, but his eyes met those of the district justice when he remarked, 'I have no objection to Mr Keane's play-writing; it is his play-acting that I object to.' This was the line the national newspapers splashed the next day in their headlines on the case.

*

It was the late 1960s and, for the playwright, a period of undoubted highs and lows. He admitted he was facing a crisis in his life. Paradoxically, this was linked to Listowel itself. As a writer, he was suffering from a loss of direction and was unsure where next to turn. On his own admission, he was not helped by the absence in the town of playwrights of his own generation. He was not helped either by the apathy shown to him by the Abbey Theatre, which returned the scripts he offered them. There were times when he felt deeply frustrated.

He could not blame the frustration on his marriage. Royalties were substantial from revivals of *Big Maggie*, and he had a steady income from his books and newspaper columns. Although, like most couples, he and Mary had their arguments, their marriage was a happy one. In fact, he was able to see the amusing side of it. 'Mary has this incredible temper, but rarely loses it,' John B. said. 'When she does lose it, my advice, friend, is to take to the wilds!' It was wrong, he thought, to let the woman do all the arguing; a man must answer back. He said he enjoyed the 'making up'.

Alcohol had become a force in his life. In the environment in which he lived, it was difficult to avoid it. He confessed he was drinking a bottle of whiskey a day. 'Around the age of forty, I got a tooth for the stuff,' he recalled. I was able to drink my brother Eamonn under the table. He hadn't the physical capacity to withstand the worst effects of alcohol.' Not that it took a personal crisis to set him off. He was fond of saying, 'No man was ever born into this world with such a passionate love of liquor as was myself. It isn't just that I love liquor for the taste of it; I love the plop of whiskey into a glass. I love to listen to it. I love to see the cream of a pint. I love the first powerful, violent impact of a glass of whiskey when I throw it back in me and when it hits the mark.'

For a time, his drinking affected his concentration and work-rate. He confessed he was afraid of alcohol on a few occasions, particularly when he overdid it. He blamed frustration as well as some bad reviews of his plays. It seemed to him that a particular breed of metropolitan critic who saw nothing good in anything had their guns trained on him. Looking back, he said he was foolish to have taken those critics as seriously as he did, when in fact he should have been ignoring them. 'After a while, I realised these people had far bigger problems than I would ever have,' he said, 'and although they had shaken my confidence, I decided in future to ignore them and think, instead, of the other critics who saw some merit in my work.'

In bad moments in drink, the playwright remembered what Maurice Walsh had advised him shortly after the success of *Sive* and *Sharon's Grave*: 'You will be the best of all of us, Johneen, if you can watch the drink.' He had deep respect for Walsh as a novelist and although he, too, had liked his glass of whiskey, he conceded it could be a destructive force. At times when she suspected he might be hitting the bottle hard, Mary would quietly remind him of Maurice Walsh's words. She knew also that his own father, William, had given the same advice; he, too, did not disguise his liking for drink.

Where alcohol was concerned, she was no alarmist, probably because she ran a bar and realised how much men could drink without showing its effects. When John B. was drinking too much or was cantankerous, she put it down to overwork or difficulties with his writing. One day, he came into the bar and announced he was giving up drink. For three or four days, he didn't touch a drop of whiskey or stout; instead, he began to eat bars of chocolate. Mary got annoyed. She recalled, 'I remember saying to him: "For God's sake, go away and take a drink." He was walking around aimlessly, banging on doors up and down the street. He needed a little drink to keep him happy. And I like to see him have a drink.'

Michael Keane was never seriously concerned about his brother's drinking. He counted John B. physically and mentally strong and able to cope. He felt he had too many interests to allow alcohol get a grip of him. Andrew Flynn could not visualise the playwright ending up in the same situation as Brendan Behan or Dylan Thomas. 'I think Mary Keane would see it didn't happen,' Michael said. 'It was a solid and binding relationship, and John B. has always been the first to acknowledge the debt he owes to Mary.'

According to Flynn, the 1960s was a period of heavy drinking in the theatre world, with people probably drinking too much for their own good. It was part of the business, like theatre gossip. 'John B. Keane, like the rest of us, enjoyed himself,' according to Flynn, 'and found theatre people good company. I don't think, however, that drink was a problem with him. If it had been, I don't honestly know how he could have written all those plays.'

During this personal crisis, Keane was encouraged by contact with Phyllis Ryan and James N. Healy and their continued interest in his work. Joining Seán Feehan of the Mercier Press for dinner, or for a drive in the countryside, was also a stimulus. The publisher was urging him to finish work on *Letters of an Irish Parish Priest*, whose central character was Father Martin O'Mora, PP. After a few months, the crisis began to lift and Keane felt his old confidence returning.

It was around this time that Keane visited Limerick for a revival of *The Field* by Gemini Productions. Maureen Toal was playing the role of Maimie, the publican's wife. One night in Charlie St George's public house, opposite the railway station, the actress was introduced to Keane by Phyllis Ryan.

'He was in his element,' she recalled. 'He and Charlie St George were great friends. I found him very witty and interesting. I could see he had a lot of respect for Phyllis; they spoke the same theatre language.'

After a while, Maureen said to him, 'Well, mate, when are you going to write a play for me?' He broke into a laugh. 'I'll do that for you,' he promised. She never doubted his word, for she had heard he had written *Big Maggie* for Anna Manahan.

Shortly afterwards, John B. attended a performance of *The Field* by the Southern Theatre Group at the Cork Opera House, in which James N. Healy played the Bull and Siobhán O'Brien was Maimie Flanagan. Larry Lyons, from the *Cork Examiner*, expressed reservations about the production and complained that Healy, as the Bull, failed to convey the menace and power which Ray McAnally had brought to the part. Healy would later say that he deliberately portrayed the Bull as a schemer and a cunning character and left the real menace to his son, Tadhg. Keane refused to make any comparisons and confined his praise to: 'a good, all-round performance by the cast.'

*

With his personal crisis behind him, Keane was working as hard as ever. He began shaping his new play, *The Change in Mame Fadden*. The veteran journalist and critic John Finegan found him in exuberant mood when he travelled to Listowel to talk to him. It was his first time meeting the playwright on his home ground. 'I remember remarking to him how fit he was looking,' said Finegan. 'He told me he often sprinted on Beale Strand with his son, Billy.'

To Finegan, he was amiable and gregarious. 'John B. struck me as someone who loved company and liked people around him,' Finegan said. 'Kerry and County Limerick were his roaming grounds, with football and fishing his biggest leisure interests.'

Finegan remembered that when *Sive* was presented by the Listowel Players at the Abbey Theatre, some of his city friends were surprised at his praise of the play, and some of his enemies were highly sarcastic, going to lengths to predict that it was a flash in the pan. Finegan had no such doubts. *Sive*, in his opinion, touched some deep chord in the national consciousness. He attributed the play's success to Keane's gift as a storyteller, the realism of his stage characters and the picturesque dialogue he gave them.

Before long, Mary Keane joined them and remarked that young Billy Keane was upstairs writing a school essay about fleas – a topic which John B. had recently explored in his weekly column in the *Evening Herald*. The subject had brought so many queries from Billy's teacher that the boy decided to write a piece embracing all the known facts.

Later that night, they were joined by Nóra Relihan. John Finegan noted that she wore the gold medal awarded her at Killarney Festival in 1958 for her production of *All Souls' Night*, the play he knew had inspired the young publican in Listowel to write *Sive*. Nora was planning a production of *The Merchant of Venice* and was proud to announce that her drama group had made a profit of £300 from performances of *Big Maggie*.

Finegan was among a small coterie of journalists and critics whom Keane liked and respected; there were others he found disdainful. He claimed the latter used their reviews of his plays to attack him personally. But he preferred to ignore them and get on with his writing. He was heartened at this time by the inclusion of a poem of his in the *Penguin Book of Irish Verse*. Entitled 'Certainty', it was from his volume *The Street and Other Poems*:

> *This is the place, I was told*
> *See the tall grass lie low*
> *They rested here and made bold*
> *Now for a certainty I know*
> *Take note of the bluebell broken*
> *The fern mangled and dead*
> *And look at this for a token*
> *Here's a hair from her head.*

Gemini Productions planned to present the première of *The Change in Mame Fadden* in the spring of 1971. The work explores the difficult time in a woman's life when she reaches the menopause, and Mame receives little sympathy from her selfish husband. In effect, she has come to accept her soulless existence.

On her first reading of the play, Maureen Toal considered Mame Fadden a very good part, though the woman herself seemed a little self-pitying in her attitude. Playing such a woman did not appeal to her, as there was no self-pity in her own make-up. At rehearsals, she began to have misgivings and regretted that Keane wasn't there to iron out a few problems. In her view, it was essential to have the author present when the play was new. She felt a responsibility towards him, insofar as he had written *Mame Fadden* for her.

The play was premièred at the Opera House in Cork, but the Dublin critics waited until it opened shortly afterwards at the Olympia Theatre. On the opening night, Maureen Toal received what she described as a 'slightly giggly' reaction from the audience, as though they were watching a comedy. She decided to fight against the trend. In the play, Edward Byrne was portraying her husband, Edward Fadden, and in one scene in which he berates her, a woman in the stalls shouted, 'Leave the poor creature alone, will you!' More giggles followed. Then another voice shouted, 'What are you doin' to that poor woman?'

The majority of the critics were not impressed. David Nowlan, a physician as well as a critic, stated in the *Irish Times* that he had been taken by the playwright's curtain speech, in which he told the audience, 'Go home now; go home and be nice to your wives.' Nowlan saw this as a worthy message of the play. In the course of his review, he observed, 'Last night a packed house roared with laughter and stamped and clapped with approval from practically the first scene in the play. It seemed almost as if they had decided even before they saw the programme that Edward Fadden was to be the funny man.'

Some of the embarrassment, he thought, arose as a result of the playwright giving his players caricatures instead of characters, or declamation in place of dialogue. 'How many total strangers would swap reminiscences of intended suicide within two minutes of meeting each other on the dockside of a provincial Irish city?' he asked. 'Yet this is what is represented when Mame Fadden meets three homeward-bound drunks one night.'

It was, he said, regrettable, because Keane – the most popular dramatist in the country – had chosen an important theme and a relevant crusade but had allowed the whole argument to go by default. Every laughing jackass in the many packed houses which the production would surely draw could go home saying that the play had nothing to do with him. 'Nonsense,' said Nowlan.

Barry Cassin, who directed for Gemini, thought the play had worked well, but it was not vintage Keane. In Phyllis Ryan's view, the play simply did not work. 'John and myself often thought of Mame Fadden,' she later said, 'and I felt then that perhaps it was before its time. I felt it required a lot more working out.'

Although she got good notices for her portrayal of Mame Fadden, Maureen Toal felt she was going against her own personality in playing the part. She was amused by the reaction to Edward Byrne. Known in the business as Teddy, and characteristically a mild-mannered man, nearly every night he had to endure derisory shouts from the audience for the way he treated his wife, Mame. 'After a few days,' recalled Toal, 'Teddy was almost afraid to be seen in the streets of Dublin in case he was recognised. The man wouldn't hurt a fly.'

21

No Laughing Matter

On a July night in Killarney in 1971, Keane made no attempt to conceal his disappointment. 'I could see he was bitterly disappointed,' Flor Dullea recalled. 'You could see it in his face and in his eyes.'

The occasion was the première by Theatre of the South (the renamed Southern Theatre Group) of his new comedy, *Moll*, in Killarney's Abbey Film Theatre. The setting of the play is a presbytery in a run-down southern parish, where a pair of easygoing curates and an even easier-going, simple-minded parish priest, have their lives changed when Moll Kettle, a woman in her late forties, is engaged as housekeeper. In practically no time at all, she is running the presbytery, winding the elderly canon around her little finger, and antagonising the senior curate with her economies in the kitchen.

Keane's disappointment stemmed from the acting. One veteran member of the cast fluffed his lines and upset the timing of his colleagues. To the playwright, the performance failed to gel and his confidence was shattered. Flor Dullea was playing one of the harassed curates, and he recalled other first nights when Keane would mingle with the cast and joke with them. Now it was different: 'There was little or no communication between us,' Flor noted. 'I think he could not accept the fact that we had let him down. He expected standards. It was the first time he appeared dissatisfied with our performance.'

When James N. Healy first received the script, he thought the writing lacked sparkle, as though Keane was tired. He suggested a rewrite of the second act and the inclusion of an extra character, in this case a bishop. When he got the play back, it was much improved. He was to play the bishop, as well as Ulick, the 'amadán'.

Keane left Killarney an unhappy man, convinced that justice had not been done to his new play. Next morning in Listowel he was to derive little consolation from the review in the *Cork Examiner*, headlined: 'FROM KEANE, A PLAY THAT IS A TOTAL DISASTER'.

Larry Lyons wrote: 'The truth is often bitter . . . I would like to record that the world première of *Moll* was a pronounced success, for the Listowel playwright was amongst his own and they were ready to give him a hand. But the truth is often bitter and I would be unfair to my calling and unfair to my readers if I did not record that while *Mame Fadden* floundered on its construction, *Moll* was a total disaster. It was a new departure for Keane, but it was not a change for the better, and after *Mame Fadden* it was another disastrous milestone, and begs the question, "Where is Keane going?" The dialogue was generally banal and there were only a few lines which brought genuine belly laughs. I cannot see *Moll* making the Abbey Theatre.'

The *Evening Herald* critic, John Finegan, put the production into perspective by describing it as 'sheer comedy' and 'a fun night in the theatre'. From the sad fate of Mame Fadden, he said, the author had, in his sixteenth piece for the theatre, turned to the highly amusing cunning of Moll Kettle. He saw her as another formidable Keane feminine creation, an intimidating person who, like Big Maggie Polpin, you secretly have to admire for her wiles.

The cast rehearsed again for the opening night at the Cork Opera House. 'We concentrated on both lines and timing,' recalled Flor Dullea, 'and I think that James N. Healy, who directed, raised the tempo, with the result that audiences in Cork saw a virtually new show. Some passages had been pruned and the action speeded up. Audiences loved it.'

But Robert O'Donoghue in the *Evening Echo* described *Moll* as 'a total disaster'. So damning were his comments that James N. Healy was impelled to reply: 'If your Saturday-night theatre pundit, Mr Robert O'Donoghue, went to see *Moll* expecting a latter-day *Hamlet*, he must be either a fool or a super-optimist, and I wouldn't like to accuse him of being either one or the other. The play was designed to entertain – this is its function; and one feels that it can be fairly claimed to have done this for very large audiences all the week – larger audiences than have been in the Opera House for many a week of summer. The average person who seeks a night's entertainment must be, and deserves to be, catered for as well as those who profess to be highbrows; and this is a point which I have always borne in mind in my long association with Cork theatre.'

In a brief reply, O'Donoghue wrote, 'There is no doubt about Mr Healy's loyalty to the element of "entertainment". In my article I indicated its validity with regard to *Moll*. What I do, and severely did, call to order was the quality of the writing. Perhaps Mr Healy would care to dispute that?'

The production continued to generate lively debate and Keane was content to allow the various protagonists battle it out in the letters page of the *Evening Echo*. In a second letter to the paper, James N. Healy stated, 'I should say perhaps that I do not doubt the sincerity of Mr O'Donoghue's view on theatre – *his* kind of theatre – although I think I may be forgiven for saying that what is missing from his criticism is a sense of proportion.'

When the comedy was staged in the City Theatre in Limerick, Keane travelled from his home in Listowel for the first night, and at the final curtain paid tribute to Theatre of the South for its outstanding contribution to theatre in the province. 'It is all the more praiseworthy because you are doing it without any kind of subsidy,' he declared.

The playwright could hardly have been happy with the Dublin critics. John Boland in the *Evening Press* was to make the surprising statement, 'Priests and their housekeepers are not intrinsically funny, and Mr Keane should have better to do with his talent than to pretend that they are.' Keane must have wondered if the critic watched television sitcoms, where monks, priests and nuns were popular material for comedy scriptwriters. 'Keane is pandering to the public's lowest common denominator,' Boland added. The playwright was to take a particularly dim view of that critique.

Moll Kettle got under the skin of *Irish Independent* critic

Des Rushe, who wasn't amused by Moll's 'bossy, brassy behaviour'. He found nothing at all funny in the conflict between Moll and the curates, and he summed up: 'Theatrically, Moll Kettle quickly becomes a great pain in the neck, and the curates become silly bores, intellectually spancelled to talk sausages and bingo.' Bingo? Did the critic not know, as Keane could have told him, that bingo receipts were building churches and church halls?

The best comment perhaps was made by Godfrey Fitzsimons in the *Irish Times*: 'There is the potential for an acute bit of social observation in the raw material as presented in *Moll*, and for even a few shafts of satire. But Mr Keane is too wise to take any such risks – it might go over the audience's heads. Instead, he shovels in a sample of every comic device in the book, and crude indeed are some of them.' Despite the poor reception accorded to *Moll*, the comedy was enthusiastically received on its tour of the southern counties, where not a few parish priests' housekeepers were living legends.

*

By now, Keane was in the driver's seat, and his new Morris Saloon was a frequent sight outside the public house in William Street, which was no longer the Greyhound Bar but carried his own name in large lettering over the front door.

The place had been refurbished and the quaint look had given way to polished wood and green cushions, but the cosy atmosphere remained. Television would not be installed until later; old-timers were not in favour of it, as chat was a priority with them. Mary Keane was particularly pleased that her husband was driving a car at last. She said he had spent a small fortune on taxis – enough to buy two Jaguars.

He began to write during the day in a small room on the first floor which he had converted into a study. Mary ensured he was allowed to work in peace. At night, he liked to saunter downstairs and through the kitchen into the bar to join the customers. If a newcomer came to see him, he might remark facetiously, 'You have a good face. Sit down.' Usually visitors found him animated, cheerful and inclined to express himself with dramatic energy.

Once, when a visitor from Dublin complained about his ailments, the playwright joked, 'Things could be worse. Take your man who owns a store in this locality. He's worth a quarter of a million pounds, but he has a bad stomach, he doesn't like drink and his wife hates sex!'

Despite his heavy work schedule, he was able to balance his life between writing and leisure. When the directors of Theatre of the South told him the company was embarking on a visit to San Francisco and asked if he would care to join them, he reluctantly had to say no. It was June 1972, and he was committed to completing a new play. The tour would see the American première of *Sive*, which was being presented along with *The Year of the Hiker* and John Murphy's *The Country Boy*.

The plays were staged at Riordan High School Theatre and attracted a good deal of interest amongst the Irish in the city. To the surprise of James N. Healy and his colleagues, the critics were less than enthusiastic in their reception of *Sive*; one critic described it as 'medieval'. But at least they recognised it as melodrama with 'hissable villains and saintly heroines'. The *Hollywood Reporter* bemoaned the fact that the organisers of the tour, the local Gaelic League, undertook virtually no publicity and the box office suffered as a result. But the paper praised the Theatre of the South and singled out James N. Healy's performance as the matchmaker in *Sive* as worthy of note. Michael Twomey considered the visit to San Francisco worthwhile and the audience reaction in the Riordan Theatre heart-warming. 'I think John B. would have enjoyed the experience,' he said.

Anita Earle commented in the *San Francisco Chronicle*: 'The brogues of the cast are simply lovely; would that local actors could tape them for study.' Paul Sargeant Clark in the *Hollywood Reporter* felt the highest achievement of 'these remarkable players is that they manage to slow down their delivery just enough to make every word of the heavy rural dialect clear and distinct, without compromising either the pace of the performances or the richness of the language.'

With the arrival of 1973, John B. had hardly a moment to himself. Seán Feehan conveyed the cheering news that *Letters of an Irish Parish Priest* was proving to be a best-seller. As Feehan said, 'The book just seems to have taken off.' He urged the playwright to 'get down to more letters.'

Keane, however, was at an experimental stage in his career as a dramatist. He travelled to Cork for the presentation at the 140-seat Group Theatre of his three one-act plays on a triple bill titled *Values*. 'I think John B. was looking for fresh modes of expression,' observed Flor Dullea, who was in the cast of two of his plays.

It was agreed that *Backwater*, which explored the relationship between an only son and his widowed mother, was by far the best of the three plays on offer. In *The Spraying of John O'Dorey*, Keane took a futuristic look at pollution, but the piece failed to come dramatically alive. The same could be said for *The Pure of Heart*, the theme of which was moral hypocrisy. 'I felt that *Backwater* was magnificent,' said James N. Healy. 'Here, John B. revealed a new depth of understanding of the human condition.'

To Keane, the experiment was a success. 'I was endeavouring to do different things in my writing,' he recalled, 'and I don't think I was disappointed with *Values*.'

For his next full-length play, he experimented with a biographical theme, and in time the Barnett family in *The Crazy Wall* would be identified by more than one critic as the Keane family of Church Street, Listowel. The wall in question had been built in the family garden during the Second World War and was, as Keane explained, 'a cross between an air-raid shelter and a device to keep out donkeys.' His father believed at the time that German bombs would fall, just as they had fallen in Belfast and Dublin.

Michael Keane had helped his father build the eight-foot wall. They began work on a Saturday morning, his father's day for experimenting, the day when he became an inventor. Once, when his father had too much drink taken, the wall leant crookedly. 'It left the Tower of Pisa in the shade,' Michael recalled. 'Next day it zigzagged in another direction. The family, including my mother, didn't mind in the slightest about the wall going up or sideways. As far as my mother was concerned, it kept my father out of the pub. Since childhood, I can recall him undertaking hare-brained schemes; he was a versatile man, but there were projects he never managed to finish.'

Eventually, when the wall was completed, it formed, along with the three adjacent walls, a shed to house various house and garden implements used by the father. Then, gradually, one by one, the walls crumbled; they were too rigid and built without variation, and soon a high wind carried away the roof. But still the crazy wall, as the family called it, remained as a lasting epitaph to William Keane's masonry.

By the early 1970s, Michael Keane was writing regularly for magazines, though he was the first to admit, 'I haven't John's creative talent.' He wrote a short story based on the crazy wall, being careful, however, to avoid identifying his father in the text. John B. read it and was taken by the title, 'The Crazy Wall'.

'I'm borrowing your title for my new play,' he said to his brother.

Michael shouted after him, 'Come back, you thief!'

At the end of his own story, Michael had written: 'Many years passed and finally the wall in our garden was razed to make way for finer and more grandiose modern structures. These buildings however had no personality, having been built by men devoid of personality, men who did not pause to quaff from the jug of contentment. In time, my father forgot about the wall; to him it was just another idea.'

In John B.'s play, the crumbling of the wall symbolises the end of his father's problems. As he explained, 'When things were not going his way, my father built a symbolic wall around himself, to shut out the harsh realities of the world; he once dreamed he was going to take off around Ireland, but it came to nothing. He wanted to write the great book, and that, too, became a futile exercise.'

Eamonn Keane argued that the wall his father built

symbolised the lack of communication between himself and his wife, although the rest of the family would not agree. When the directors of Theatre of the South decided to première the play, they were aware of the unease among the Keane family regarding the 'delicacy of the theme'. They were assured by John B., however, that there was no opposition to staging the play.

On Wednesday 27 June, John B. made the journey to Waterford for the first night and came away describing it as 'a marvellous opening night'. Larry Lyons, of the *Cork Examiner*, was in agreement; he commented, 'You have broken through tonight, Mr Keane.' It was a compliment from a man who had described *Moll* as 'a total disaster'. Keane was particularly impressed by Dan Donovan's portrayal of the central character, Michael Barnett.

In the *Irish Independent*, Des Rushe did not hesitate to draw a distinct comparison between the Barnett and Keane families: 'It is probably the Keanes. There are a father and a mother and four sons, and the play has Mr Keane breaking new ground by being unabashedly biographical. He washes some family linen in the back garden of the Barnett home, and a couple of characters are more than identifiable. Young Lelum Barnett, for instance, is determined to be an actor, and in Liam O'Mahony's performance is strikingly like Eamonn Keane in appearance. Paddy is a younger brother obsessed with writing poetry, and suggests John B. Keane himself, despite the age discrepancy.'

Rushe saw the wall as a symbol of Michael Barnett's reluctance or inability to face up to realities. 'The situations Mr Keane creates are full of incipient revolt and conflict,' he added. 'But the potential is not explored to anything like the full scope, because the playwright's lack of craftsmanship leads to incidents lacking in credibility.'

Reflecting on the biographical nature of the work, John Finegan in the *Evening Herald* thought that John B. Keane was taking a stern look at his own upbringing. In a programme note to the Waterford presentation of *The Crazy Wall*, Keane seemed to go to great pains to emphasise that the family in his play could be drawn from all the families of the time in the 1940s, though he did concede that the strongest echoes were from his own family.

The play was not well received by the critics when it opened in Dublin at the Gaiety Theatre. This large theatre seemed too big for a work of such a domestic nature, and inadequate stage sets did not help the production visually. For a Keane first night, there was a curious lack of excitement. Furthermore, Dan Donovan, who had made such a fine impression as Michael Barnett in Waterford, was forced to withdraw and was replaced by James N. Healy. To Keane, Donovan's absence weakened the production.

Critic Desmond MacAvock in the *Evening Press* probably made the most salient point, when he commented, 'While one suspects that the play has a deep significance for the author, this is not transmitted to the audience. Yet I feel there was evidence that deep within there was a good play lurking.'

On reflection, James N. Healy believed that, unlike Hugh Leonard with *Da*, Keane had pulled some punches in *The Crazy Wall* and had stopped short of probing his father's character to the full. He thought this was deliberate; John B. had probably taken the feelings of his own family into account. 'I don't think he would do anything to hurt his parents,' Healy said.

Nonetheless, there are scenes in the play in which Michael and Mary Barnett are in conflict. At one point, she tells her husband, 'I started out life in love with you but it died slowly, day after day, month after month. You watched it die and you were content to do nothing about it. You dodged the reality of it like you dodged everything else.' Michael Barnett replies, 'You can't mean all this. If I was so awful, why bother with me at all?'

Members of the Keane family who attended the Gaiety production made no fuss. 'I regarded it as a play, nothing more,' said Michael Keane. 'Actually, I think it worked better as a short story.' Likewise, Denis Keane treated it as a piece of theatre and refused to read 'family realities' into it. Their sister Peg, who remained close to her mother, insisted that her parents' love for one another had never waned. She remembered her father telling her, '"I never loved anybody like I loved your mother." Dad would never say a bad word about her. He used to say she was a pure and good woman. For her part, she loved to go walking with him, and I don't think the communication between them ever broke down.'

It was said that Hannah Keane did not much care for *The Crazy Wall*, and this was understandable. On the other hand, Keane himself remains convinced that it is his best play and would like to see it get an imaginative new production. Anna Manahan, who played in it years later in Howth, found the final scene a problem. Otherwise, she liked the play. 'I think John B. was very courageous to write it,' she said.

*

Despite his lack of success with *The Crazy Wall*, 1973 ended on a high note for Keane. In his speech accepting the presidency of Irish PEN, he both surprised and amused the members. He apologised for all his 'indiscretions' down the years and said he now hoped to mend his ways. Only Keane would have dared make such a public confession.

The seal of office was bestowed on him by his fellow townsman and author Bryan MacMahon at a dinner in the Royal Dublin Society in Ballsbridge. MacMahon recalled that he had taught John B. in Listowel National School. Since Maurice Walsh had also been president of Irish PEN, he felt it was unique for three north Kerry writers to hold the office. He had no doubt that John B. Keane would fill the position with distinction; he was a man of the people, as well as a poet, essayist and playwright.

MacMahon was amazed by the power of PEN. When he chaired a PEN international conference in Dún Laoghaire, which nine hundred delegates attended, he saw the useful links forged and the goodwill generated among those present.

Accepting his seal of office from the outgoing president, Keane said, 'We are in a time which is revolving around violence; we are moving towards an era of unprecedented violence, and where does the writer stand in this time? I would respectfully suggest that it is time for the raising of standards, a time for the forging of a new respect for human life and dignity.'

He was appalled by the violence in Northern Ireland and, in view of that, was proud of the strong links maintained in Irish PEN between Dublin and Belfast. He also expressed worry at the growing violence relating to crime in the south and said there was no room for complacency.

'It was a vibrant time for Irish PEN,' recalled Barbara Walsh, then treasurer, 'and J. B. Keane was to make a valuable contribution. Like the rest of us, especially our secretary Desmond Clarke, he saw great merit in our links with Belfast, as it fostered a valuable cross-border spirit between poets and writers. In those years we all worked extremely hard, and the membership included most of the outstanding literary figures in the thirty-two counties.'

22

WRITERS' WEEK

For Keane and other north Kerry writers and poets, the launch of Listowel Writers' Week would, it was hoped, bring them closer to the people. For too long they had been people apart. In time, one of their proudest boasts would be that the local community, instead of regarding them as 'freaks', came to accept and respect them, perhaps because the pen was a savage and satirical weapon on the bardic side of their heritage.

Keane welcomed the idea; he believed there was a need for a week with the focus on writers and books. When broadcaster Tim Danaher invited him to a meeting, he replied almost immediately: 'Dear Tim, In haste, I'm writing the last few lines of the first play to really satisfy me. With you to the last.'

It was Séamus Wilmot, like Danaher a native of Listowel, and for twenty years registrar of the National University of Ireland, who helped get the event off the ground. Danaher had invited Wilmot to his home in Dublin, where, with friends, he was launching a radio recording about Listowel. Afterwards, Wilmot said to him, 'We should do something about that place down there in Kerry. You're a young man, go on, do something!'

Danaher didn't take undue notice of this command, but several weeks later Wilmot telephoned him again to ask if anything had been done. As the broadcaster made excuses, Wilmot said, 'Now, no excuses, get down to it.' Together they drew up a list of proposals for a festival of the arts and circulated it to prominent people in County Kerry.

Eventually, on a cold November night in 1970, they joined a couple of dozen people, including John B. Keane, around an oil stove in a hall just off Market Place in Listowel. After a lively discussion, it was agreed that a festival of the arts in Kerry would be held the following May.

'The idea caught the imagination of all those present,' recalled Tim Danaher, 'and I remember Séamus Wilmot made an eloquent speech.' In time, Keane would think up the title, Listowel Writers' Week. At the first event in May 1971, the emphasis was on Kerry writers and poets, and Keane read a few of his own poems along with Brendan Kennelly, Bryan MacMahon and Séamus de Faoite. There was a screening of *The Quiet Man*, which was based on Maurice Walsh's short story of the same name, and Father Tony Gaughan talked on the social and political history of Ireland.

Not surprisingly, the townspeople warmed to the idea and voluntary workers gave their assistance. The event survived its early 'teething pains', as Séamus Wilmot put it, and gradually attracted people from Dublin and elsewhere. 'It became a prestige festival,' said Tim Danaher, 'and writers and artists wanted to be part of it.'

When Keane was asked in the early 1970s where he thought the event was going, he replied, 'Where it is going to I'm not sure. But it is beginning to take positive shape. It can give employment to a writer whose voice might not otherwise be heard. It can help to channel a talent in a positive direction. Its influence on young people could be profound – we give them a feeling of theatre and writing early in life. I think it could produce a major writer.'

On one occasion, he chaired a theatre discussion with Alun Owen, Brian Friel, Phyllis Ryan and actress Kathleen Barrington. To show that the week was embracing the thirty-two counties, a discussion was held on the arts in Northern Ireland, and among the speakers was Seamus Heaney. Keane welcomed this cross-border contact and saw it as a valuable merging of North–South minds.

The novelist Benedict Kiely caused a traffic jam when lecturing on Maurice Walsh outside a pub on the road to Ballybunion. Hugh Leonard and others ran useful workshops; in Keane's view, the week served a positive purpose in bringing together writers and publishers, and the value of book fairs was seen at first hand. As a playwright, he welcomed the provision of a second theatre, the Lartigue, which had opened in the old Castle stable and, although small, was ideally suited to experimental work. Danny Hannon found time to contribute fittings to the theatre and hoped to create an open-air Elizabethan-type amphitheatre in the flagged and cobbled stableyard.

By now, Writers' Week had managed to break down all apparent barriers between strangers and townspeople, writers and holidaymakers. The event combined serious literary business with high – often eccentric – gaiety. To Keane, the social side of the festival was as important as the working sessions. As he said, 'We wanted visitors to enjoy their stay in Listowel, and to me they always did so.'

At late-night drinking sessions, poets, playwrights, novelists and artists chatted earnestly; occasionally an argument would become overheated and a bearded poet might have to step between a play producer and an aggrieved dramatist. To Tim Danaher, however, the event had blossomed and he was quick to praise others, in particular Luaí Ó Murchú, who, he said, with 'charm, blandishment, cajolery and Northern guile' had gathered round him a committee whose dedication made the dream come true.

For some, the week was paying off. A Killarney housewife heard her winning play on RTÉ; two short-story entries were published in the literary pages of a national newspaper, and a group of budding writers who attended the week now met once a month in Dublin to analyse and criticise their own work. To John B. Keane, the discovery of writers and artists was becoming a welcome function of the week. He was a strong advocate of the introduction of fresh thinking into the arts.

As time went on, he admitted, he found the social side becoming strenuous. 'Before it starts I always wish the week was over, but when it's on I revel in it,' he said. 'It gives me a great opportunity to renew old acquaintances with other drunkards!' He attributed the success of Writers' Week to the region more than to the town itself. North Kerry, he said, had a tradition of ballads, poetry and storytelling and, in more recent times, plays and novels. Yet as he walked through the square in Listowel or along the road by the Carnegie Library, he might pause for a moment to take a deep breath and remark, 'Writing is in the air in a place like this.'

Although Listowel's characters were no more outlandish or outspoken than those of any other place, what made them different was the raciness and the speed of language they used. It moved at an astounding pace, and it was more than colourful. Keane liked to recall the story of a man who came into the bar looking for him: 'I was told he had a moustache by a man at the counter,' he said. 'When I asked what kind of moustache, he said, "'Twas as thin as you'd draw with the stroke of a biro." People here don't settle for ordinary language; it's full of imagery arising naturally out of conversation and the provocation of those involved.'

During Writers' Week, he was bombarded with questions by Irish and overseas visitors on his views on subjects ranging from Arthur Miller to bachelors on the land. Asked about Listowel, he told a young woman, 'It's the type of town where you'd be brought down to your size very quickly. If you decided to go above yourself, you'd get your comeuppance around every corner. And there's a little bit of begrudgery. I'd be surprised if there wasn't, but behind it there's total goodwill.'

With a twinkle in his eye, he explained how to survive in a small town. 'There are things you learn while living in small towns,' he explained. 'If you are to survive at all, you have to know that everything you tell someone in confidence or say behind someone's back will always come back to you. It's the nature of men and women to spread the news they're not supposed to spread. Of the two sexes, man is the greater gabber. I will always be less inclined to believe a man.'

Visitors could never be sure whether to take him seriously, for at heart John B. remained a prankster, as the characters in his pub well knew. There was, however, one occasion when he was more than serious: during Writers' Week one year, he was charged for refusing to admit a garda to his public house at 12.30 AM. 'We had actually stopped serving customers forty minutes earlier, and when the guard arrived they were about to leave,' recalled Mary Keane. 'We had been full with visitors, and the singing and the chat dragged on until after midnight.'

The incident upset Keane. It was the first such incident

during Writers' Week, and he felt that raiding the premises was uncalled for. In court, he received the benefit of the Probation Act.

*

Phyllis Ryan was a frequent visitor for Writers' Week and happened to be in Listowel when *Letters of a Matchmaker* was launched at the book fair. She found the book hilariously funny and came to the conclusion that it could be successfully adapted for the stage.

On her return to Dublin, she was told that Ray McAnally's production of the American play *Kennedy's Children*, at the Eblana Theatre, was in trouble. McAnally had booked the Eblana for sixteen weeks, but already the play was proving a disaster at the box office.

The irony was that the play had been a great success in the West End, and when McAnally saw it there he decided it would pack them in in Dublin. But Dublin playgoers, as Ronnie Masterson later observed, 'shunned it like the plague.' They got the notion that it was exploiting the late President Kennedy's children, and so must be cheap, when in fact it had nothing to do with the Kennedy family. Now Ronnie and Ray were in danger of having to sell their house to meet the mounting debts.

One afternoon, when Phyllis Ryan visited the Eblana Theatre, she brought with her a copy of *Letters of a Matchmaker*. She met the McAnallys and Barry Cassin and began to enthuse about Keane's book. As she listened to Ray's tale of woe about *Kennedy's Children*, she suddenly said, 'Here, why not adapt this for the stage and take off *Kennedy's Children?*'

McAnally expressed doubts about whether John B. Keane would give permission. 'I'm sure he will,' remarked Phyllis. 'From experience, I know he's sympathetic to theatre people in difficulties. I suggest you call him as quickly as possible.'

A few hours later, McAnally telephoned the playwright in Listowel and told him of his dilemma. Straightaway, Keane said, 'You have my permission to adapt the book for the stage. Go ahead and do it if it gets you out of trouble.' He even waived a percentage of the author's royalties.

Ronnie Masterson bought three copies of *Letters of a Matchmaker* and gave them to her husband. Ray and Barry completed the adaptation in five days. It was to prove an immediate success at the box office, providing Ronnie and Ray with an opportunity to play a variety of parts, including Fionnuala Crust, Dicky Mick Dicky O'Connor, Lena Magee and Claude Glynne-Hunter.

A few playgoers found the piece too bawdy, and some walked out of the Eblana Theatre in protest. For the most part, however, the play's Rabelaisian humour was enjoyed. The McAnallys brought it on a tour of the provinces and enjoyed an even bigger success than in Dublin, although Keane's ribaldry again sent a few nuns and priests rushing headlong out of theatres.

This ribaldry is particularly to be found in Fionnuala Crust's somewhat desperate letters to matchmaker Richard Michael Richard O'Connor. Having paid him the sum of £20, she has married one Mickeen Snoss but, to her disgust, he turns out to be 'a lifeless latchiko with as much spark in him as a taovode of spairt.'

'I wanted him to go to a doctor to see after his apparatus but he told me he'd let no man living look at it till they were washing him for the day,' Fionnuala concludes in her letter. 'So you see I would be well entitled to a refund of my money, for you contracted to supply me with a partner who would be well-geared to fulfil his part of the bargain.'

Later, she writes again to O'Connor: 'I tried your recipe and went back to Mickeen Snoss. He was with the doctor and he was told there was no cure for his ailment and 'tis me that knows it for didn't I give the past three weeks under the one quilt with him. I'd be better engaged sleeping with a corpse. Now like a good man will you forward my money by return of post.'

The playwright's humour is not for the puritan mind, though it was obvious during performances of *Matchmaker* that women more than men complained of the bawdy language and sexual innuendo. Men, for the most part, found the piece frank and funny.

Keane has never been reluctant to call a spade a spade. Once, when he was showing a visiting journalist around Listowel, he explained the origins of the name of the River Feale, which, he said, was named for a seventh-century aristocratic lady who drowned herself in it in mortification at being caught swimming there naked by an illicit admirer. Not far off, an eminence rises up over the town by the name of Ballygrennane. 'It is said,' says Keane, 'that if you spin a Listowel man around anywhere in the world, his penis will point to Ballygrennane.'

*

Keane caught up with *Matchmaker* in Limerick, and thought McAnally and Cassin had done a fine adaptation of his book. He was an admirer of the actor's brilliance and stage technique, and chuckled at his adroit use of accents. Today Ronnie Masterson feels indebted to Keane for his generosity. 'You can take it from me,' she stated, 'that he saved our bacon at that time. Ray had a lot of time for John B.'

The book became a best-seller for the Mercier Press, and publisher Seán Feehan counted it among the funniest pieces ever written by Keane. In an amusing introduction, the playwright wrote: 'Poets, they say, are born not made. The same cannot be said of matchmakers. As will be seen from the following correspondence, they are not created overnight. Only circumstances can make a matchmaker. In an ideal world there would be no need of such a person. Men and women would be paired off, the brave deserving the fair and, at the other extreme, every old shoe finding an old stocking.'

Phyllis Ryan had by now received from Keane his latest play, *The Good Thing*, and it struck her that he was determined to turn the tables on men. In the play, two sisters decide to get their own back on their unfaithful husbands: Eve, the younger of the two, goes to bed with a stranger after drinks on the town, while her sister succumbs to the charm of an 'old flame'. A third sister, Maudie, has married a road sweeper who becomes violent when drunk. As 'the Good Thing', Maudie, whose blatant sex appeal belies her pure and single-minded devotion to her husband, cannot understand how any man could assume her to be 'an easy lay'.

When Maureen Toal read the play, she considered it both funny and touching but had reservations about playing Maudie. True, she was an interesting character with some sex appeal; on the other hand, Maudie's personality ran counter to her own. During rehearsals, she began to see Maudie as something of a bore and in no way 'a Good Thing'.

Des Nealon was surprised to be cast as her husband, Mickie. He couldn't see himself bringing conviction to the part. 'I was a benign kind of guy,' he said, 'and here was Mickie, a nasty and vicious individual when drunk, so I expressed my doubts to Barry Cassin. But he assured me I could play the role convincingly.' Nealon at that time considered himself overweight and he felt this might make the character more credible. The playwright, in his opinion, had painted an accurate picture of Mickie. He knew such men, whose personalities changed after heavy drinking.

On the same night that the two 'liberated' sisters go off with their men, Maudie is beaten up by her husband in a fit of drunken jealousy. This enrages her sisters so much that later they try to persuade Maudie to leave Mickie and amuse herself with a night on the town. But Maudie is content with her impoverished existence and finds her husband tolerable in his sober state.

The *Irish Times* critic, David Nowlan, observed that neither the author nor the play was helped by the audience's insensitivity, and this may have been what made the players appear uneasy. Maureen Toal's Maudie was at its best when played 'wide-eyed and indignant for laughs,' Nowlan commented. As director, Barry Cassin did his best in a brusque production with the play's 'uncertainty of style' and the author's 'arbitrary and sometimes stilted action,' the critic continued.

Maureen Toal was surprised when a few Kerry people came to the play and told her they knew women in their own locality like Maudie; she wondered if Keane had based his play on one of them. When she mentioned this to the playwright, he dismissed the claim. 'They're talking nonsense,' he said indignantly. 'I did not base my characters on women I know in Kerry.'

Phyllis Ryan was surprised for another reason. A number of theatregoers complained to her that Irish women don't try to retaliate against unfaithful husbands. She said that, on the contrary, *The Good Thing* was not contrived: Keane was depicting a situation that could quite easily happen. His understanding of women and their attitudes was, she felt, incredible. She liked to recount the story of the actress who, having seen her fifth Keane play, remarked proudly, 'Thank God at least one man cares enough about women to do a bit of research on the subject, and thank God he writes roles for women that you can really get your teeth into.'

When *The Good Thing* was toured, it was, in the words of Phyllis Ryan, received with shock and disbelief. The general reaction was that 'it couldn't happen here', that a man might stray now and then, but sure wasn't that his nature?

As a visitor to Listowel Writers' Week, the critic Robert Hogan had come to know the playwright. He had made a study of his dramatic writing and could speak authoritatively about his plays. It would be impossible, he said, to have discussed sexuality in plays in Ireland before the 1970s, and in light of that, Keane's achievement was noteworthy. In *The Good Thing*, he had taken up the ferocious sexual problems, the frustration, the boredom and the disillusionment that so often set in after ten years of marriage. Sex had been discussed in Irish novels much earlier and more frequently than it had been in plays, so playwrights like Keane were now getting the balance right.

Hogan was amongst those who admired Keane's humour and charm – a charm, he said, which never deserted him. It was a brake against eccentricity. He was concerned though about the playwright's career, now that he was approaching fifty. He wondered where he would turn to next. Could he continue to produce more essays, stories – and a play perhaps every year? Was he too creative for his own good?

What he really wanted from John B. was what he called 'the Big Play', and he urged him to take time in writing it. He had faith enough in him to make this personal appeal, for already he had seen much to praise in *The Year of the Hiker*, *The Field* and *Big Maggie*.

Could Keane devote enough time to come up with the Big Play? On the face of it, he had more than enough commitments. Nonetheless, in January 1974 he was nominated as a member of the new Arts Council by the then Taoiseach, Liam Cosgrave, and agreed to take his place at council meetings in Dublin.

When he learned that the editor of the *Evening Herald*, Brian Quinn, had also been appointed to the Arts Council, Keane wrote to him, 'I must applaud the good sense of Liam Cosgrave to nominate us both.' They joined a seventeen-member council that was chaired by Geoffrey Hand, professor of legal and constitutional history at University College Dublin, and included Seamus Heaney, actress Kathleen Barrington, sculptor John Behan, Belfast art-gallery owner and former unionist MP Tom Caldwell, architect Andrew Devane and Dr Tom Walsh, founder of the Wexford Opera Festival.

According to Brian Quinn, Keane surprised some of the council members by his practical approach and his remarks, which were very much to the point. When members began to theorise unnecessarily, he became impatient. He had firm views on what he believed should be implemented and wanted ideas expedited. And he was interested in forging good North–South cultural relations.

In time, the members would travel to Belfast to meet with their counterparts in the Northern Ireland Arts Council and discuss ways of combining their resources to further the arts here. 'Cross-border cultural links are essential in this small island,' Keane would say. 'In Irish PEN and, again, in Listowel Writers' Week we encouraged such links, and I think I can say they were mutually beneficial.'

The playwright enjoyed exchanging views with artists working in other spheres, and agreed with Brian Quinn that the new council was as good as any in the history of the state. But, like its predecessors, it too received its share of criticism from aggrieved artists, publishers and theatre companies.

23

CRITICS – 'A DISGRACE'

James McGlone is a studious American academic with a deep love of theatre, particularly Irish theatre. In the late 1970s, he discovered Keane's plays and proceeded to produce a number of them at Seton Hall University in New Jersey, where he was professor of drama.

Having directed *Sharon's Grave* with his students in 1977, he decided to stage *The Field* and wrote to the author in Listowel, drawing a comparison between a passage in the play and a short scene in Sean O'Casey's *Juno and the Paycock*. Unaware that Keane sometimes took time to get round to his copious mail, McGlone got no reply. In later years, he said wryly, 'Maybe I embarrassed John B. in the first place by making the comparison at all. I can only assume it's not always the best thing in the world to tell a playwright why his work is good!'

Aspects of *Sharon's Grave* fascinated him. He considered it earthy and elemental, with the dramatic power stemming from the characterisation. The mood reminded him of Shakespeare's *Richard III*, and in the crippled Dinzie Conlee's character he saw facets of the king. With the support of Eoin McKiernan's Irish American Cultural Institute, McGlone was now able to engage a leading Irish actor to play the Bull McCabe in *The Field*. In this case, it was County Armagh-born Michael Duffy. McGlone had met the actor a few months previously when he toured the States with his one-man show woven around Northern Ireland theatre.

Performed as theatre-in-the-round by McGlone's Celtic Theatre Company, Keane's play proved a popular success and, in New Jersey, stimulated interest in his work. McGlone recalled that Duffy played the Bull less menacingly than Ray

McAnally, yet in its own way it was a powerful portrayal.

Keane was profiled in the *Star-Ledger* and his background as a publican-cum-playwright was traced to the time of *Sive*. In the same paper the critic Bette Spero praised Michael Duffy's performance and emphasised that the play was much more modern in its outlook and tone than J. M. Synge's *Playboy of the Western World*. 'It is crisply written,' she noted, 'and there are gentle touches of satiric wit streaming through the more serious thoughts.'

McGlone was determined to pursue his artistic policy of inviting guest players from Ireland. As the stage director of the Keane plays, he found that the students welcomed the opportunity of working with leading Irish professionals. He contacted Keane in Listowel and extended an invitation to him to address the drama faculty in Seton Hall University about his life and work. For his part, the playwright was pleased to learn that McGlone was faithful to the instructions in his scripts and said he hoped in time to visit Seton.

For his next Keane play, the director chose *Big Maggie* and counted himself fortunate to be able to engage Marie Kean, who had created the title role in Ireland. At this time she was playing in Noel Coward's *Blithe Spirit* on Broadway with Peter O'Toole, and through a friend McGlone contacted her. 'I talked with her for twenty minutes and, having explained myself, Marie seemed to trust me and in a few days called me to say she was willing to play the part. Imagine my relief!'

According to the artistic director, the audience loved her performance. 'You see, Jewish mothers are like Maggie Polpin,' she said, 'so people in the audience identified with her attitudes. The thing about Maggie is that she is actually right; her kids are in a mess. It is up to her to sort them out.'

Writing in the *Star-Ledger*, Bette Spero commented, 'Marie Kean is magnificent. Her impeccable speech, rapid movement, riveting determination and gorgeous mother-lode of truth make her an awesome spectacle.' The critic saw Keane as 'a marvellous, realistic playwright with an incisive style', but his work, she said, was little known outside Ireland, so New Jersey theatregoers could thank Seton Hall University for staging him in America.

In 1979, McGlone contacted Keane again and told him he intended staging *The Year of the Hiker*, with Éamon Kelly as the Hiker Lacey. When it was found that the actor was unavailable, Keane recommended James N. Healy to McGlone. 'I think you'll be delighted with James N.,' he told him. Earlier, Healy had been profiled by Bob Davis in the New York *Irish Echo* when he toured his solo show. Davis described the Cork actor as a versatile performer, equally at home in plays and musicals.

On the first night at Seton Hall, James McGlone thought Healy was a revelation as the Hiker. 'He came on stage as an unlikeable, self-pitying old man who took his punishment from his sons,' McGlone recalled, 'but as the play progressed, you began to sympathise with him more and more, and by the end of the evening you were inclined to say to yourself, "Gee, this is a nice guy." And when the cast begin to sing "Red Sails in the Sunset" before the final curtain, it breaks your heart.'

The more Keane works he staged at Seton, the more McGlone became mystified by the Irish drama critics. The way some of them had treated the playwright's work was, in his opinion, a disgrace. He deplored their begrudging approach to Keane's plays; most of the time they were overcritical and unsympathetic and scarcely seemed to understand what Keane was striving for in his writing. He had no doubt that Keane had something important to say, and he had got it across theatrically.

Subsequently, when he produced *The Crazy Wall*, McGlone wrote in a programme note, 'When we began promoting John B. Keane's plays, the Dublin theatrical cognoscenti considered him a primitive and his plays mere popular entertainment. With the passage of the years, his work has become the staple of the Irish National Theatre at the Abbey. You will pardon us then if we seem like proud members of a family basking in the reflected glory of one of its favourite sons.'

If McGlone regarded *The Crazy Wall* as 'a neglected gem in the Keane crown' and *The Man from Clare* as having a mature theme, the production of *Moll* was one of the playwright's works that failed at Seton. Anna Manahan was engaged to play Moll Kettle, and the New Jersey papers explored her background. 'J. B. Keane trusts actors and gives them "space" within his plays to work,' she was quoted as saying. She stressed that he had always written good parts for women, and Moll was a good comic role.

Critic Bette Spero thought that not enough was seen of Moll to allow Anna Manahan show her full range of talents. In what the audience saw, she was 'spirited and precise and extremely funny when she teaches two young priests how to give a sermon.' The trouble was that Moll was just too one-dimensional to become truly interesting as a human being. 'Her interfering interloping, obviously designed to garner laughs, becomes too pat,' Spero said.

The McGlones – James and his wife Virginia – made periodic visits to Ireland, and in Listowel they were warmly welcomed. 'John B. Keane is a man hard not to like,' McGlone said some years ago. 'He is witty and a born raconteur, but he leaves the direction of his plays to the director. He has a fine grasp of Irish drama.' For her part, Virginia McGlone found that the playwright possessed unusual charm and great warmth of spirit. 'Meeting him in his home town was a real thrill for me after seeing nine of his plays in America,' she said.

*

For his next theme, Keane travelled no further than Ballybunion. In *The Buds of Ballybunion*, he deals with rural holidaymakers who visit the resort each September after the harvest is secure. They stay in special houses known as 'buds' houses, where they are provided with rooms, a fire and a cook. Keane came to know some of them and was fascinated by their mode of holiday living.

'The same people would come every year to the same places,' he said. 'They were mostly older members of families – bachelors, spinsters and widows. Many of them would be refugees from intolerance at home, where a daughter-in-law would have scant patience for the older women. They all brought their own food with them, and then while the bacon was being boiled, the cook would tie different-coloured threads to each piece to indicate its owners.'

To Keane, these people had beautiful styles of singing and dancing. The kitchen was the focal point of the house. There, the rosary was said, the card game of Twenty-five was played, and polkas and sets were danced. The local people looked upon the 'buds' as a source of amusement, but although conservative, they were never dull. They were viewed as relics from another century, which in a way they were. At the end of the Second World War, their style of holiday had disappeared.

Keane thought they were worth remembering, and it was one of the reasons he wrote his play. It was his first new play in four years and would be the last staged by Theatre of the South. He emphasised that the story had plenty of romantic interest. 'There is a lot of loneliness among the people which ends in romance,' he said. The music for the work was recorded by the Cork traditional group Na Filí. It was generally held that Keane needed a success with a new work, for not since *Big Maggie* had he made a profound impression.

It was an exuberant Keane who travelled to Dublin with Mary for the opening at the Olympia Theatre, however. The mime artist Marcel Marceau had packed the theatre for two weeks, and the playwright told friends that it would be a hard act to follow. But the theatre was nearly full for the occasion; indeed it was almost like old times as he was greeted by a legion of Kerry people, including Mick McCarthy of the Embankment, always a regular Keane first-nighter in Dublin. Denis Keane arrived with John and Peg Schuster, and there were familiar faces like Phyllis Ryan, Barry Cassin and Ray McAnally.

'It's been four years since I've had an opening night in Dublin,' Keane reminded friends in the bar of the Olympia. 'But I think this is my most entertaining show to date.' He was as nervous as ever on this first night, and there was laughter when he remarked, 'Wouldn't all of you be nervous if you had to follow Marcel Marceau?'

If he had expected a dramatic 'comeback' in Dublin, he was to be disappointed. He may have read too much into the enthusiastic reception the première of the work had received in Clonmel shortly before, for on this occasion the critics saw little to enthuse about. Frances O'Rourke in the *Sunday Press* seemed to echo the majority of her colleagues when she wrote: 'It says a lot for John B. Keane's dramatic and writing skill that his newest play can survive its clumsy construction, shallow character development and blithe disregard for unity. The world about the Buds, an assorted group of visitors to Ballybunion in September 1945, is colourfully written, sharply observant about some aspects of Irish life, and moving where Keane manages to get under the skin of his characters. Flor Dullea, as Tom Shaun Shea, the lively bachelor too shy to declare his lifelong love for the lady of the guesthouse hosting the Buds, has one of the best parts, and plays it effectively. But for all the pluses, there are minuses; for every character, there is a caricature – e.g. the spinster sisters, or James N. Healy's "hairy man".'

On reflection, Flor Dullea had happy memories of the play, although he admitted that in rehearsal he reckoned it would be a flop. But it came to life on stage. In one scene he asks the landlady, played by Marie Twomey, to boil his egg hard, but when he tops it, the yolk shoots out at him. So he puts the top back on the egg, hands it to the landlady and says, 'Boil that again, girleen.' The audience broke into laughter in Clonmel, and after that they decided to keep it in the scene.

Another line that roused the audience was when the actor Charles Ginnane remarked, 'I won't tell my sins to any farmer's son with a roundy collar on his neck.' There was something sentimental about the theme that appealed to Flor Dullea – perhaps its sheer nostalgia. When it opened in the Opera House in Cork, Maureen Fox in the *Examiner* wrote in the course of her review, 'In the past, J. B. Keane has, more often than not, displayed sensitivity for characterisation, but last night's performance was tainted by a crude and caustic portrayal of Irish men and women who, even to the extent that they existed in the past, are deserving of more from this experienced playwright.'

Keane would have liked to see *The Buds of Ballybunion* revived. 'It is a tender play that gets inside the hearts of people,' he contended. He was not alone in thinking so. In a letter to the *Cork Examiner*, a Cork woman living in Dublin wrote,

'This is J. B. Keane's loveliest play, written primarily out of the sweetest emotions, mainly affection. It is full of wit, hilarity and tenderness.' The play's warm mood is encapsulated in the words of the song sung by Mary O'Dea, the landlady, in the final scene:

> I walk along a sandy shore beside a silver sea,
> Where every wave and ripple there remind me love
>   of thee,
> And when at night the stars are bright beside the
>   pale moon's glow,
> I'll dream of Ballybunion and the Buds of long ago.

It was true to say that Keane had experienced mixed fortunes throughout the 1970s. The decade closed without him having achieved what he had set out to do in theatrical terms, and certainly not the Big Play that Robert Hogan had hoped for, although Keane was still enthusiastic about his biographical drama *The Crazy Wall*.

During the 1970s, it was noticeable that he was finding it difficult to fill the big Dublin theatres with his new plays, as he had done in the 1960s. The themes no longer appeared to be attracting the Keane aficionados of earlier years, and staged in theatres such as the Gaiety and the Olympia they tended only to show up the production's shortcomings, such as inadequate lighting, unimaginative sets and some obvious miscasting. Nevertheless, his loyal friends never despaired. They had witnessed both Brian Friel and Hugh Leonard go through 'bad patches' when nothing was coming right; those playwrights had pulled out of those spells, and they expected Keane would too.

For the Listowel dramatist, there were compensations. Prompted and cajoled by publisher Seán Feehan, he completed his *Letters of an Irish Minister of State*, a hilarious account of Tull MacAdoo, Minister for Bogland Areas. It will be remembered that in *Letters of a Successful TD*, the same Tull spends as much of his time writing to his wayward student son Mick as he does at his constituency work. Now the further exploits of new Minister Tull MacAdoo seemed to be essential reading for every ambitious TD.

During the 1970s, Mercier Press had also published Keane's latest book of short stories, *Death Be Not Proud*, and a few of the stories were read in the foyer of the Peacock Theatre before lunchtime plays. Abbey actress Kathleen Barrington, who was among the readers, says they were thoroughly enjoyed. She still has a copy of the book, signed, 'Love, J.B.'

One of the most moving stories in the collection is 'The Hanging', which explores the circumstances that lead to Denny Bruder taking his own life. The opening line evokes the dark mood: 'There is no sight so grotesque or pathetic as the dangling frame of a hanged man.' It is a story of betrayal, after Bruder has forged a loving relationship. Keane exposes the small-town mind, which can be at once sly and secretive and, in the case of Bruder, cruel. It is written in a simple but effective style. For the Peacock reading, it was pruned, with an eye to the clock.

In another story, 'The Change', Keane reflects on the leisurely mood of rural life:

> The village slept. It was always half asleep. Now, because there was a flaming sun in the June sky, it was really asleep. It consisted of one long street with maybe forty to fifty houses on either side. There were shops, far too many of them, and there were three decaying public houses, the doors of which were closed as if they were ashamed to admit people. No, that isn't quite true. The truth is that passing strangers upset the tenor of normal life. The locals only drank at night, always sparingly, and were therefore reluctant to accept habits that conflicted with their own.
>
> In the centre of the roadway a mangy Alsatian bitch sunned herself inconsiderately and that was all the life there was. The day was Friday. I remember it well because my uncle with whom I was staying had cycled down to the pier earlier that morning for two fresh mackerel. Mackerel always taste better when they are cooked fresh.

24

THE CHASTITUTE

Bachelor farmer John Bosco McLaine is one of Keane's most comic as well as most tragic creations. We first encounter him in *Letters of a Love-Hungry Farmer*, a man with a troubled and unfortunate love life, haunted by the spectre of being the last in his line, and in desperation seeking a suitable woman to be his wife.

'John Bosco,' Keane explains, 'suffers from the same ailment that afflicts many of his age group in country places – he is without a wife, mistress or regular copulatory companion. He shares a religious legacy that has consigned him and thousands like him to nights of stark loneliness and endless futile dreams.'

To describe him more accurately, Keane coined the word 'chastitute', and in *Letters of a Love-Hungry Farmer* he points out that 'chastitute' is the name given by the local parish priest to those without holy orders who choose celibacy before marriage, love affairs or promiscuity. 'Or in brief, he is a man who has never lain with a woman,' as the author puts it.

With *Letters of a Love-Hungry Farmer* proving to be a best-seller, Keane was searching for a suitable theme for a new play. It struck him that John Bosco might after all be a ready-made peg on which to hang his new work. He approached the subject with newfound enthusiasm. By the spring of 1980, he had finished the play to his satisfaction and decided to give it to Theatre of the South. He felt that James N. Healy would suit the part of the middle-aged farmer John Bosco McLaine.

Eventually, when Healy and his directors read *The Chastitute*, they were less than enthusiastic and believed it needed a lot of revision; there was also crudity in the dialogue that had to be considered. It was a surprise decision by Theatre of the South, for the actors made no secret of their enthusiasm for a new Keane work. As Flor Dullea said, 'We always looked forward to presenting a John B. première, and we didn't like to miss out, as had happened with *The Field*.'

As he had done with *The Field* years before, Keane turned instead to Phyllis Ryan's Gemini Productions. Phyllis had no hesitation in accepting the play and told the playwright that she planned to present the première at the Opera House in Cork, which would hardly please Theatre of the South, particularly if *The Chastitute* proved a box-office success.

Cork-born Donall Farmer, who had played in the television production of *The Field*, in which Geoffrey Golden was the Bull McCabe, got a phone call from Phyllis Ryan; she told him that John B. Keane had written a new play which Barry Cassin would direct, and asked him to play the title role of John Bosco McLaine. The actor, who had been directing a television film for RTÉ in Kerry, returned to Dublin to read the script. 'I loved it; it was a great vehicle for me,' he said.

Martin Dempsey was cast as Father Kimmerley. He was inclined to view *The Chastitute* as a tragicomedy, with John Bosco McLaine as a rather sad figure. He was greatly taken by his own part, especially the confessional scene in which John Bosco comes to tell him he has 'a notion of entering Holy Orders'.

The play opened at Cork Opera House in June, with Donall Farmer as the 'eternal loser' – the bachelor who can't get off with women – Cecil Sheehan as the local matchmaker, Ronnie Masterson as the Chastitute's aunt, David Byrne as the ladies' man, and Maria McDermottroe and Ann Sinnott as the women he pursues. The action opens with a long soliloquy by John Bosco McLaine in which he asks the audience, 'Look at me and tell me what you see. Go on.'

Donall Farmer knew this was a potentially dangerous opening line. On the first night in Cork, a well-known Corkonian sitting in the front row shouted, 'You're a hard man, that's what you are!' 'That got us off to a great start,' Farmer recalled.

On the second night, Keane arrived at the Opera House

with what he described as a 'posse of Kerrymen'. Farmer thought him understandably nervous. 'He is very shy anyway,' he recalled, 'but he hadn't had a success for a number of years.'

The audience response was enthusiastic, and at the interval Keane felt that the play would do well in Dublin. Donall Farmer could not recall the playwright congratulating him after his performance. 'John B. has his own way of letting you know that he appreciated your performance,' Farmer said. 'He doesn't go in for the "Lovely performance, darling" remark. He has certainly never said darling, at least not to a man.'

At the end of the play's first week, Keane appeared on television on *The Late Late Show*. Before leaving Dublin, Martin Dempsey and Donall Farmer filmed the confessional scene; this was screened during Keane's interview. The bookings soared after the show, and when the company opened a fortnight later at the Olympia Theatre in Dublin, even the boxes were filled night after night.

'The boxes were so close to the stage,' recalled Donall Farmer, 'that you could see people rocking with laughter.' He would have preferred a more upbeat ending to the play, but it had a certain charm, he said. Martin Dempsey felt there was more in the play than was realised by the production. He thought the playing tempo was too fast, with the result that the full effect of John Bosco McLaine's key opening speech was lost. Keane himself was not entirely satisfied and thought that one or two improvements could have been made in the casting.

He admitted that the play was a money-spinner for him. 'I was getting over £1,000 a week in box-office royalties, which was phenomenal money in those days,' he recalled. 'It took the pressure off me.' He agreed that he might look again at the ending of the play. As he admitted, 'I think the audience expected something else.' In the final lines of the last scene, John Bosco says, 'I'm going to blow my brains out.' That took many in the audience by surprise.

As one of the 'new wave' Dublin theatre critics, Fintan O'Toole, was to note in later years, much had changed in the twenty-one years separating *Sive* and *The Chastitute*. By 1980, the rural notion that cities were bastions of perversity against which rural society had to hold on to its traditional values had become entrenched. John Bosco, seeking to lose his virginity, is beset in the play by three types of person: fast women, who are unthinkable as marriage partners; frigid women, who refuse to satisfy him; and townie men, who whip away the available women with their confidence.

Even the matchmaker in *The Chastitute* is no longer a dangerous and distasteful figure, but a harmless and ineffectual comic who spells out the goal of John Bosco's search for a woman. 'What are we looking for?' the Chastitute says. 'Isn't it only someone to make our beds, wet our tay, and keep us company for the rest of our days with maybe a leg thrown over now and again?' But as O'Toole observed, 'The ravages of the new rampant sexuality are encountered by John Bosco in his search for a mate; indeed, sex has been loosed on the Irish countryside and has gone too far, denying unfortunate farmers like John Bosco the chance of happiness. "Modern damsels," points out Mickey the matchmaker, want only "booze, sex and discos."' O'Toole found the men in Keane's play 'cornered, cowed and embittered' by the failure of women to play their parts.

To O'Toole, the playwright was capable of exerting considerable force when he wrote about the old world of arranged marriages and simple peasants, but as the world became a more complex and difficult place and the idea of a simple rural locality sheltered from outside interference vanished, John B. ended up with a cranky and bewildered despair.

Keane would not have agreed with such a judgment. Although he had certain reservations about the casting of *The Chastitute*, he saw it as a theatrical success and a step forward into the 1980s. More good fortune lay ahead. The Abbey Theatre, it seemed, was again showing an interest in him. As he said, 'By now I had almost forgotten that the Abbey existed – or, at least, existed for John B. Keane's plays.'

Joe Dowling had been appointed artistic director of the National Theatre and, to his dismay, found that since the new Abbey building had been opened, no play of Keane's had been staged there. With the backing of the board, it was decided to stage a Keane work in the Abbey in 1980.

Basically, this was Dowling's decision, though he recalled that there was an admission at the theatre that a Keane revival was long overdue. The notion that the Abbey should not stage Keane because he was too popular seemed to Dowling 'an absolute nonsense' that had to be rectified. He argued, 'If you have a national theatre that ignores one of its most prolific and rooted playwrights who deals mostly with the issues of the country, you cannot call it a national theatre.'

The play chosen for the Keane revival was *The Field*, which Patrick Laffan was to direct. 'It was,' said Dowling, 'very much a case of testing the water.' From Keane, Dowling found that, because the Abbey had neglected him for seventeen years, there was an element of 'Let's see how it goes' in his response.

Joe Lynch was cast as the Bull McCabe. Two days after rehearsals began, Lynch met Dowling and Abbey Theatre manager Martin Fahy coming down the staircase. 'The play is off,' they told him. He was taken aback and asked what had happened. Dowling told him that Pat Laffan was ill.

Lynch had arrived from London to play the Bull and the Abbey management offered to pay his salary. Instead, he suggested they take Paul Brennan out of the cast and allow him to take over as director of *The Field*. The play went on, even though Lynch thought the setting of the field looked like 'an allotment in Inchicore.'

Des Nealon, who played William Dee, the outsider who is murdered by Bull McCabe and his son Tadhg, recalled that Joe Lynch did not play the part as a vicious individual but with a quiet menace. Friends of Keane, however, thought he looked too middle-class in his crombie overcoat, giving the impression of a smug and successful man.

Lynch insisted that his interpretation was based on some experience of the land. He remembered bringing cattle to fairs in Charleville in his youth. 'Cattle traders,' he recalled, 'wore high-laced shoes of a colour for working cow-dung, and narrow trousers that came down over the laces. They wore a frieze overcoat that was water-resistant and had pockets you never heard of for the concealment of money. In the left arm, they carried a sally twig, not a heavy stick, because you wouldn't want to mark a cow you were exporting to England.'

To Lynch, the Bull McCabe is 'no gobshite'. He has a mind like a computer, and so has his son, Tadhg. 'They can look at a beast and figure out his exact value,' Lynch said. The actor had grown up beside a rented field for holding cattle; such a field had to be extensive, well-watered and well-fenced. Without such a field, the Bull McCabe was lost. In law, he believed, a man like the Bull would have a case.

Des Nealon found Lynch 'wonderful to play with. When he waved his stick in my face, it was frightening. He really lived the Bull.' The scene in which the Bull whispers an Act of Contrition into William Dee's ear drew laughs from the audience, although to Nealon it was one of the most telling moments in the play. 'It was very daring of Keane to write this scene,' Nealon recalled. 'I know that actor after actor has fought the laughs in the scene.'

Night after night, he watched Lynch fighting the laughs, until he finally killed them. He brought his lines down to a whisper until the power and emotion of the scene carried it. To the audience, no doubt it appeared ludicrous for the Bull to whisper a prayer into the ear of the dead man. But to Nealon it was credible. 'The death is accidental, and the Bull and his son do not intend to kill William Dee but to frighten him,' he said. 'They are only trying to beat the man up, but Tadhg loses his head and kills him.'

They had rehearsed the scene with a stunt coordinator. Nealon was kicked to a sequence of counts. But on the first night he angled himself the wrong way and Colm Meaney, playing Tadhg, cracked one of Nealon's ribs. The actor had to go on stage for the next six weeks in plaster.

Keane came away from the first night with reservations about the production. Although he refused to be drawn into making comparisons between the Ray McAnally *Field*, as playgoers liked to call it, and the Abbey revival, he said later that the young director, Paul Brennan, should have contacted him about the production. 'I would have been willing to discuss certain aspects with Paul,' Keane said, 'but I was not consulted.'

Keane had known Patrick Laffan since the early 1960s, when the Abbey presented two of his plays, and he was disappointed when he had to withdraw. He felt that Laffan had an instinctive feeling for his work and that his direction of *The Field* would have been interesting. Nonetheless, the revival of the play was considered both an artistic and a commercial success, although Eamonn Keane 'never came to terms' with Joe Lynch's crombie overcoat.

Joe Dowling felt fully justified in reviving the play. As he recalled, 'Of course Keane was neglected for too long by the Abbey. People didn't regard his work as important; they saw it as commercial and tawdry – and it's not true. I think at this time the Abbey started taking him seriously, and we were able to get him recognised again as the major writer he is.'

It was ironic that the Abbey was rediscovering the Listowel playwright when other Dublin and Cork companies had been presenting his plays successfully for years. Looking back, Anna Manahan recalled that it was the establishment who refused to acknowledge his worth; he would have come back into fashion earlier if the Abbey had not delayed so long in reviving *The Field*. But the Irish people as a whole, she felt, had never let him down, and she remained convinced that Phyllis Ryan was the greatest influence on his career as a dramatist.

As Keane came back into fashion, Barry Cassin was wryly amused. When he read 'serious critics writing serious articles' about Keane's plays, it seemed to him that it had taken them a long time to discover what Phyllis Ryan had recognised almost immediately. There was a time in his own experience when John B. Keane had been laughed at by those who considered themselves leaders in the intellectual field. He once attended a university lecture when the lecturer, speaking about drama, dismissed a play with the words, 'It's about the standard of a J. B. Keane.'

At the time, Cassin remembered, there was a certain intellectual snobbishness, a feeling in urban circles that we should be striving to get away from our roots. In the 1960s, people had become self-conscious about their roots, and to them Keane's plays recalled a peasant past. He could understand such attitudes but he never had any doubt that Keane's plays would survive – at least the best of them.

Keane, who years before had said that the Dublin literati

bored him, never allowed critics or intellectuals to get between him and his writing. He liked to say that 'Nobody ever accepts a writer, he accepts himself.' He didn't want to be regarded as an intellectual and he was pleased that, in spite of the personal fame he had achieved, he had retained the friendship of those who knew him in north Kerry. He went to pains to emphasise that his friends were 'small farmers, big farmers, Kerry footballers, fighters', men whose friendship he cherished, and if he presented a side of himself as a famous man and a famous writer, he would be in danger of losing that friendship.

Nonetheless, it was also true to say that he was quite at home walking through the cobblestoned squares of Trinity College with Brendan Kennelly or discussing playwriting in the bar of the Abbey Theatre. John B. Keane was a man of many parts, though he was essentially a man of the people.

25

BIG MAGGIE IN NEW YORK

Big Maggie was to be a $300,000 off-Broadway production in the autumn of 1983, with a subsequent transfer to another theatre. It was the news that John B. had awaited for years and he did not intend his play to go on without him. He was not unaware that both Brian Friel and Hugh Leonard had in their time taken Broadway by storm with works like *Philadelphia, Here I Come!* and *Da*.

The backer for the production was Hugh O'Lunny, the Cavan-born owner of O'Lunny's bar in Manhattan. He had been approached by the father of actress Robin Howard to invest in the play. He checked out the actress who was to play the role of Maggie Polpin and found that she was an accomplished performer, so he reckoned the show was not as risky as it seemed.

Lester Ostermann, who had a good track record, was the executive producer, and he invited actor Dónal Donnelly to direct. Donnelly had built up a fine reputation as an actor and had starred in *Philadelphia, Here I Come!* and other successful Broadway productions. He cast the production, believing the play to be 'a passionate piece of writing', although he had never seen it performed on stage.

Keane and his wife Mary arrived in New York for the previews. Donnelly said, 'We wanted his advice. He was tremendously encouraging, as was Mary. I remember them both being terribly warm to everyone, and in no time at all John B. had the whole cast relaxed. My memory of him was that he was just constantly beaming, and loving New York and the whole experience.'

On the first night, the production played to a full house in the 199-seat Douglas Fairbanks Theatre on 'Theatre Row' off

Broadway. 'It was tremendous to feel the enthusiasm around you,' recalled Hugh O'Lunny. As always, Keane was nervous; it was something he could not disguise. He wanted a success in New York and he found the warm response of the audience around him encouraging.

'They loved the play,' said Mary Keane, 'and the applause at the final curtain was as good as anything the play had got in Dublin or Cork. I was hoping it would be a success for John's sake; he had waited a long time for this kind of night.'

But at the party that followed in Rosie O'Grady's pub on Seventh Avenue, the play's fate was devastatingly sealed when the newspaper reviews were delivered. *Big Maggie* received a partial acceptance from Clive Barnes, the *New York Post* critic, but it left the *New York Times* and the *Daily News* critics cold. Barnes may have found the play to be in the great tradition of Irish theatre, but Frank Rich in the *Times* regarded it as soap opera. 'Mr Keane,' he wrote, 'is incapable of investing any character with depth or ambiguity.' In the *Daily News*, Douglas Watt was more blunt. 'We are told *Big Maggie* is one of the most successful plays in Irish history,' he wrote. 'If so, Irish theatre is in a sorry state.' He summed up the play as 'a kitchen-sink comedy with pasteboard characters. Keane's speech, imagery and humour lack the soaring quality we have come to expect from the better Irish playwrights.'

Hugh O'Lunny saw that the reviews were devastating for Keane. 'The fact that the play wasn't appreciated or understood upset him as much as anything else,' O'Lunny recalled. Dónal Donnelly realised how important it was the have the imprimatur of the *New York Times* for a production; he knew how Keane must feel, for he had seen other playwrights, including Brian Friel, shattered by reviews in the past.

'It's not Frank Rich who wields the power,' Donnelly remarked, 'it's the paper. I thought if the play was well-received by the *Times*, it would get a long run. It was foolhardy to think any other way. Big musicals can run over the *Times*, no matter what the paper says. It is impotent against these juggernauts. But works of theatre, which have to be taken seriously, must have the paper's imprimatur for serious playgoers. I'm just sorry that the *Times* did not take an objective view of it.'

Lester Ostermann wanted to take the show off immediately to save backers losing more money. O'Lunny, however, prevailed in keeping it going for as long as possible. It ran for fifty-three performances.

O'Lunny felt that if the production had been staged by the Abbey Theatre Company instead of by Irish-American actors, it might have come across more successfully. The cast, he felt, had not extracted the humour from the play. The critics seemed to believe that all English-speaking cultures were the same, when in fact they were very different. It was his first experience of being close to a theatrical production. He had wanted to help what he was assured was a great play, which would be good for Irish culture and Irish theatre. In hindsight, he felt that John B. had allowed the production too much leeway. Nonetheless, audiences who saw the play thoroughly enjoyed it.

'That was the sad thing about it,' O'Lunny recalled. 'If the play had received no reviews, it might have done better. I think the cast felt that they too had to share some of the blame.' Robin Howard was in tears. 'I thought the show was getting better every day,' Howard said. 'We would have made it if it had run a little longer.'

The curtain fell for the last time after the Sunday matinée performance on 6 November 1983. 'It was an afternoon of cheering and stomping,' recalled Dónal Donnelly. 'We ended on a high note.' The Irish papers reported that Hugh O'Lunny had lost $300,000. 'My mother back in County Cavan thought I was bankrupt,' he said. 'So did one of my aunts in Swanlinbar, who kindly offered me money.' Today he confirms that his personal investment in the show had been $29,000.

Looking back, Keane remarked that his play had done 70 per cent box-office business; in a bigger theatre, that would have seen the show through. 'It was a terrible disappointment to me. It was like having all the hairs of your head pulled out together.' He knew *Big Maggie* was good enough, but he also realised that there's a lot of luck in the theatre. His one regret was that he had not become more involved in the production, even if this had entailed going to New York for the rehearsals.

'I should have been in there with the cast and director,

seeing to every detail,' he admitted. But it was not his way of working. He had always been content to let professionals stage his plays to the utmost of their ability. Mary Keane thought that if Marie Kean had been cast as Big Maggie, it might have added more weight to the production.

A year later, Keane was back in America to accept an honorary degree from Marymount College, New York. James McGlone decided to rent a theatre in New Jersey at the same time, to stage a production of *Sive*. Keane attended one of the performances by McGlone's Celtic Theatre Company and was guest of honour afterwards at a dinner at Cryan's Beef and Ale House in South Orange.

McGlone liked to quote Michael Judge's comment that, unlike some other Irish playwrights, Keane would be remembered a hundred years hence because 'he writes for the Irish people.' McGlone, a self-confessed traditionalist, commented, 'He writes from the gut. He is not to be found in the salons of Dublin.'

*

Keane shrugged off his American disappointment as best he could, helped by news from the Abbey Theatre that they planned to revive *The Man from Clare*. It was an apt choice for the year 1984, when the Gaelic Athletic Association was celebrating its centenary. He was pleased that Patrick Laffan would direct the revival, and he agreed to do some rewriting. 'He came to Dublin and we lunched at the Gresham Hotel,' Laffan recalled. 'I think I asked him for about a dozen new lines.'

Ray McAnally was cast as Daigan, the football-team manager. It was the actor's first role since undergoing major heart surgery. He was not sleeping well, and Laffan knew he was riding his bicycle in the middle of the night in the Phoenix Park for exercise. But at rehearsals he got right inside the part. Later, at one of the previews, he insisted on taking out his dentures, believing it would help the character. But the audience couldn't understand a word he said, even though his Kerry accent was very good. After that, he put his dentures back without argument.

The production, which packed the Abbey, was to start a Keane renaissance. 'I think it was something to do with the vitality of the dialogue,' Laffan suggested, 'or maybe a new generation of Irish people were interested in him.' It appeared too that critics like Fintan O'Toole had begun to see genius in the playwright. 'I feel they claimed too much for him, more than John B. would claim for himself,' Laffan said.

Éamon Kelly was cast as Morrisheen Brick, the football hero's father. He has a line to his son, 'Do you know what's nice? Girls you'd see through the windows of motor cars. They're here one minute an' gone the next.' It was a line, Laffan recalled, which always brought the house down.

To Éamon Kelly, *The Man from Clare* was an interesting play in that the theme of a fading footballer could be applied to an actor or musician who was growing old. The Abbey production was extraordinarily successful. Yet he felt that the Abbey could never put it in their history books that they had brought Keane to the forefront. So far as he was concerned, Phyllis Ryan had done that.

Kelly knew that the playwright had learned a lot as he went along about construction and craftsmanship. From the first day he came to prominence in the Irish theatre, the Abbey should have said to him, 'Come to Dublin and work in our theatre for a year.' That would have helped his craft. As it was, Keane had to learn the hard way, by trial and error.

The critic Con Houlihan, who came from Castleisland, wrote, 'If John B. Keane failed to evoke the worlds of hurling and Gaelic football, it would be almost as strange as if a French person wrote a novel and didn't mention wine.' To Keane, the production was a celebration of Gaelic football, staged in a more vibrant manner than the original Abbey production in the earlier 1960s. At the time, he told the journalist Charles Hunter, 'My early dealings with the Abbey were not happy, not a bit happy. I held my own and they discovered I wouldn't go away.'

At this point, Keane sensed he might not write any more plays. 'I'm just about at the age where a man can write a couple of novels,' he said. It was understandable. He had exhausted most of the rural themes, and the few that came immediately to mind seemed to him more suitable for a novel. Although the new popularity of his work at the Abbey pleased him enormously, he still found it hard to fathom why they had ignored him for seventeen years. Ironically, he was now among the very few playwrights capable of packing the national theatre, and this had not gone unnoticed by the board.

As a result, Joe Dowling found little difficulty in persuading the board members to agree to another Keane play, *Sive*. He was helped by the fact that the theatre itself was in financial crisis, and he admitted that he was having his own problems with the board. He asked the young director Ben Barnes to direct *Sive*. Barnes had successfully directed plays for the Abbey and the Peacock and had lectured on Beckett in Japan, where his production of *Rockaby* was presented. 'Ben was from Wexford, and I thought his work had a terrific rooted quality, which I felt at the time a lot of young directors were unable to achieve,' said Dowling.

Dowling called Keane in Listowel and told him that he had a young director who was his choice to direct *Sive*. Would he meet him? Keane agreed, and Ben Barnes travelled down to Listowel. Barnes came completely fresh to *Sive*. When he read the play for the first time, he was amazed by its power and captivated by the nuances of the language.

In Listowel, the young director met a genial, though cautious, Keane. As ever, he would try to be of assistance, but he had no idea what was in Barnes's mind. When he talked to him, however, he was impressed by his thoughtful approach and his willingness to listen. For his part, Barnes admitted that he, too, was cautious, but soon found a level at which they could communicate.

'I think it was refreshing and invigorating for him to work with someone completely new to his plays,' Barnes said, 'and it struck me that he found my serious approach gratifying. At the time I was a relatively inexperienced director, so I was anxious to have access to his mind and tap into his inspiration.' Together, they walked the beach at Ballybunion and talked for hours about *Sive*'s characters and the background to the play.

To Barnes, it was essential to meet Keane in his own environment. 'I looked on it like a pilgrimage,' the director recalled, 'and in time I became a regular visitor to the Listowel

Arms Hotel. I did good work down there. John B. was relaxed and helpful. I think he's like a fish out of water when he comes to Dublin.'

Instinctively, Keane felt this was the beginning of an important liaison. He counted him an intelligent young man with an agile mind. As he said, 'It is very easy to work with a fellow who likes your work. But he is a terrible man for bloody detail, and I'm forced to admit he is probably right. There is a considerable amount of careless writing in my plays, because some of them were written in a hurry. Ben leaves nothing to chance and he seeks clarification. No matter how bad the play Ben is presented with, it won't flop.'

Although the production of *Sive* was delayed – a mistake, in Joe Dowling's view – it finally went on in June 1985 and was ecstatically received by an audience that in the main consisted of a new generation of young playgoers. It proved an auspicious first night, with the professional theatre strongly represented, along with leading civic and business figures. It was a far cry from the old days at the Queen's Theatre, when even important first nights lacked excitement.

Corinne Martin, a young Dublin actress, played Sive, with Marie Kean as the grandmother and Catherine Byrne as Mena Glavin. Éamon Kelly, who was Pats Bocock, with Macdara Ó Fátharta as his tinker son Carthalawn, recalled putting venom into the parts. On the opening night, Ó Fátharta struck the bodhrán with such force that his knuckles went through the instrument. Kelly recalled, 'He never stopped. He just kept up the rhythm on the rim of the bodhrán.'

Although old-timers would hold that no cast could equal that of the original Listowel Drama Group in *Sive*, the consensus was that the Abbey company had done Keane proud, even if the stage set looked absurdly modern. Keane had no complaints. So far as he was concerned, the company had brought all its resources to the play. What was just as important, a new generation of playgoers had discovered his work. *Sive*, because of its sheer dramatic surge, would endure long after some of his other plays were forgotten.

26

THE FIELD IN MOSCOW

Five weeks ago in this parish, a man was
murdered – he was brutally beaten to death. For
five weeks the police have investigated and not
one single person has come forward to assist
them. Everywhere they turned, they were met
by silence, a silence of the most frightful and
diabolical kind – the silence of the lie. In God's
name, I beg you, I implore you, if any of you
know anything, to come forward and to speak
without fear.

This is part of the bishop's powerful plea to parishioners in
Act II of *The Field*, when he pleads with them to cooperate
with the police in solving the murder of William Dee. In the
first production of the play, in the 1960s, the bishop, as played
by Barry Cassin, could be seen in his purple vestments in the
pulpit; it proved one of the most telling moments of the
production.

When the Abbey Theatre revived *The Field* in February
1987, the audience found that the character of the bishop
was removed from the stage and replaced with a disembodied
voice. 'The scene loses its impact when the actor is unseen,'
wrote John Finegan. 'Here we are left,' observed Des Rushe
in the *Irish Independent*, 'with the audience looking at sixteen
faces while the voice of Desmond Cave delivers the words
over the public address. It is close to embarrassment.'

Phyllis Ryan said, 'I felt a dreadful loss when they hadn't
the bishop on stage. You see, the visible presence of the bishop
is powerful and his words lose much of their effect when you
don't see him saying them. It was a mistake to omit him.'

The omission of the bishop on stage was a decision made by director Ben Barnes with the blessing of Keane. It became a talking point in theatrical circles and there seemed to be no logic for the change. Looking back, Keane said he was prepared to make the concession to Barnes because his direction was very subtle. As the bishop's lines came over the address system, the shadow of a crucifix was shown.

'I think that Ben was trying to prove the futility, really, of the bishop and the church in trying to get people to talk,' Keane recalled. 'I do agree, though, that in the first production Barry Cassin was a superb bishop on stage. If the play is revived, I will be insisting that the bishop's scene is done as I wrote it.'

This was one of the few significant changes suggested by Barnes, however. While he felt that *Sive* was overwritten and needed pruning, *The Field* stayed more or less the same. At the Abbey's first night, the then Taoiseach, Charles Haughey, came to see it. As his car drew up outside the theatre, Keane, in a well-cut suit, stepped forward to greet him with a touch of humour. He counted Haughey among his political friends, although he insisted, 'I'm no Fianna Fáiler!'

Keane admitted that he was nervous, behind the smiles. 'I'm always shaking on opening nights,' he told columnist Brenda Power. 'Memories of past disasters come back to haunt me.' The fact that this was the second production of the play by the Abbey only made him more apprehensive. 'The second time around is like a grandchild,' he said, 'and you always worry more about grandchildren than about children.'

He dreaded doors that stick on the first night, actors who miss their lines, and critics. 'Irish critics can often be bitchy. I think that kind of verbal thuggery speaks of some deficiency in themselves, something wrong with their love lives. But I've never met an Irish critic who wasn't at least literate.'

Times had changed. A ticket for a Keane first night at the Abbey was now an item to be coveted. Fellow playwrights Hugh Leonard, Tom Murphy and Bernard Farrell arrived to wish him luck. So did such diverse personalities as Bernadette Greevy, Gay Byrne and Barry McGuigan. The United States ambassador, Margaret Heckler, waxed enthusiastic at the prospect of meeting the playwright whose 'personality was as legendary as his plays'. But a man from the BBC waited ticketless in the foyer.

Brendan Kennelly had written an introduction for the programme, extolling *The Field* for its 'emotional depth and riches'. Keane need not have been nervous. The audience was enthusiastic and the critical response positive. In the *Irish Times*, David Nowlan referred to the play as 'one of the best Irish plays of this century'; nonetheless, he felt that the theatricality in Barnes's production was that of metropolitan Europe rather than rural Ireland. Yet the play survived 'to send shivers down the spine of another generation of theatergoers.' In the *Sunday Tribune*, Fintan O'Toole explained that Keane's plays 'tell us a lot about how we got to be where we are now' and said he felt that Barnes's production presented *The Field* as 'a play about a whole society in transition' and did it superbly. It was 'a meticulously intelligent and well-acted production of a fascinating play,' O'Toole wrote.

John Finegan in the *Evening Herald* thought that Keane's 'most potent and bravest play' had got 'a tingling, splendid revival'. Niall Tóibín played the Bull with 'almost frightening power'. Nowlan found Tóibín 'original and cunning'. O'Toole thought he played him as 'smaller than life, an ordinary man whose actions are based on the absolute belief that he is right, a man who substitutes violence for the imagination to comprehend the changing world around him.'

The Abbey revival proved extremely successful, and was revived again during the summer. 'Not for the first time', wrote John Finegan, 'has John B. Keane come to the aid of the national theatre.' It must have caused the playwright some wry amusement that interviewers were now beating a path to his door. He regaled them before the first night with his views on audiences, the literati, the metropolis and the early antagonism towards his work.

He recalled to Mary Leland, the Cork writer, some of the remarks that journalists and intellectuals had made about him in the early days. One columnist had written that he would be conspicuous at a gathering 'because of his pinstripe wellingtons'. He was considered 'a bit of a literary gombeen', an impression reinforced by resolutely sticking to the environs of his native town. He had found 'a pot-shot element' in Dublin – 'people who liked to take the mickey out of rustics.'

He confessed, 'When I met these people, they were only barely removed from the cow-shit themselves – and there's nothing wrong with that.' He told journalist Michael Sheridan, 'I have always found a resistance to my work from the pseudo-literati, who on many occasions would lie behind my back. For example, I was accused of being anti-Irish because I was involved in the Language Freedom Movement. Although I have been writing plays for thirty years, the theatrical establishment has always considered me to be a bit of an upstart.'

It was a view which Aodhán Madden, himself a playwright, was to echo in the *Irish Press*. For twenty years, he pointed out, the author of *The Field* wasn't taken seriously by the Dublin arts politburo. 'He was raw, unsubtle, sentimental, his plays furrowed muddy tracks into neurotic Irish consciousness,' Madden commented. 'If we came from backwoods, we wanted to forget it pronto. Our self-delusion could better be served by imitations of Syngian romanticism or the mean-city angst of Beckett. Keane was plastic statues and bar-room bathos. *Sive* was thus deemed irrelevant; arranged marriages just didn't happen any more in Gay Byrne's Ireland. And how could the Bull McCabe fit comfortably into the tarmacadam of EC-subsidised farming?'

Madden saw an irony in the Abbey revival of *The Field*. 'The mandarins of taste have come to realise that Keane, after all, does have something to say to a modern audience,' he remarked. Keane would say that the Abbey renaissance in respect of his work was important to him, yet he was aware that people still tended to look at him from their own particular point of view. He believed they often viewed him through distorted lenses.

*

International recognition soon came Keane's way. When members of the USSR Ministry of Culture and Government visited Dublin, they asked that the national theatre's current productions, *The Field* at the Abbey and Tom McIntyre's surrealist *The Great Hunger* at the adjoining Peacock, be staged in Leningrad and Moscow.

The plays might not have been the Abbey's first choices for the national theatre's first visit to the Soviet Union, but the theatre directors went along with the Soviets' decision. The two companies, together with a representative press corps, set out for what was described as 'The Journey from Two-Mile Inn to the Moscow Arts'; the Two Mile Inn was where the party spent a night before boarding an Aeroflot flight from Shannon to Leningrad on 8 February 1988.

Had Keane made the journey to see his play performed in two of the most famous theatres in Russia, he might have acted as a mediator between the two companies and the travelling journalists. Whereas Éamon Kelly and his wife, Maura O'Sullivan – who played Dandy, the Bull's first cousin, and his wife in *The Field* – were the soul of good humour, some members of the company were, to the journalists, prone to temperament. Kelly recalled the unease among the party and thought some of the journalists were hostile. 'People who set out as friendly reporters ended up as war correspondents,' he recalled.

In Leningrad, the journalists were allocated the best rooms at the Europskaya, the former nineteenth-century Hôtel d'Europe. At the first press conference, they questioned the choice of plays for this historic tour, and the temperature became decidedly icy. The actors were allocated a hotel restaurant which closed its doors before midnight; the journalists dined in the hotel's art deco restaurant, which had chandeliers, white linen tablecloths, and private booths which could be sealed off with red velvet curtains.

To Éamon Kelly, there was 'almost the same reaction to the lines that we got at the Abbey.' Des Nealon played the priest (he had played William Dee in the earlier Abbey production). He had a line to Máire O'Neill's Mrs Butler, the owner of the field: 'Place yourself in God's hands and all will be well.'

'No matter how I said that line in the Abbey, it got a laugh,' Nealon recalled. 'I hammered it; I threw it away; I barely spoke it. But still they chuckled or laughed. In contrast, when I spoke the line in Moscow and Leningrad, there was a hush in the audience. They totally related to *The Field* in Moscow; they understood it straightaway. I found an enormous respect for the part of the priest I was playing.'

Nealon, like the other players in the companies, was surprised by the enthusiasm of the audience and the sight of even the stagehands applauding. 'People were screaming for autographs outside the theatre and running up to us with their programmes,' he said. 'It was a novel experience for all the company.'

For Éamon Kelly, performing on the original Moscow Art Theatre stage was a memorable experience. He found the acoustics perfect. 'You hear your voice coming back to you,' he recalled. 'And to think you were playing on that stage where so many famous people strutted their hour away! It gave me the feeling of an old parish priest in Knocknagoshel saying Mass in the Vatican, a kind of long-term fulfilment. There is something very special about the Moscow Art Theatre. I was happy to play there before I finally pass from the theatrical scene.'

'What a pity,' lamented Nealon, 'that Keane wasn't in Moscow. It was an opportunity lost.' As Kelly put it, 'It was great experience for us to go there and to bring Keane's best play there. I would have liked him to have joined us on stage at the final curtain.' Ben Barnes, like the Abbey directors, was disappointed that John B. could not join the tour. The playwright would later say that he decided not to go for personal reasons.

27

MAGGIE'S MONOLOGUE

In one of his last decisions as artistic director at the Abbey Theatre, Joe Dowling revived another Keane play. He believed it was time to complete the trilogy that had begun with *Sive* and *The Field*. The man who agreed with the decision to revive *Big Maggie* was Noel Pearson, chairman of the Abbey board, and now also involved in films.

Pearson had no illusions about the theatre; he kept a constant eye on the box office and often judged plays on their box office appeal. He was only too aware that two consecutive flops plunged the Abbey into deep financial crisis. For that reason, *Big Maggie* struck him as a likely winner, provided he could get the actress he wanted for the title role.

By now Pearson had become friendly with Keane and they hit it off extremely well. The playwright found that the ebullient Pearson was good to do business with, possessed flair and talked the same language as him. Keane came to have an unstinted admiration for him. When Pearson told him that he had an actress in mind to play Maggie, Keane said, 'I hope she'll be as good as my other Maggie Polpins.'

During the filming of *My Left Foot*, which he was producing at Ardmore Studios, Pearson approached Brenda Fricker, who was playing the part of Christy Brown's mother in the film. The actress recalled that she was following her usual custom of collecting her food at the buffet counter at the studios and going to sit at the bar to eat alone. 'I have a rule during lunchtime when I'm working that I don't do anything except have my lunch alone,' she said.

Pearson came and sat beside her. 'Would you like to play Big Maggie at the Abbey?' he asked.

It was a quarter to two. Brenda retorted, 'Don't you dare

intrude on my lunch hour!' So he sat there until one second past two. 'Then he asked, "Would you be interested in playing Big Maggie at the Abbey?" And I said yes.'

It was six years since Brenda Fricker had been on the stage. She had reportedly been hurt by the fact that the Dublin theatre had ignored her for more than a decade. During that time she had appeared in such films as *The Ballroom of Romance* and *The Woman Who Married Clark Gable*; she was also playing the motherly, caring Nurse Megan in the long-running Thames Television series *Casualty*.

Still, she was not coming entirely new to Keane. She had played the daughter, Mary Madden, in the first production by Phyllis Ryan of *Big Maggie*, when Marie Kean had created the role of Maggie Polpin, the woman who wins her freedom through the death of her husband. 'The play was being rewritten on the backs of envelopes,' Fricker recalled. It was one of her first professional jobs, and she remembered, 'It was the time when, if you had a very good house for a show, you got an extra pound in your pay envelope.'

Ben Barnes, who was faring extremely well with Keane plays, was to direct the new production of *Big Maggie*. He sensed that the general atmosphere of the 1960s, when the play was written, had impeded the playwright in his writing. The play was about a woman whose sexual lifestyle had been conditioned by the confessional – a woman seeking to come to terms with the menopause and her private lusts while punishing her children for her misalliance as they try to come to terms with their own sexuality.

Once again, Barnes made the trip to Listowel and for a few days made the Listowel Arms Hotel his base. For hours, he discussed *Big Maggie* with Keane, either in the playwright's first-floor study or on the strand in Ballybunion. He found the exercise stimulating as he sought to unravel Maggie's character in detail. Keane would say, 'There's a bit of my mother in Maggie, but the majority of Maggie came from a matriarch I knew in this town. A powerful woman who dominated her family completely and made successes of all of them. I suppose you could say she was a materially successful woman, but romantically her life might have been a failure.'

Barnes was keen to dramatise the social tensions in the play, and the sparring between Maggie and Byrne, the stonemason with designs on the widow, became less central than in the earlier productions. Furthermore, Barnes felt that Keane had been very restrained when writing *Big Maggie* originally and began to wonder whether the Kerryman would write in things he had held back in the original work. After discussions, they thought perhaps a monologue for Maggie at the end of the play would be effective, although Barnes agreed that it would be a radical change.

To Brenda Fricker, it was an inspired idea. When the monologue was written, however, she thought it 'far too long and a little bit too purple', though she realised it explained 'a lot of what he must have been thinking about Maggie when he wrote it.'

Fricker had found Keane 'kind of shy' when she had played in the original production; now she was to come to know him better. She had seen other actresses, like Doreen Hepburn and Ronnie Masterson, play the part of Maggie, and believed she herself was the only actress with a Kerry background to play the role in a professional production. In fact, she had worked it out that she and Keane were distant cousins. 'My mother was a Murphy from Kerry,' she said, 'and if you are a Kerry Murphy you are related to everybody else in Kerry.'

In her early days, she became nervous when a playwright came to rehearsals. Now, by her own admission, she was cheekier and tended to take Keane's presence at rehearsals for granted. She didn't need to talk to him about the character because she had appeared in the first production in the 1960s. As she recalled, 'I had grown up in Kerry, so I knew these women intimately. I didn't need to talk to John B. about that, just about the new ending.'

She asked him if he would mind if she edited the monologue a little bit. At the end of one rehearsal, they went up to the Gresham Hotel to discuss the speech. The hotel staff refused to allow Brenda bring her dog into the hotel. Keane was angry, but she reassured him, 'It doesn't matter. I'll put the bowler in the car.' They went back to the hotel and began drinking pints of stout together.

Keane wanted to relax, but Fricker was anxious to revise the final speech. 'John B. kept dodging the subject,' she recalled. 'He was kicking away from me every time I tried to bring the script out of my bag. Eventually I did bring it out, and we spent hours going through it. I fought over bits and pieces. He kept bits I didn't want; he let me take bits out I didn't want. It was an even match.'

To the actress, the speech, though a beautiful piece of writing, had been too long. She knew how she was going to play Maggie Polpin. 'I'm not reluctant to play baddies, but I don't think she was a baddie,' she said later. 'She was a woman cursed with four layabouts – her kids – who were complete wasters. All she could do was kick them in the ass and get them out of the house and try to live a bit of life for herself. I tried to fill her out more, and I tried to make her not bitter. But you can never tell if it has worked.'

To Barnes, who was directing, Keane's women were the backbone of the Irish social structure. 'The men are weak and the women are strong,' he noted, 'rather like in *Juno and the Paycock*, in which the Paycock goes out to the pub while Juno makes the decisions.'

There were still divided opinions during rehearsals about the monologue which was to close the play. Barnes admitted that this 'was controversial, but necessary if only to avoid the original ending, which was repetitive.'

'I thought the audience should hear it,' Brenda Fricker recalled. 'But it was a bugger for me to turn around at the end of a play when you are exhausted and suddenly take a deep breath and walk down and do half an hour to the audience.'

She asked both Barnes and Keane to let her try it at the Abbey previews. 'If it works, you can keep it in,' she told them. They reckoned it did work, but in her view, 'Half the audience loved it, the other half hated it.' To Keane, her performance was stunning: the voice, the expressive face, the eyes that conveyed so much meaning.

On the first night, Fricker's portrayal seemed even more powerful. A stark figure dressed in black, she lorded the stage from the moment she uttered her first word in the graveyard. For the monologue in the final scene, she walked down to the front of the stage and the light closed in behind her. In total silence, she began, 'I'm alone now, but I'm free and not too many women can say that. But I need not to be alone and that's the beauty. A woman need never be alone as long as men crave what she has, and that never gives out.'

Like the audience, the critics were divided about the inclusion of the monologue. Brian Brennan in the *Sunday Independent* saw it as 'a direct appeal by Maggie to the audience for understanding (or sympathy, perhaps).' But to David Nowlan in the *Irish Times*, it was 'a gratuitous solo' in which Maggie, the drama over, 'tells us just what blighted her life.' Nowlan felt 'as theatrically bludgeoned as Maggie's family, all driven from their Kerry nest, are supposed to feel in "real life".'

Fintan O'Toole saw Big Maggie as Keane's Mother Ireland. Like Ireland after the departure of the English, she is tasting freedom with the death of her husband: ''Tis only now I know what freedom means,' she says at his graveside. He regarded Maggie as an embodiment of the old order of sexual values, a woman motivated by concern for the welfare of her children. She is the old order that Keane wants to see modernised, a woman who must be criticised because her sternness stands in the way of a more flexible approach to sex and marriage, which is needed for the good of society. Like Kate in *The Year of the Hiker*, Maggie has failed to keep her husband sexually satisfied and he has sought solace elsewhere. Maggie's daughter Katie says, 'My mother didn't sleep with him for years, and when she did I doubt if she was any good to him.'

O'Toole was among the new generation of critics who were championing Keane's plays. He believed the new ending offered Maggie Polpin 'at least the tragic blessing of self-awareness.' It was a 'powerful monologue in which Maggie analyses her sexual self, her relationship to her body and to men and the way in which the Church has moulded that relationship,' he commented. O'Toole found dark corners in the play worthy of Strindberg, and he noted that the production had resisted the temptation to fill them in.

Joe Dowling went to see the production and described it as 'a marvellous evocation of the time.' Brenda Fricker was 'extraordinary,' he said. David Nowlan commented that 'Ms

Fricker's performance is remarkably sustained and controlled, with none of the hyperbole that was evident in earlier characterisations.' Gerry Moriarty in the *Irish Press* thought the new monologue compelling but unnecessary, 'because the story allows us to know intuitively the dark religious and social forces that shape and restrict Maggie.' He was nonetheless overwhelmed by Fricker's 'magnetic performance.'

Keane was left to wonder how the Abbey production might fare on Broadway. In his view, such was the impact of Fricker's performance that he could scarcely see it fail. It packed the Abbey, and the controversy about the new monologue continued among Dublin's theatrical fraternity.

*

Keane returned to Listowel a happy man. The critical acclaim afforded to the production of *Big Maggie* naturally pleased him, and he would remember the 1980s as his 'years at the Abbey'. In July 1988 he celebrated his sixtieth birthday. 'I don't feel sixty,' he joked to the locals in his pub. 'I can still walk ten miles a day.' He preferred not to dwell on age but to get on with his work.

Except for his greying hair, some extra pounds round the waist, and a fuller face, he looked fit and well. In his view, there was no such thing as a working day. It was 'non-stop, you never left your work alone,' he said. In his opinion, you might get away from it for an hour, but if it was going to be any good, you had got to keep returning to it.

Mary said, 'People really don't realise how many hours John spends writing; he is no more a publican than I don't know who. He's rarely inside the bar. He comes outside it every night and we all love to see him coming, and I'm a sort of go-between there. I think I'm sometimes Moll, the Moll in his priests' play. She's all the time protecting the parish priest, and I think I'm another Moll here.'

Mary enjoyed running the pub. She said it kept her close to people and hardly a day passed without friends dropping in to chat with her. It was a changed house now. Billy, their eldest son, had a solicitor's practice in the town and, in a typical gesture, Keane handed him the keys of a new house he had built for Mary and himself. Mary thought it was too early yet to leave the public house and 'retire in style'.

John Keane and his brother, Conor, had become journalists and were attached to papers in Kilkenny and Limerick. Joanne Keane was studying to be a teacher. 'Dad never tried to influence us in our choice of career,' recalled Conor Keane. 'I had joined the Limerick Leader before he knew about it. He wanted us to be as independent as possible. I think we all have his sense of humour and love of football.' Conor's abiding memory of home was the presence of his father. 'Dad always seemed to be around; it was a strong and reassuring presence,' he recalled.

Keane had expressed disappointment at having missed out on wearing the Kerry football jersey, but he had the satisfaction of seeing his sons, John and Conor, wear it with distinction for the Kerry minor team. John was so promising that he played in some friendly games with the Kerry senior team. It was an achievement that made his father intensely proud. John B. liked, too, to drink a pint of stout with his sons. 'You get to know them better that way,' he said, 'and I think they come to appreciate your trust in them.'

Joanne was twenty-one, and close to her parents. In the family circle, she did not look upon her father as a famous playwright, but simply as a parent. In Listowel, she found they accepted him as one of their own; she understood that, just as she knew that elsewhere she would always be regarded as John B. Keane's daughter. She never ceased to be amazed at how well-known he was.

Among her father's virtues, Joanne counted a generosity of spirit: she felt she could ask him for anything and probably get it. Most times he was cheerful around the house, but when he was engrossed in his writing, he was pensive. Because of his passion for Gaelic football, he sometimes avoided watching a big game on television for fear of getting too excited; instead, he would ask Joanne to tape it so he could watch it later. On one occasion, she stopped the tape at half-time; when he found out, he flared up and stormed out of the room. 'But, as always, the beauty was that in a few minutes he had forgotten all about it,' Joanne recalled. She found that, curiously, it was little things that tended to annoy him most; the bigger things seldom did. When he had had a few drinks, he tended to talk endlessly in Irish; then, when no one was listening, he would slip away to bed.

William (Billy) Keane chose law as a career in spite of his father's warning that it was very demanding. 'I think he wanted me to be a teacher like his own dad, William, but he accepted my decision. I've had a happy upbringing and a more liberal one than most boys could expect in a small town like Listowel. Growing up, I was brought to rugby internationals at Lansdowne Road as well as big football games at Croke Park, and we were left with no hang-ups about religion, sex or censorship.'

Billy admired the discipline his father brought to his writing and the long hours he devoted to it; he saw how utterly engrossed John B. became with the characters in his plays and novels. 'During those times, he was more thoughtful,' Billy recalled. 'I would like to see Dad and my mother, who has also worked hard, devote time now to travel and generally relax more. But will they? I'm not so sure. Writing is integral to Dad's life, just as the pub is to my mother. She just likes meeting people and talking to them.'

Billy's younger brother, John, once played for the Kerry minor footballers in an all-Ireland final against Dublin; it was a source of regret that his father was not there to see him, even in defeat. But John understood. He realised that the excitement might be too much for him. One of his cherished memories of growing up was the confidence instilled in him by his father. 'Dad gave us lots of freedom to get around and also encouraged self-expression,' John said. 'I suppose it was a matter of trust. It was something all of us appreciated.'

To John, the house exuded warmth and cheer, and he saw that his father was not slow to demonstrate his affection for their mother. 'They had their arguments like everybody else,' John recalled, 'but Dad sometimes hugged and kissed my mother. It was spontaneous and tended to show the humour he was in.'

When Keane was awarded a literary prize from the Irish

American Foundation, he handed the cheque for $10,000 to John. When Gay Byrne asked him on *The Late Late Show* why he had done such a thing, the playwright simply replied, 'John's my son.' He didn't elaborate, nor did Byrne make a comment.

Mary Keane regretted the children's departure from the home in William Street. It wasn't the same place without them, she felt. But Joanne often came home at weekends, and so did John and Conor when they could. It remained a close-knit family. By now, Keane's mother, Hannah, had died peacefully in her eighties. He had tried to visit her each day, and he knew she derived satisfaction from his successes.

At sixty, John B. could say he had achieved everything he had set out to achieve, and more. In particular, seeing Richard Harris play the Bull McCabe was very fulfilling. He had no serious regrets, although he often felt outside forces working for and against him. 'I think I have an invisible Celt's tail,' he said, 'which sometimes whips me around and around irresistibly. My regret is that I often could not control this tail.'

Reflecting on life itself, he had learned that tolerance was the great virtue. 'The man who can go 51 per cent of the way towards accepting another's point of view is a great man,' he said. He admitted he had made sacrifices to be a writer. 'I was regrettably isolated for long, long periods from my wife and family, but that's writing,' he said. 'There were too many curtailed holidays, too many years of pain and frustration as I was learning my trade. The rewards came late in the day, but my ships are starting to come home in the end.'

It was a source of satisfaction to him to have achieved success in the spheres of poetry and the short story, as well as as a playwright. And his novel *The Bodhrán Makers* had become a best-seller, with sales running into many thousands. His output continued to be remarkable: scarcely a year passed without a new book of short stories or a novel. He had not abandoned dramatic writing, in spite of what some theatre people imagined. He was revising his new play, *Vigilantes*, and hoped to have it staged.

To his friends, who remained intensely loyal to him, there

was a palpable sense of contentment about him; he was mellower, even if a little restlessness coloured his life. He admitted that much of the old turbulence had disappeared, though he was still capable of showing a troublemaker the door of the pub in William Street. He liked to think he had the 'old demon' drink under control, yet he still enjoyed a few pints of beer with the locals in the pub or after football matches in Tralee and Killarney.

He had not lost his sense of humour or his spontaneity, although as one Dublin journalist put it, 'At sixty, J. B. Keane is still the scourge of the sham, the hypocrite and the pseudo-moralist.'

28

THE FIELD ON SCREEN

'If the film is going to be made, the only person who's going to make it is you.'

Noel Pearson recalled Keane's words when he telephoned him in Listowel, asking for the screen rights of *The Field*. The deal did not interest the playwright. Pearson said that Keane asked him for 'whatever you feel, and I'll have the contract back to you in twenty-four hours.' The contract was delivered and within twenty-four hours the playwright had signed and returned it. He said that he was favourable to the suggestion that Ray McAnally play the Bull McCabe.

It was Jim Sheridan, the director of the film *My Left Foot*, who had first told Pearson of McAnally's idea to make a film of *The Field*, with himself playing the Bull. Others had considered the film project previously, among them Jack Phelan and Gerry Coulson; there was even a screenplay. The producer Arthur Lappin had also discussed with Pearson and Sheridan the idea of making a film.

Lappin called up Jack Phelan to tell him that there was now interest in a film of *The Field*, but Phelan's option had lapsed. 'By the time I found Noel Pearson, he had actually bought the option,' Phelan recalled. Pearson knew that the play had been optioned on several occasions, but, as he put it, 'it had never happened.'

As with most film productions, the course of pre-production did not run smoothly. Contrary to newspaper reports at the time, there was no substance in the suggestion that Marlon Brando might play the Bull McCabe, though Sean Connery was seriously considered for the part. McAnally's name, despite his achievements, was not strong enough internationally to front a film that was to cost $7 million.

'The film would not have happened,' admitted Noel Pearson, 'with just McAnally. The finance didn't come until we got Tom Berenger as William Dee.'

Jim Sheridan began writing the screenplay. Initially he had talks with McAnally, then went to Listowel and met Keane. It was not Sheridan's first association with the playwright. He had once appeared at the Peacock, in an Irish-language production, as Dan Pheaidí Aindí, and had met Keane briefly when touring the amateur drama festival circuit with a production of Marlowe's *Doctor Faustus*.

'We were called the Slot Players, after the church of St Laurence O'Toole in Sheriff Street in Dublin,' Sheridan recalled. 'It was 1972, and I directed the play with the Seven Deadly Sins wrapped in muslin cloths. When they danced, the muslin fell off and various parts were exposed. The devil was costumed in a ski diver's suit with his hair down to his waist.'

Sheridan remembers presenting the play in Killarney. 'It was such an outrageous production, we should have come last,' he said. But John B. Keane was in the audience. 'At the end of the show,' Sheridan continued, 'I remember this big fellow standing up – it was John B. – and saying, "They'll win the trophy!"' Sheridan and his group were placed second and reached the final in Athlone. As he commented later, 'When John B. said something like that, we definitely had to get second.'

When Sheridan moved to New York, he staged *Matchmaker* at the Irish Arts Centre. It had earlier been adapted by Ray McAnally and Barry Cassin from Keane's book *Letters of an Matchmaker*. 'I had to call John B. to ask if we could do it. Instead of the usual response, "I'll have to talk to my agent", John B's attitude was, "Ah, send me whatever you think is fair."'

Keane's attitude to business is coloured by his experience of running a pub, Sheridan concluded. 'He knows that business is difficult and that you have to be positive,' the director recalled. 'Whereas most people are trying to figure out how they are being screwed, he is a treat to work with.'

Sheridan believed that the first time the playwright read

the film script for *The Field*, he was shocked. 'I think he thought it was quite wild,' the director said, 'and that changing the ending was like taking your life in your hands.' But he maintained contact with Keane during the rewriting. For his part, the playwright was not anxious to become involved in the film script and was prepared to leave that to Sheridan.

McAnally saw the Bull as a darker character than either the play or the film script portrayed. According to Pearson, 'He didn't like the script, yet he didn't dislike it. He said he didn't want to be in a situation where he would have to argue all day on the set.'

'Ray was really tired at the time,' said Sheridan. The last meeting between Sheridan, Pearson and McAnally was adjourned. Pearson told Sheridan, 'Let's go away and think about it.'

'Ray may have had reservations about the script,' said Pearson, 'but he looked exhausted, he looked dreadful, that day.' McAnally was to deliver his reservations in writing to the film duo and they were to answer them. But the meeting they were to hold on the following Friday never took place: McAnally died on the Thursday.

Ronnie Masterson, McAnally's widow, felt that Ray was not physically capable of appearing in the film at the time. He also disliked the ending, showing the Bull driving the cattle into the sea. He could not accept that as a climax, nor could he equate it with the Bull's character. 'I'm sure he would have said no to the script,' Masterson said.

*

Richard Harris had been offered the role of the local priest by Pearson. In the script, the priest had become 'a Max von Sydow type of character,' according to Pearson, and his sermon to the congregation was to have been 'a lot crazier'.

But Harris did not want to play the priest; he wanted the part of the Bull McCabe. Four weeks after McAnally's death, he began calling Pearson. 'He drove me mad,' says the producer. 'Nobody wanted him, including Jim Sheridan. Granada (who were among the film's backers) demanded he audition. They even sent a woman to the Halcyon Hotel in London, where he stayed, to look at him physically. They didn't believe he was off the drink. It became a comedy.'

Pearson finally decided that Harris was so obsessed with playing the Bull that he would ask Sheridan to go to meet him. The director had reservations: Harris had been ill with a gum infection, and on their last meeting 'he looked like he was dying,' Sheridan recalled. But when they met again at the Halcyon, the problem had been cured. 'He was still quite thin, but physically he is huge,' the director said. 'He gave me the full lash in his hotel. I could see he was mad to do the part.'

Harris had not made a cinema film for some eight years, however, and Granada did not consider him bankable. At their suggestion, they had already got an American, Tom Berenger, for the part of Dee. Then John Hurt came in to play the Bird Flanagan. 'I think John B. thought Harris would be good,' said Sheridan, 'but it was really a decision between Noel and me, and in the end we said, "Let's go."'

The film of *The Field* was made on location at Leenane in Connemara. Harris worked 'unbelievably hard' on the film, according to Pearson. 'He worked like a slave,' the producer said. John B.'s brother Eamonn had hoped for the part of the Bird Flanagan, but Pearson thought he was not physically capable of taking on the role; instead, he played a smaller part.

Pearson recalled that Eamonn was complimentary to Hurt, who himself had not wanted to take on the part of the Bird. Hurt said, 'He had played the part himself on stage, yet he was nothing other than encouraging.' They acted together in the critical dance-hall scene. 'If you have played a part and somebody comes from abroad to play it, it is very easy to be difficult,' Hurt continued. 'But Eamonn was never that.'

Some three weeks into the filming, John B. Keane arrived on location with the film-maker Muiris MacConghaile, who was making a documentary on the playwright. Arthur Lappin, who was line producer on the film, said, 'I had the feeling Keane wasn't all that interested in the process.'

MacConghail directed the interviews for the documentary

at the hotel at Leenane. Brenda Fricker found Keane looking 'very dapper and wearing this wonderful camel-hair coat.' His first question related to her dog. 'Where,' he asked, 'is W.B.?' W.B. (named after Yeats) was with the actress, and Keane wanted to know if he was allowed into the Renvyle Hotel. Brenda was happy to tell him that W.B. was welcome there.

Keane and Harris had exchanges on camera about the character of the Bull, but Harris dominated the conversation.

'*The Field* is Ireland to me,' declared Harris.

'The land is his heritage,' said Keane.

'That's right!'

'And it's the thing he passes on.'

Harris launched into his own interpretation of the part and of the character of the son, Tadhg; he also discussed his belief the Bull had condemned his dying mother to hell by saving the hay before sending for a priest.

Keane admitted to differences of opinion with the actor, though he affirms that 'they didn't last.' According to the playwright, Harris, like himself, was a fairly volatile fellow.

When the film went into the editing stages, Keane began to read reports of disagreement between Harris and Sheridan. 'It's the worst thing in the world to show an actor the rough cut of a film,' Sheridan said. 'You have slaved for eight months on it. You've cut it, you've fine-tuned it. You think it's perfect. Then they watch it and they go crazy. Daniel Day-Lewis's reaction when he saw *My Left Foot* was: "I thought there was more there." It's always like that.'

In London, at the screening for Harris of the rough cut of *The Field*, at which Sheridan and the editor, J. Patrick Duffner, were present, Sheridan heard Harris jangle the coins in his pocket. 'Not only did he jangle the money,' the director recalled, 'he shouted, and then asked everybody what they thought.' Harris's main objection, Sheridan recalled, was that a scene in which the Bull carries the body of the American had been removed. 'The few points he made, however, had validity,' the director admitted.

While the film was being completed, Eamonn Keane died. Arthur Lappin recalled that he had seemed in very poor health during the filming. 'I think Richard was very happy Eamonn was playing in it,' Lappin said later. 'Eamonn, Eamonn, my friend,' Harris had called him in the MacConghail television documentary.

At the location near Leenane, the Bull's cottage was at the top of a short, steep hill. Lappin remembered, 'Every time Eamonn came up the hill, his breath had gone completely. I felt we should have carried him.'

Eamonn died early in January 1990. His son, Feargal, spoke at the funeral in Listowel, quoting lines from *The Great Gatsby* that were favourites of his father: 'He had come a long way to the blue lawn and his dream must have seemed so close he could hardly have failed to grasp it. But he did not realise it was already behind him, somewhere where the vast fields of the republic roll on under the night.' John B. Keane admitted that Eamonn's death, and other deaths in his family, affected him – and his work – profoundly.

*

The film of *The Field* was given its première at the Savoy in Dublin. Richard Harris did not turn up, but Keane was there with friends and relatives from Kerry. The première was a charity affair to raise money for the Abbey Theatre.

The day of the screening, Keane asked Noel Pearson at the Gresham, where the pre-première drinks were served, 'How many tickets will I be getting? I need seventeen.' Then he wrote Pearson a cheque for £1,700.

The première was a splendid affair presided over by Taoiseach Charles Haughey. It was a night, as Keane's friend the poet Brendan Kennelly described it, 'of pomp and formality redeemed by drink and debauchery.'

Keane's true opinion of what he saw on the screen that night is not clear. He said, 'I thought Harris did a marvellous job of acting as Bull McCabe. There are parts of *The Field* with which I wouldn't agree. It's a bit stage-Irishy in places, but by and large I was pleased with it.' He added a rider: 'It made a real impact on me, but I also had a good share of drink taken.'

The makers of the film were themselves dubious about Keane's views on it. 'He said something cryptic to me at the première,' said Jim Sheridan, 'and I can't remember what it was. He knows what he thinks of it; I don't.'

'He never talked about the finished film to me,' said Pearson. 'I don't know if he was happy. I have a sneaking suspicion that he wasn't over-the-moon about it. It's hard to be happy when you have written a stage-play and then it's taken away and cut up for the screen, and you know it's going to be seen by a lot more people than the stage-play.'

'He wasn't altogether unhappy when we met at the première,' John Hurt recalled. 'John B. is intelligent enough to know that there has to be a development from stage to screen.'

Keane told Arthur Lappin, 'I don't think I'd be that pushed about seeing it again.' 'He wasn't being critical,' added Lappin. 'He said it in the nicest possible way. But the film was not the play that he had written.'

There were others, like Phyllis Ryan and Ronnie Masterson, who were both puzzled and disappointed by the omission from the film of the midnight conversation between the Bull and his son, Tadhg, as they await the coming of the stranger. The pair are huddled together at a gateway beside the field; the Bull unwraps a small paper parcel and hands Tadhg a sandwich:

Bull	I enjoy a crow as much as the next man. The first up in the morning is the crow and the soonest under the quilt.
Tadhg	I seen a few water rats today.
Bull	Crafty sons of whores!
Tadhg	They say that if the seed of man fails, the rats will take over the world.
Bull	They're crafty, sure enough. But I could watch crows if there was time given for it. I often laughs at crows.
Tadhg	Can they talk to one another? I'd swear they have a lingo all of their own.
Bull	Who's to say? Who's to say? Anyway I have something else in my mind besides the antics of crows.

To Phyllis Ryan, the conversation is very poetic and has a magic of its own. More than once she had remarked to John B. Keane on the scene and the effect it had on her. Ronnie Masterson can still recall the scene vividly in the play, as the light shines on the field and the Bull begins to speak about crows in a low voice. The passage was eerie and full of foreboding, she felt. Although it is a scene that appeals to Keane, he was prepared to leave editorial decisions to Jim Sheridan.

*

When the Hollywood Oscar nominations were announced on 13 February 1991, *The Field* was not among the nominations for Best Picture, but Harris was nominated for Best Actor.

To secure an award, a production company must bring their film to the attention of the more than four thousand members of the Academy of Motion Picture Arts and Sciences. The film which overshadowed all others in 1991 was *Dances with Wolves*, which had already collected a number of trophies in the previous three months.

By the weekend before the Oscar ceremony, Best Actor nominees Kevin Costner, Jeremy Irons and Gerard Depardieu had still to arrive in Hollywood. Only Harris was in town; one reporter described him as being 'almost driven' in his quest to establish his role in *The Field* as his best achievement. 'I got nominated against major names, major studios and major dollars,' the actor declared. 'My only worry is that only half the members of the Academy will have seen the film and will know how to vote for it.'

From his Beverly Hills Hotel, Harris began sniping at Noel Pearson, accusing him of letting down the film in the run-up to the awards. He blamed Sheridan, too, and the company distributing the film. 'Enough voters haven't seen the film,' the actor fumed. 'There is no way we can win anything.'

When Jeremy Irons won the Oscar for his role in *Reversal of Fortune*, Harris was dignified in defeat and told reporters, 'It was an honour just to be there.' As Irons was named the winner at the ceremony, Harris, on camera, smiled and applauded.

Noel Pearson would say later that the distribution of extra video copies of *The Field* 'wouldn't have mattered in the slightest.' He considered it a 'big surprise' that the film had got so far. 'The nomination is hard work and hard to get,' he remarked. 'The award is down to people liking it – to votes.'

Back in Dublin some weeks later, Harris continued to insist that *The Field* was a masterpiece of cinema. 'A flawed masterpiece, certainly – but then so was the *Mona Lisa*.' He believed that 'larceny was committed on Jim Sheridan.' The director had deserved six nominations and at least three Oscars for the film, according to Harris.

Keane had not travelled with the Irish contingent to Hollywood, just as he had not travelled to Moscow. 'If the film or the screenplay had been nominated,' said Pearson, 'I would have made sure he came to Hollywood. But I don't think he feels comfortable outside Listowel. He's a home-bird.' Sheridan, however, believed he should have been invited to Hollywood. 'He was really chuffed *The Field* had made it with an Oscar nomination,' the director recalled.

After the event, many views were aired about the merits of the film. Arthur Lappin felt that 'in many ways Richard Harris had an undue influence' on it. 'The enormity of the character of the Bull that emerged was to some extent a product of Richard's input,' Lappin remarked. Brenda Fricker wondered why Harris had made so many pronouncements – good and bad – about the film before its release. 'I think that is very unprofessional,' she said. 'You keep your mouth shut until the film is released, and then people can exchange views.'

The actress had gone to Hollywood to present the Best Actress Award to Kathy Bates for *Misery*. 'I went because I had to go,' she said. 'Ray McAnally was dead, Daniel Day-Lewis was being difficult about doing interviews, so I was the only one left.' She understood the reason for Keane's absence from the ceremony. 'I think he is a very shy man,' she said. 'He's also king of the castle down there in Listowel, and perfectly content. So why put yourself in a stressful situation if you can afford not to?'

Two months after the Oscar ceremonies, critic Richard Pine told an audience at the Writers' Week in Listowel that the best thing that could be said about *The Field* as a film was that it was loosely based on an idea by John B. Keane with extra material on loan from *The Quiet Man, Ryan's Daughter* and *Man of Aran*. The producers of the film, 'for quite legitimate reasons of their own', he noted, had delivered the Bull McCabe to the Hollywood box office. 'But in doing so,' he continued, 'they have pandered to the image of Ireland as a failed, clientelist society, cap-in-hand to the coloniser.'

In Muiris MacConghail's television documentary about *The Field, A Clear Eye and Open Hand*, Richard Harris gave his interpretation of the film's climax. 'The Bull McCabe was too big to die of any ordinary thing,' Harris said. 'He couldn't die of a heart attack, he couldn't die of cancer or with a bullet: a bullet would be too small. He had to go, he had to be captured by the elements because he is elemental. And so the end of the movie when he wanders off into the elements to fight the elements, he is absorbed by the elements . . . and you can't have a bigger death than that.'

All Keane would say was that it was a gripping film, but he continued to have misgivings about it. It was not a happy time for him. Grief had overtaken him and was affecting his writing. Within the space of a few years, he had lost his sister Kathleen, who was a Reverend Mother in a Kerry convent, his mother Hannah, and his brother Eamonn, who on his deathbed in a Tralee hospital had whispered, 'Thanks for everything, old boy.'

A few months later, John B.'s brother Bill, who lived in England, died. This came as a particular shock to the playwright. John B. was resting in bed one morning when Mary brought the mail up to him. After returning to the kitchen, she heard a loud cry from upstairs and thought that the playwright had been taken ill. It transpired that Bill's widow had written, telling of his death. 'I was stunned,' he said.

The death of Keane's son John's wife, Sandra, was another cruel blow. A pretty and vivacious girl, she was a fine traditional dancer, and John B. looked upon her as one of the family. 'Sandra was a sweet young girl,' he recalled. 'I took her death as badly as did her husband, John.'

John B. found it almost impossible to concentrate on

writing. He attempted a novel but left it aside; he struggled through his new play, *Vigilantes*. At one stage, he feared he might not be able to write again for years. Friends, however, rallied around. 'They were great,' Mary said. 'Slowly the gloom lifted from him.'

'It was a terrible time for me,' he said. 'Grief can kill the creative urge. Anything I wrote during those dark months is flawed and needs revision.'

29

KENNELLY, HIS FRIEND

A week before the Oscar ceremonies in Los Angeles in March 1991, John B. Keane's thoughts were far from Hollywood and *The Field*. He had promised Brendan Kennelly he would attend his daughter Kristel's twenty-first birthday party in Ballybunion.

Kennelly had advertised the party as being from 9 PM until 4 AM. At five minutes to nine, Keane arrived at the Cliff House Hotel with his daughter, Joanne. 'He was like a young fella going to a party,' said Kennelly. 'He was ready to go.'

Three hundred guests crowded into the hotel, including some of Kennelly's teachers from the national school – one of whom, over eighty years old, danced the night away. The band played music from the 1950s and 1960s. Keane got up on stage, took the microphone and sang songs of the period like 'Sioux City Sioux'.

The youngsters watched Keane, Kennelly, Kennelly's old teacher, Johnny Walsh, and others of a past generation dancing foxtrots and tangos, and even the twist. Keane was the MC. 'The kids loved him,' said Kennelly. 'He has that special magic and personality that many writers don't have who insist on being playwrights or poets with a capital 'P'. John B. is not like that.'

Around two in the morning, the old-time dancing switched to disco. The lights were dimmed and the young people got up to dance. 'We stood back and looked at them,' Kennelly recalled. 'A bridge had been created between the generations, and a lot of that was due to John B.'

Kennelly's friendship with the playwright had an odd beginning. In the early 1950s, Kennelly was playing for his native town of Ballylongford against Listowel in the football

282

semi-final of the North Kerry League. 'We were the small village and they were the big town,' recalled Kennelly, 'yet we were shaking them. They brought on this substitute, and the first thing I noticed about him was his knees. He had the knobbliest knees I had ever seen in a footballer.' A fellow player remarked to Kennelly, 'He's a chemist and a Listowel man, and he's a dirty footballer.'

The footballer was John B. Keane. Kennelly found Keane a good midfielder: 'Those knees were strong,' Kennelly remarked. Ballylongford won the match by a point, scored at the start of the second half by Kennelly, 'due to a bit of advice from Johnny Walsh,' as he put it.

To Kennelly, Keane's knees were the Homeric attribute of his frame. 'He wears long johns, and under pressure he will lift the underwear and the trousers and show you the knees,' Kennelly said. 'And they are a wonder. I always connect them with his writing – knobbly, rhythmical, the knees of a midfielder. They would terrify you.'

One day some years later, Kennelly, in his first year at Trinity College, was working during the term holidays in his father's pub in Ballylongford. Keane, who had just published *Sive*, came in with his friend Johnny Walsh. They drank pints and Kennelly talked to them, telling Keane he was writing poems.

'Have you any there?' Keane asked.

'I have them upstairs,' Kennelly replied.

'Then bring them down.'

The young Kennelly went to his room and collected some of his poems, which Keane stuffed in his pocket. A few days later, the aspiring poet received an encouraging and helpful letter about his work.

The two men became friends and Kennelly went to view Keane's plays during the ensuing years. He always saw the poet at work. Like Ibsen, Keane had begun by writing verse, but gave it up to write plays and novels. 'But giving up the writing of verse doesn't mean giving up being a poet,' Kennelly noted. 'His plays are, in the deepest sense, poetic plays that could only have come from a man who spent a lot of time trying to work with language. He is often accused of being a careless writer. In fact he can be gloriously precise. I may be prejudiced but I attribute a lot of the imagery and the wonderful rhythm in his plays to poetry.' Some later works, such as *The Buds of Ballybunion* and *The Roses of Tralee*, depart from this; they are of a comic nature. 'But where the apprehension is deep, as in *The Highest House on the Mountain* and *Sharon's Grave*, there is poetry,' Kennelly continued. He admits that some of Keane's work was written quickly. 'But a lot of his critics fail to take into account that he is an extremely careful craftsman,' he said. 'He rewrites his plays a lot, worries about them, broods about them.'

During the mid-1960s, Keane called Kennelly in Dublin to talk to him about *The Field*. 'The play wasn't going right for him,' Kennelly recalled. It then had the title *The Field by the River*, and Kennelly suggested he drop the words 'by the River'.

'I remember going into a phone box in Baggot Street and ringing him,' Kennelly said later. 'I was still a student and it cost me money to ring Listowel. But I just wanted to say, "You've got a great play there. Stick with it."' 'That's just what I need,' Keane assured him. Those encouraging words, Keane was to say afterwards, helped him overcome his uncertainty at that time.

The Field, for Kennelly, is one of the great Irish plays, written out of experience and knowledge, even though the implications of it have never, he says, been fully examined by critics. He believes there has been confusion between the actual murder, on which the play is reputed to be based, and the play itself. 'The Bull is ironically named,' Kennelly said. 'He is an unemployed bull and the whole action of the play is a substitute for sex. The sense of heredity which Richard Harris talked about in his interpretation of the Bull, while being very acceptable, is perhaps not the full story. The connection between sexuality and acquisitiveness is strong.'

Kennelly sees a poetic rhythm in Keane's major plays. 'When a Keane character is fully realised, like the Bull in *The Field*, you get this wonderful language in a rhythmical pitch,' Kennelly noted. 'You could take a lot of the lines out of *The Field* and find the hidden metre. In the deepest sense, Keane, like Arthur Miller and Eugene O'Neill and Tennessee Williams, is a poetic playwright. If poetry means the lucid comprehension of complex feelings and ideas, and rendering them in clear language, then these fellows are poets.'

Kennelly cites Flann O'Brien's dismissal of J. M. Synge as a classic example of the dismissal of rural writers by urban writers in Ireland. 'The wonderfully urbane and urban writer dismisses the sing-song,' Kennelly said. 'Yet Synge is one of the great playwrights of the century and O'Brien one of the great novelists. But the mutual incomprehension is inbuilt.' He admits that Keane's plays to some extent refer back to the early Abbey tradition, of which audiences had grown tired.

'A lot of Keane's plays are set in kitchens,' Kennelly continued, 'yet what critics failed to perceive was the freshness of the characterisation.' Keane had received good reviews through the years from such critics as John Finegan and Séamus Kelly. 'Maybe it's a mistake to assume there was a universal dismissal of him, though certainly there was a feeling that he was not of the first rank,' Kennelly said. 'It took thirty-five years for Keane to create the impression that here was a playwright capable of great work, and finally people are admitting to it.'

Of Keane's popularity, he observes: 'If you put on a Keane play in any part of rural Ireland, it will pack out, and this is not true of most other playwrights. You can achieve popularity with something that is less than excellent. I don't think it follows with Keane. His very accessibility, his easiness of character, his readiness to write for the papers, seems to put some critics off. They want their writers to be isolated and suffering in some way, whereas Keane seems to be a relatively happy man.'

In his writings, from the thrilling and the excellent to the quickly produced work lacking depth, Kennelly finds in Keane a love of nature. 'The years he spent going to the Stacks mountains were a positive influence,' Kennelly noted. 'I would say he was opened up there to paganism and Christianity interlocked. Paganism is naturalness, and Keane loves nature. It is very rare for a rural Catholic – or for any Catholic – to cut through the forces that were instilled into us from the

285

catechism and to appreciate nature – naturalness. Part of an Irishman's education is his struggle to be natural.

'Keane has Adam's ears, and I think he has Adam's eyes. In other words, if we regard our great mythological figures like Adam and Eve and Abraham and the prophets as aspects of ourselves that we have lost, then our struggle is to return to the primordial freshness that created us in the first place. Keane has that kind of drive. He has the drive to be utterly natural. It's in Rousseau, it's in Patrick Kavanagh, it's even in George Orwell within an urban setting. It comes easy to Keane.'

Kennelly suggests that, when the Bull stands back and talks to the priest about 'one law for you and another law for me', behind that remark is Keane's love for a fellow man who is a law unto himself. 'Scratch a lot of Irishmen and you'll find a tolerance of law, the law unto themselves,' according to Kennelly. 'That is why Keane's plays have reached the Irish people. He is a critic of values, but ultimately he loves his characters.'

Kennelly places *The Field* with *The Playboy of the Western World*, *Juno and the Paycock* and *Waiting for Godot* as one of the great Irish plays. The Listowel man wrote in the play of the closed marriage. 'The Bull walks into a home where for twenty years the woman does not speak,' Kennelly commented. 'That must be a terrible thing. Before the newspapers woke up to the articulate conscience, a lot of the homes of our people were true prisons.' In Keane, as in O'Casey and Synge, there is the strong, powerful woman in a male-dominated society. 'It is the conspiracy of a morality that is kept in place by the priest and the teacher and the husband,' Kennelly noted. 'The act of love becomes the act of burial, and the woman is buried. I can see how strong women would rise up against that morality and assert themselves against the social fabric created by that morality. A powerful individuality is the only thing they have to offer against a quietly tyrannical system.'

Keane did not go to Hollywood for the Oscar ceremonies, nor to Russia for his play, 'because they wouldn't let him sing,' jokes Kennelly. The truth, he suggested, is that Keane 'knows his world, and the glittery world is not for John B. There is a sense in which he is too real for a lot of people. He doesn't change, whereas lots of us change in different contexts. He is one of those who change least with external pressure. He is himself, and it is very hard to define him. He is quicksilver.

'John B. loves Listowel, he loves the rhythm, he loves the streets, he loves the people. Yet there is always the element of the detached poet about him. The modern writer, like Sartre or Camus, is often outside his society. But he is both outside and inside. I think he has a very sane realisation of his own nature, and certainly that nature is utterly unpretentious. He never makes plans for himself; he actually diverts attention from himself. His conversation is funny. It's diversionary. He's witty, shrewd, great at anecdotes. Yet his eyes are observing. He's in his pub not as a bar worker but as an observer.'

*

It was a particularly happy day for Brendan Kennelly when Keane arrived at Trinity College, Dublin, to be accorded the distinction of being made an honorary doctor of literature. In a reciprocal gesture, the playwright donated his papers, including the handwritten manuscript of *Sive*, to the university. As he said later, 'I thought I owed them this, so I gave them everything I had.'

Some people believed that he should have been similarly honoured by the National University of Ireland; that he wasn't is a source of disappointment to his friends. Not that Keane had ever intended to preface 'John B.' with the word 'Doctor'. As one local in the Keane pub quipped, 'I'll take no drink from Dr Keane!'

On the wall of the pub today is another reminder of the friendship that binds the Keanes of Listowel and the Kennellys of Ballylongford. Framed in glass is the poetic tribute by Brendan Kennelly on the occasion of the death of Eamonn Keane. It is simply entitled, 'In Memory of Eamonn Keane', and it reads:

Now and then we met in the streets of Dublin.
Once in Stephen's Green he stood, courteous and
    kind,
Talking of George Fitzmaurice, 'a dedicated, shy
    man.'
Eamonn had a laughing, fiery mind
And as subtle rich a voice as I have heard.
He stilled the ranting traffic with that voice
And freed the ancient magic trapped in every word,
Making the hectic city stand still and rejoice.

With what sweet ease the man could conjure
People, images, scenes to please the blood.
He was a pure artist, celebrant-loner,
Yet few could charm a company as he could.
The child that most men kill he nurtured in the heart
And to the end remained a vulnerable lover
Paying the price of fierce fidelity to art.
Peace to your spirit, Eamonn, Eamonn, love
    forever.

Forever may your spirit stroll through Gurtenard
Where you were happy once and saw a hawk
Bulleting to kill a singing skylark.
You are beyond all singing and all talk .
Now but we will not forget
A voice that could bring ease to God's own pain.
You spent the lot but we are in your debt
Knowing your like won't grace the earth again.

30

A New Era

The Abbey Theatre had by now completed the trilogy of Keane plays, so what alternative avenue was open to him? The playwright had no clear idea. Fortune smiled on him, however, when Arthur Lappin and Ben Barnes launched their theatre company, Groundwork. Although the company's first choice of play was *The Righteous Are Bold*, they eventually got around to a Keane season at the Gaiety Theatre.

Lappin and Barnes were friends and wanted to work together. Lappin, a former banker and the business side of the partnership, felt that Barnes had not received the credit he deserved for his Keane productions at the Abbey. 'These had grossed £1.5 million,' Lappin noted, 'and Ben saw only a very small part of that. For his script-editing alone, he was worth more than they paid him.'

The Keane play they chose for the Gaiety was *The Year of the Hiker*, which had not been staged in Dublin for some years. Barnes was worried about its ending; he considered it too sentimental and hardly acceptable to audiences in the 1990s. He travelled to Listowel to discuss the problem with the playwright and found him agreeable to change, which meant a reconstruction of the final scene to pave the way for what the director described as 'an uneasy reconciliation between the Hiker and his son, Joe.' As Barnes was to say later, 'We wanted to put the father–son relationship very much back at the centre of the work.'

Mick Lally had gained an impressive reputation with the Druid Company in Galway and, in Keane's view, seemed ideal for the part of Hiker Lacey. Years before, he had played the commercial traveller in an Irish version of *Big Maggie* at An Taibhdhearc in Galway. He recalled that when they performed the play, the playwright was not popular in that part of the country because of his involvement with the Language Freedom Movement. Lally had his own opinions on this, however. 'I think that John B. had more of a benign attitude to the language than some of the other people in the LFM,' he said. 'I think his attitude was more egalitarian. He did genuinely feel that compulsory Irish was bad for the language.'

Lally knew that Keane was the author of a one-act play, *Faoiseamh*, which he had seen staged a few times during his university days. The story, he recalled, concerns a man who emigrates to England and dies there. When the family arrive to collect the body, they discover he has another family.

In subsequent years, Lally visited Listowel for Writers' Week and chatted with poets and playwrights in Keane's public house. He remembered a certain actress remarking, 'God, they must love John B. here. They've even named a pub after him!' When he first met Keane, an almost instant camaraderie developed and they talked in Irish and English. Lally approached the part of Hiker Lacey carefully and set out to portray him honestly and truthfully. He admitted that his own rural background helped, and in Galway he had seen individuals like the Hiker, especially during race week. There was something of the romantic wanderer in him; it was a motif that recurred in Irish writing, for instance in Synge's *The Shadow of the Glen* and in Boucicault's *The Shaughraun*.

According to Lally, the difference with Keane was that in *The Year of the Hiker* you had, as the story unfolded, a complicated domestic scene with which the Hiker is unhappy. To his surprise, Lally discovered later that women considered it a very chauvinistic play, in which the male attitude was dominant. 'It was a woman who said that to me,' he recalled. 'She was amazed to see a man who was so destroyed by two women.'

During the run of the play at the Gaiety Theatre, the actor scarcely met John B. and he had to wait until its presentation at the Opera House in Cork to have a conversation with him. 'I think he said something like, "Fair play to you, well done." He was as offhand as that. I don't think John B. is the sort of man who is going to tell you how wonderful you were, darling.

The words "fair play" were good enough for me. I think he felt a good job was made of the Hiker and he was quite happy about my playing. He is an easy man to talk to and people find him good company. That's a good situation for a writer to be in, because people will reveal aspects of themselves.'

He agreed that the pub had been an important factor in the playwright's life, but even outside the pub he was essentially his own man in the way in which he was able to commune with people. Lally sought to pinpoint the secret of his success. 'It is the way he sets out to tell a story in his plays,' he said. 'There's a raw simplicity about them, yet a complete honesty and truthfulness. John B. is an actor's playwright because most of his characters are wonderful characters to play, and this includes the Hiker Lacey. His characters are alive, and in fact they are very much there, as the play is written before you start to do anything with them as an actor.'

The publicist Gerry Lundberg was entrusted with selling the show to the public. In this field he had few peers. Since John B. and his wife, Mary, were staying at the Westbury Hotel nearby, he reckoned it would be a novel idea to transport them to the Gaiety in a horse-drawn cab for the opening night of *The Year of the Hiker*. The playwright, sensing that this would be a boost for his play, agreed to cooperate. By the time the cab drew up outside the theatre, a band was playing and a large crowd had gathered.

This was a far cry from the dull opening nights in the 1970s, when little glamour attached to *The Rain at the End of the Summer* or, later, *The Crazy Wall*. Keane was being pushed into a new, media-conscious era, when he could expect leading figures from many walks of life to grace his first nights. Lundberg's invitation list included Gay Byrne. If Byrne liked what he saw, he usually told listeners to his popular morning radio show. In the business, it was accepted that one favourable word from Gay Byrne could offset five bad notices from the critics.

The Gaiety box office ticked over for *The Year of the Hiker*. The enthusiastic response set Ben Barnes thinking about Keane's remarkable drawing power. He felt that audiences identified with his themes and characters; it was the laughter of recognition rather than the laughter of derision. Yet the real strength of Keane's plays was in the language. It was poetic, racy and authentic. In due course, eighty thousand people paid to see *The Year of the Hiker*, and in spite of some begrudgery, the great majority enjoyed the playwright's work.

Barnes knew that in some quarters there was criticism of his reconstruction of the final scene, but he had no regrets. It worked, and that was enough for him. Playgoers told him they were touched by the reconciliation scene between the Hiker and his son, Joe, and the Hiker's words as he dismisses Simey's uncompromising attitude towards him:

> Oh, he'll be examining a cow some day and he'll ask the owner how old she is and the owner will say, 'I'm not too sure but she was born in the Year of the Hiker!' (*Joe laughs*) Or it might be a horse and the man that owns him will say, 'I bought him, and he a colt, in Cahirmee (*Pause*) the year they buried Hiker Lacey (*Pause*), the Lord have mercy on him!'

Keane recognised the risk factor in staging plays in a big theatre like the Gaiety and, for that reason, felt indebted to Lappin and Barnes. But, as Lappin pointed out, they did not intend 'to kill the goose that laid the golden egg' by concentrating on Keane. Just now they were more concerned with getting an option on his plays and, with this in mind, the pair set off by road for Listowel. Along the way, their sole topic of conversation, Arthur Lappin remembered, was how best to approach the playwright, for they had no idea how he would take them.

Keane walked the short distance to the Listowel Arms Hotel to meet them. He was in one of his cheerful moods. He had come to have complete trust in the Groundwork directors, and saw them as young men committed to the highest professional production standards in the theatre. Lappin, for his part, knew that the playwright loved to get business out of the way so that he could relax and chat over a drink. To his astonishment, the business was dispensed with in two minutes.

'We just sat down,' Lappin recalled, 'and John B. looked at us and said, "Let's get this out of the way first before we drink any more." On the option question, we suggested five years at X pounds and asked if that was all right by him. He nodded and said yes. We then insisted that for his own sake we would do a contract on the deal. I don't think he ever read it; he took the piece of paper and signed.'

To Lappin, Keane depended on his memory a lot; as he soon discovered, this could lead to confusion. Having completed the five-year option deal on his plays, and the 'Letters' series, Lappin found that at least one director of another Dublin company had notes from the playwright to prove that it could stage *Matchmaker*, the stage work based on his *Letters of a Matchmaker*, and was going ahead. 'We were a bit annoyed,' Lappin said, 'and discussed the matter with John B. But we decided to let things be.'

*

In the summer of 1991, to the surprise of many, Lappin and Barnes revived *Moll* at the Gaiety Theatre. Neither producer made apologies for the quality of the play. Barnes, who admitted that it did not have the undertones of Keane's other plays, rated it as 'good fun', 'a summer show' and 'a good night out'. 'It is a farce, really, a punter's play, and we are not making any apologies.'

Lappin agreed about the play's farcical nature. 'It is a farce in the sense that there is no pretension to any major social content,' he said. But their Groundwork company had, as Lappin said, 'a very detailed session' with Keane before rehearsals began, and the producer found that he had improved the script 'enormously'. Brian de Salvo was signed to direct it, with Mick Lally in the role of the canon, Barry McGovern and Ronan Smith as his curates, Pat Leavy as the housekeeper and Derry Power as the bishop.

Many years previously, the play had been offered to Cyril Cusack. 'I had written to John B.,' Cusack remembered. 'Egocentrically, I had wanted very much to do a play about a priest, and having read John B's *Letters of an Irish Parish Priest*,

I thought he was the man to write it. He said he already had the idea in mind.'

Cusack recalled that, later, the playwright sent him a play 'which consisted of three or four priests in their presbytery'; it wasn't satisfactory from his point of view. Yet he felt Keane was capable of creating a parish priest 'who could touch on our human condition in its various aspects – comic, pathetic, tragic and so on.' Of Keane's works, *Big Maggie* had made the biggest impression on him, and Brenda Fricker had been magnificent as Maggie. He regarded the monologue as unnecessary, however: it was, he said, 'a concession to the sexual drive that was happening all round, an apologia for Maggie's sexual instincts and needs.'

Cusack could understand Keane's resentment towards the Abbey early on in his career. He agreed that he hadn't been welcome there, in spite of his great popularity throughout the rest of the country. In the canon of Irish dramatists, he placed him high on the list, but in a different category to Synge and O'Casey. Like Brian Friel, Keane was both prolific and successful, but he lacked Friel's inventiveness and originality.

To Cusack, Keane's pub in Listowel was obviously a source of inspiration to him so long as he was not, as Cusack put it, 'incarcerating himself there.' He regretted that he had never been asked by the Abbey to act in a Keane play. He had counted *The Year of the Hiker* as good theatre, and *Sive* as a product of – and a progression from – the tradition of melodrama.

Keane and his wife came to Dublin during the rehearsals for *Moll*. 'Staying at the Westbury, he could work during the day and meet friends and family at night,' said Lappin. 'It's like an excursion for him, though John B. is now very much at ease in Dublin. I think he feels he is receiving the critical acclaim he deserved years ago.'

Keane had been kept out of the establishment, and Lappin found him embittered towards the Abbey and the GAA. 'He was put down, I think, because he was perceived to be dangerous in the way he dealt with some of our sacred cows,' Lappin recalled. 'If Irish writing is sombre and outdated, it gets due regard, but if it is purely skittish or humorous, it is not acceptable.'

It was noticeable that Keane was becoming more involved in the production of his plays. Around the table with Barnes or Lappin, he would suggest a certain actor for a role or how a stage setting might be improved. 'Arthur and Ben revitalised John B.,' said the publicist Gerry Lundberg. 'During rehearsals of *Moll*, he seemed a new man: he had got over the painful grief that had so deeply affected him, and I found him most cooperative in giving press interviews. But if anyone in the press rubbed him up the wrong way, he could really put them down. But that was rare; most times, he went out of his way to facilitate newspaper people.'

Lundberg noted that the playwright, perhaps because of the deaths of his two brothers, was watching himself carefully and drinking less than in the past. Sometimes he refused to stay for dinner after a show, saying he had to leave early next morning for Listowel. 'But he would do anything to publicise his plays,' Lundberg recalled. 'And there was no bullshit about him: he admitted he was making money, and he was happy making money.'

In Arthur Lappin's view, the playwright was 'nobody's fool' when it came to money. He remembered the first question he had asked him on the opening night of *The Year of the Hiker*: 'What's the advance?' Lappin had no idea. Yet both he and Ben Barnes reported that Keane was very reasonable with them, and the option agreement with him was 'not penal'.

Moll had a chequered history in the theatre. When first staged by Theatre of the South, it had been panned by the critics, though subsequently it was to prove popular enough, though not so much in Dublin. The response to the new production at the Gaiety was a revelation, however. In spite of the snide remarks of most critics that it was 'slight' and 'inconsequential', it caught the public's imagination and was to prove the most commercially successful play in the Gaiety's history, earning a hefty six-figure sum in box-office receipts.

Keane was elated. The hard work he had put into revising the piece had, as he said, 'paid off handsomely'. Even Barnes was surprised by the phenomenal response. 'I expected it would have a good summer run,' he commented, 'but I didn't think that it would attract people in their thousands week after week.' Before the curtain came down on the final night, Lappin and Barnes were wondering which Keane play to tackle next.

*

While *Moll* was packing audiences into the Gaiety, Phyllis Ryan's Gemini Productions was touring the country with *Matchmaker*, the two-hander, with Frank Kelly and Anna Manahan playing a variety of comic parts. It had been a typical Keane opening night at the Tivoli Theatre in Dublin, with the family represented by Denis Keane, who arrived at the theatre with Peg and John Schuster.

After that, it became a record-breaking tour, with Gemini being invited back more than once to Limerick, Athlone and Castlebar. Unlike at the Tivoli, where some people walked out because of the bawdiness, scarcely anyone protested in the provinces. 'So far as I remember,' recalled Phyllis Ryan, 'one nun walked out in Cashel. Everywhere else it was laughter at John B.'s lines. *Matchmaker* has a great magic about it.'

Frank Kelly agreed. 'This was a little world I could inhabit,' he said. 'Once you inhabited the text, you could not think outside of it. Keane has a terrific sense of irony, which is the stuff of comedy.' Since he was playing Dan Paddy Andy, the matchmaker who had been well-known in the Listowel area, he felt apprehensive when Phyllis Ryan told him that they had been invited to stage a single performance of the show in the town.

The Arts Centre, the former St John's Church, seats one hundred people, and for *Matchmaker*, every seat was occupied. Keane and his wife came along, accompanied by their daughter Joanne and her boyfriend. 'It took us a while to be accepted by the audience,' recalled Kelly, 'and this did not surprise me. Gradually, however, we won them over.' During the performance, Phyllis Ryan noticed that Keane was laughing heartily. When she remarked on this to him later, he admitted, 'I had forgotten some of my own lines.'

In a typical gesture, after the show, Keane invited the cast to a private party in the pub in William Street. It was just like a reunion, remarked Phyllis Ryan. It was thirty years since she and John B. had first met in Dublin. Yet their friendship was as enduring as ever, and in conversation the playwright often spoke of his indebtedness to her. Now, over drinks, they sought to pinpoint the reason for the nationwide popularity of *Matchmaker*. 'I think it brought back to people some home truths, but in a hilarious way,' Anna Manahan said. 'It's the characterisation,' decided Phyllis Ryan. 'You see, these characters are disappearing from our lives, so people want to enjoy them before they go altogether.' Keane sipped his pint of beer, and reflected, 'Maybe it's the language they speak. Sure isn't that, too, disappearing from our world?'

It had been a decade since Phyllis Ryan had staged a new play of Keane's and she was tempted now to ask him for another, but for some reason she let the opportunity pass. The fact was that he was concentrating on writing novels and short stories. *Durango*, his new novel, was with Mercier. It dealt with a cattle drive over the Stacks Mountains, and Keane was enthusiastic about the storyline. This enthusiasm was justified, as, in time, the book would become a best-seller, prompting at least one critic to suggest that he write more novels, even if this meant forgetting about playwriting.

*

It was by now after midnight, as Keane retailed funny stories, or listened to the others recall episodes on the tour. They could not help noticing that he had not changed. 'He could have been talking to us thirty years before,' said Anna Manahan. 'We were the Dublin company coming down to perform his play, and he appreciated it.'

Since the playwright had not referred to his performance of that night, Frank Kelly assumed he had played it well. He was at ease in Keane's company, and he knew that behind the playwright's affability there was an original mind at work. If you considered plays like *The Field* and *Big Maggie*, you could describe them as strong drama which would endure long after more sophisticated works were forgotten. If *Sive* and *Sharon's Grave* were melodramatic, this did not in any way lessen their impact. He remembered touring eleven US cities with *Matchmaker*, and the audience response was no different from that in Ireland. This suggested to him that Keane's folk humour had a universal appeal. If that was immortality in theatrical terms, then John B. Keane had achieved it.

PART FOUR

THE LAST ACT

31

The Unexpected

As a member of Fine Gael in north Kerry, John B. Keane had more than a passing interest in politics; indeed, he found time to canvass for party candidates at election time. Once, though, when a member of the republican Fianna Fail splinter group Aontacht Eireann asked how he fancied his chances in the general election, the playwright quipped, 'Well, Joe, if you can swing the Jewish vote in Knocknagoshel you have it made.'

It was by now the early 1990s, and there was speculation that he himself might contest the presidential election, although his friends understandably asked how he hoped to find the time. As a writer he was still as prolific as ever and the decade ahead promised to be most productive. He quickly ended any further speculation about his future when he succinctly announced, 'I looked at myself in the mirror this morning when I was shaving and I didn't see a president.'

In the meantime, publications bearing Keane's name regularly appeared. In 1992, his first novel for Mercier Press, *Durango*, a stirring adventure tale about life in rural Ireland during the Second World War, went on sale; this was followed shortly afterwards by *The Ram of God*, another of his popular collections of humorous essays. A year later *The Contractors* was published; the action in this book is set in the England of the 1950s and offers provocative insights into the lives of Irish labourers and building contractors. Evidently he was drawing on his own experiences, for in the book he explores the conditions under which the labourers worked, their accompanying frustrations, drinking habits, violence and deep longing for their homeland. In his plays *Hut 42* and *Many Young Men of Twenty*, Keane had already dealt with this theme, which was close to his crusading heart.

The Contractors was enthusiastically received by reviewers for its honesty and well-drawn characters, most notably that of Dan Murray, who becomes a contractor by an innovative, if questionable, device. John B.'s 'Letters' series, which he had begun in 1967 for Mercier Press with *Letters of a Successful TD*, was by now a resounding success, and in 1993 the ninth in the series, *Letters to the Brain*, was published by Brandon. At the same time, he continued to contribute his weekly columns to the *Evening Herald* and the *Limerick Leader*, and attend revivals of plays such as *Sive*, *The Man from Clare* and *Big Maggie*. Conserving his energy did not seem a priority, though he did enjoy his leisure time, going to Gaelic football and rugby matches, taking walks and, when called upon by the media, fearlessly commenting on the burning issues of the day.

To the disappointment of professional theatre managements, he did not write a major new play. It was by now well over a decade since he had written *The Chastitute*, and though from time to time it was said that a new play was imminent, it never materialised. Perhaps the novel now held greater fascination for him; success was proving an undoubted spur. Nevertheless, it was doubtful if he would achieve the same fame or experience the same excitement in this literary genre as with his playwriting. But this didn't seem to bother him.

Meanwhile, it was over thirty years since Barry Cassin had directed Keane's third play, *The Highest House on the Mountain*; Cassin was by now among those theatre people who were surprised that no important new play was forthcoming. As the director said, 'Thirteen years seemed to me a long time between new plays for John B. I mean, anyone who wrote as much as he did could, I felt, go on writing more and more of them. In the business, we had all hoped he would come up with another *Field* or *Big Maggie*, but as we know, writers work at their own pace and in their own time.'

In John B.'s case, it was the writing of a new novel that had mostly occupied his time. *A High Meadow* was published by Mercier Press in 1994; at 340 pages, it is quite a lengthy work. *A High Meadow* tells a highly entertaining, if unusual, tale about farmworker Eddie Drannaghy, known as 'the Ram of God', and his twin brothers Murt and Will. A tragicomedy, it is also humorous in a sexy way; in Mollie Cronane, Keane has created a female character as steely and persuasive as Maggie Polpin. The seduction scene between Mollie and 'the Ram' is not only funny but oddly chilling. One imagines that A High Meadow is the kind of book that, read by farmers, might well cause them to miss milking times.

*

It was around this time that Keane read a medical piece in the Irish Times that outlined the symptoms of prostate cancer. He admitted it made him ponder, so he decided to have a check-up in a Cork hospital, where the condition was diagnosed. Initially John B. was scared but eventually he came to terms with the disease and vowed to fight it every inch of the way. In the months that followed, he talked about the cancer openly – at least twice on the Gay Byrne morning radio show. Later, his lifelong Listowel friend Tony Guerin would laugh and say, 'As far as I could see, John B. was intent in taking the mystery out of the disease. And as time went on, I think he succeeded in achieving this – which was no bad thing, for fellows began to look out for the symptoms.'

In the ensuing months, John B. experienced highs and lows, with the daily newspapers occasionally telling readers about 'his latest health scare'. But in typical style, he soldiered on bravely, though he did admit in 1995 that he had felt uncomfortable after two operations. 'God, they nearly killed me,' was how he put it. Nevertheless, he remained determined to keep up his spirits, and he seldom if ever lost his sense of humour. Coming up to the production of his early play Sharon's Grave at the Gate Theatre, the playwright as usual welcomed visiting journalists to his pub in William Street, believing as always that revivals of his plays needed some pre-publicity.

When one young journalist asked him about his health, he straightaway issued a warning, 'Never ask a fellow about his operation, because he'll bore you to death. I remember one morning I was walking back the street and one fellow nailed me. "How are you?" he said to me, but he was only looking for an opening to talk about his own operation. Jesus, I had to run from him. But cancer is no fun, my friend, and I am very lucky so far to have survived.'

He did admit, however, that some of his routine had changed. For example, the late-night writing sessions were put on hold. Inevitably, he was asked whether he was working on a new play, and when it was likely to be staged. For the first time, he talked about a play of his which Garry Hynes, artistic director of the Druid Theatre Company, wanted to stage, but made the point that it wasn't quite ready. 'This was a work entitled *Vigilantes* which he had spoken to us about previously and he reckoned its theme was controversial, though he didn't want to divulge it,' Hynes recalled. 'It seemed at the time that he wasn't sure whether it should be premièred at all.'

As was customary, John B. chatted with the journalists outside the bar area and offered them a round of drinks. They were agreeably surprised at how forthcoming he was: he never shirked a question. He told them persuasively he had one big regret – that he never wore the green and gold of Kerry football – but that for the most part he felt fulfilled and had no real regrets. 'I married the woman I love,' he said with a smile. 'I achieved all I wanted to achieve, I was lucky to escape death, I'm moderately well off and I never lost a friend.' After the slightest of pauses, he looked at them and mischievously added, 'Having said all I want to say, will ye feck off now.'

As 1996 arrived, he drank less but enjoyed himself every bit as much. He rested when he felt tired, and under Mary's attentive eye wrote only by day – something he had seldom done previously. As he reflected, 'Some of the best lines in my plays came to me in the stillness of the night when I was alone with my characters. At that hour, I was never lost for inspiration.' He was already looking forward to a revival of *The Field* at the Gaiety Theatre and was determined to make an occasion of it. Sometimes he joked and said he had to make the best of borrowed time, but one felt that he meant it. That May, he and Mary brought a party of 120 friends from Listowel and Dublin to the first-night revival. John B. appeared in lively spirits and shook hands at the interval with prominent theatre and screen personalities as well as the American ambassador, Jean Kennedy Smith.

While there was never any doubt in his mind that Ray McAnally's portrayal of the Bull McCabe was the greatest he had seen, he was always generous when other actors played this towering role. That night, he shook hands with Pat Laffan and told him that his performance as the Bull was convincing, at times even frightening in its impact. He had kind words also for cast members such as Pat Kinevane, John Olohan, Maria McDermottroe and Mark O'Regan; he also made it his business to walk across the foyer to welcome playwrights Bernard Farrell and Hugh Leonard and actor Mick Lally. The evening was reminiscent of those first nights years before when the ebullient Keane and his supporters had taken Dublin by storm. Despite the uncomfortable nature of his illness, he looked fine, and many friends were not slow to reassure him. While such exciting first-night revivals tended to tire him now, his well-wishers felt they were the tonic he needed.

In December of that same year – 1996 – he was back on the Gay Byrne show to talk about his latest book, a collection of Christmas pieces called *The Voice of an Angel*. In the course of a friendly chat with the presenter, he revealed a recurrence of the cancer for which he had been treated and, on the advice of his consultant, was now considering a course of radiotherapy. As though anxious not to sound morose, he typically joked, 'I can tell you, Gay, that the treatment will not inhibit me from consuming a lot of porter between here and my expiry, which will be a long time off, I hope.'

Around this time, Tony Guerin, a garda detective based in Dublin, continued to meet the playwright either in the city or in Listowel, and found him the best of company. Despite his condition, he could see that John B. was bearing up well and had no intention of throwing in the towel. 'John was the kind of man I'd do anything for and I knew he'd do the same for me,' Guerin asserted. 'I remember that one day in the spring of 1997 he told me he was going to have a course of radiotherapy in a Cork hospital and wondered if I'd drive him there once a week. I told him there was no problem, that I'd be at the door of the pub when he wanted me.'

As it turned out, Guerin – no mean wit himself – found the subsequent journeys a rare experience. 'The weather that spring was, as far as I can remember, sunny, and Mary would pack a basket for each of us and along the road we'd stop at some nice spot and have a picnic,' Guerin recalled. 'All the time, John B. would be reciting poetry, telling me stories and enjoying himself, despite his occasional discomfort. After a while, the council workers got to know we were making the trip to Cork, and as we drove past in the car they'd wave at John B and shout "Good luck" after him. I could see by his smile he appreciated the gesture, for he knew the men were sincere.'

One afternoon, Guerin told his celebrated passenger he was going to write a play. 'I thought it was best to let him know,' Guerin said, 'but he showed no surprise at all, except to tell me that I was a natural storyteller and I'd probably have no trouble with dialogue. He was sincere in what he said, and it was a fillip to me. He already knew I had written two novels that remained unpublished.' Eventually, when two of Guerin's plays were premièred in Listowel, John B. and Mary went along to see them. For his part, Guerin felt he got to know him better on the journeys to and from Cork. 'I used to find it amazing that he never complained or whinged about the cancer,' Guerin remarked. 'Instead, he tried to be cheerful and hopeful in his outlook, but the man had exceptional faith in God and I suppose, like his good humour, it kept him going. We'd exchange stories and he might sing a song as we made our way through Knocknagoshel and on to the Cork road. At times I felt my passenger wasn't going for hospital treatment at all but was on a pleasure trip.'

*

John B. would have good cause to remember 1998. Patrick Mason, the artistic director of the Abbey Theatre, had recommended to his board that the playwright be awarded the Gradam Medal for his considerable contribution to Irish theatre. Recalling the rejection of *Sive* by the Abbey in the late 1950s, Mason said it was an infamous decision. James Hickey, the chairman of the Abbey board, stated that past recipients of the award were Brian Friel, Tom Murphy, Éamon Kelly and Tomás MacAnna. John B and his wife Mary were present on that August evening, and the playwright looked to have mellowed and to be in a forgiving mood as he responded in typical fashion: 'If Terry Rogers had been standing in the Abbey foyer at the old Queen's Theatre in 1959, he would have given 500 to 1 against my getting any kind of award.'

With a pint of beer in his hand, the playwright looked relaxed as he mingled with the gathering of theatre people. He could say that the Abbey had made things up to him by reviving his plays and forgetting about the past. By now he held honorary doctorates from Trinity College Dublin and Marymount Manhattan College, New York, as well as honorary life membership of the RDS. Moreover, in 1988 he had received the American-Irish award for literature, he was a former president of Irish PEN, and he had been a member of Aosdána since the early 1980s. He made no secret of his pride in receiving public recognition.

Barry Cassin, meanwhile, continued to meet him occasionally on his visits to Dublin and remembered that he always put on a brave face. 'On such occasions,' Cassin recalled, 'I might say to him, "John, I'm very glad to see you look well." He'd shrug and say, "I took plenty of rest today."' To Tony Guerin, his friend was fighting the cancer tooth and nail and was determined to keep up his daily walks around Listowel and his beloved Feale river and his affable chats with locals. It was a routine that was helping to keep his spirits up. He still attended revivals of his plays in Cork and Dublin and to most people he appeared to be his old vibrant self. The publication of his short stories by Mercier Press gave him personal satisfaction, but it appeared that no new full-length play would be forthcoming. The Abbey Theatre did try to commission one from him, but he wasn't interested in commissions, however well meant, as he felt this policy would put unnecessary pressure on him. He was prepared, though, to meet newspaper deadlines for feature articles and stories.

Keane was by now the most fêted playwright in the land. In February 1999, as a kind of belated seventieth birthday party in his honour – and also as a fund-raising event for the new Listowel Literary and Heritage Centre – glowing tributes was paid to him. Six hundred people, representing all walks of County Kerry life, as well as friends from outside the county, were present in the Brandon Hotel in Tralee. John B., while looking proud as well as happy, at times seemed overwhelmed by it all. The event was the Kerryman Newspaper Group's idea. The playwright could not have asked for more; he was particularly pleased that more than £40,000 was raised for the Heritage Centre on the night. Mary, as usual, was staunchly by his side, listening silently to the tributes, and smiling when someone recalled humorous stories. By now, their eldest son, Billy, was running the family pub, giving his parents more time for relaxation.

But neither John B. nor Mary would hear of retirement. Any such prospect was simply anathema to them. When a young reporter quizzed her on the subject, she told him, 'Writers don't really retire, sure they don't. They keep tipping away all the time.' Shortly before, she admitted she had worried because John B. hadn't written a single thing for two or three years and she wondered if it was the illness that had affected his energy and sapped his inspiration. 'But then it happened,' she said with a smile. 'I call it a minor miracle. One morning I was climbing the stairs from the pub to the dwelling quarters when I heard the unmistakable clatter of his old typewriter. It was music to my ears to hear it again. He hadn't written in ages since the operations and treatments. All the tension went away from me the minute I heard the typewriter. I said to myself, "This fella's back" – and he was.'

Watching John B. during his illness had not been easy for Mary, but they had the greatest of neighbours and there was nothing these people wouldn't do for the playwright. Looking back in particular on the two most difficult years of his illness, she tended to be philosophical, with her characteristic common-sense outlook on life. As she said, 'I suppose every family goes through their own hard times, don't they? You have to take the rough with the smooth. You have to go through the bad times to appreciate it when things are good.' Around this time, in the late 1990s, she was more hopeful than ever that John B. was improving; she felt he was winning his fight back to health.

*

At the Tralee gala banquet in his honour in the Brandon Hotel, there were friends who had known the playwright since he played minor football, and some glorious reminiscences were exchanged. Nóra Relihan, who played Mena in the first production of *Sive*, summed up: 'The year 1959 and the play called *Sive* marked the beginning of the legend which is John B. Keane.' On the same occasion, Brendan Kennelly mused in the *Kerryman*, 'I have always thought that even the most complex writers possess, among their talent, one single deep-rooted talent, which drives them and inspires them. In John B.'s case, that single, deep-rooted talent is his ability to write and sing beautiful and moving songs. The man would sing at the drop of a hat. And he has a lovely voice. He must be one of the hardest-working and most disciplined writers I have met in any country. He has always had this strict disciplined approach: he puts in the hours; he writes and rewrites; he needs deadlines; he produces all the work in time. He realises that in the world of writing, as in so many other spheres, there is no substitute for hard work. Inspiration is 99 per cent perspiration.'

Kennelly, academic and poet, summed up: 'John B. is a connoisseur of pleasure, he takes enormous pleasure in eating and drinking, in talking and singing, in the past and in the present, in football and work, in town and country, and in his endless preoccupation with the minds and hearts of his fellow human beings. This deep, thoughtful pleasure gives a humane depth to his insights and their expression. And he is married to a great human being, Mary. She is largely responsible for the fact that he is still living, writing, drinking, eating, talking, laughing, remembering, loving. She is an unfailing source of strength and support, a bright, witty, wise woman, with a heart full of tolerance, kindness and understanding.'

*

Meanwhile, a new century arrived. Like everyone else, the playwright toasted the millennium with a raised glass, a song and a story among his own people in his William Street pub.

309

That year, he had managed against the odds to write a light comedy for the theatre, *Matchmake-Me-Do*; he told friends that it was written solely to make people laugh. He thought the country needed some laughs after the recent political scandals. 'I've written enough tragedies in my time,' he added. 'It's my ambition now to write one more really good comedy for the stage, but I don't have the same energy that I used to.' *Matchmake-Me-Do* was premièred in August at Dublin's Tivoli Theatre. The playwright, accompanied by Mary and family friends, looked his typical self as he met people in the foyer and shook their hands. It was the tonic he needed, and it would do him nothing but good.

Back in Listowel he resumed his routine, and when asked by friends how he felt, he'd shrug and say, 'I have good days and bad days.' And he might even joke about it. 'D'you know,' he said, 'my illness seems to be taking a welcome holiday from pestering me these last few weeks.' He was determined to keep up his regular walks. It was the manly spirit that Tony Guerin had talked about and so greatly admired in the playwright.

As the weeks slipped into months, it was noticeable that fewer people enquired about his state of health, believing perhaps that he was holding his own. It was only in the spring of 2002 that word began to circulate among his friends that the great man wasn't too well, but some of them still refused to accept that he was dying. He himself already had been told the truth. John Spillane, managing director of Mercier Press, recalls his last conversation with the playwright: 'I visited him in the Bon Secours Hospital in Cork on the day he was told that he had just a short while to live. He was very philosophical and said that he had been told nine years earlier that he probably had about ten years to live and felt he hadn't done too badly on that score. He was supposed to remain in hospital but he decided – and was determined – to go home to Listowel to be in his own bed and to be with his family without further delay.'

To Spillane, the playwright hadn't lost his sense of humour in the hospital; despite the circumstances, John B. and himself enjoyed a couple of good guffaws. The chemistry between them was very good and went back over many years; Spillane regarded him as much as a friend as an author. 'I was always conscious how accessible he was,' Spillane noted, 'not alone to all of us in Mercier but to any tourists or visitors or fans who wanted to talk to him; they only had to drop in to the pub and there he was. I imagine that was probably unique in the case of major literary figures.'

John Spillane agreed that Keane's illness affected his output, for apart from the Christmas story collections, there was little else written during that period that the company was aware of. Despite that, there was never any problem or delay in the editorial or proofing process between editor Mary Feehan and himself. In fact, Spillane said that, up to John B.'s illness, it had been a very productive time for the author, with a large literary output, including revised versions of plays in collaboration with Ben Barnes, and the signing of a lucrative American film deal for his novel *Durango*.

*

In the middle of May, John B. was still able to go outdoors, although Tony Guerin sadly noted a deterioration in the writer's condition. Soon it would be Writers' Week, the highpoint of Listowel's cultural year. For years, John B. had been a hard-working member of the Writers' Week committee and was rarely known to have missed a fortnightly meeting. Now, as his condition worsened, the committee members were saying, 'We hope John B. lives to see the Week through.'

One remembered that the same thing had happened in Wexford in 1988, when Dr Tom Walsh, the founder of the town's international opera festival, was dying in the local hospital while his admirers wondered if he would see the event through. He managed to do so but passed away peacefully shortly after the final curtain fell in the Theatre Royal. One sensed the same sombre atmosphere in Listowel; this atmosphere was conveyed by *Irish Times* literary correspondent Eileen Battersby. 'John B. had experienced bad spells before,' she wrote, 'and survived them, so we were hopeful he'd be with us for Writers' Week. However, coming up to the opening of the event, one could hear people anxiously ask, "How is he?" and "Any word?" and people prayed he would survive, and indeed most of us were hopeful he would.'

Meanwhile, David Browne, chairman of the Writers' Week committee, had visited John B. and been told by the playwright, 'No matter what happens to me, I want the Week to go on as usual. Give it your best, give it your almighty best, man.' Leaving the room, Browne felt that if John B. passed away, his loss would be devastating. Father Kieran O'Shea, a close friend of John B.'s for forty years, regularly dropped in to the house to talk to him. 'He knew he had only a short time to live, and I remember him pointing upwards and saying quite simply, "My next appointment is with the man above." I was caught for words, but he was in like a flash and quoted from Keats's 'Ode to a Nightingale'. The authors of this book had met Father O'Shea while researching this book's first edition and were struck by his admiration for Keane's writing and talent; on that occasion, he had suggested some local people we should meet. Keane and Father O'Shea shared a healthy sense of humour and a deep love of the hinterland of Listowel.

Tony Guerin had travelled from Dublin to be with the playwright and spent hours in the house with him. 'I reckoned 'twas his humour that was keeping him alive,' Guerin recalled. 'As we sat together in the sitting room upstairs with some of his grandchildren nearby, he'd try to be as cheerful as he could. He loved his grandchildren and they loved him. And all the time Mary scarcely ever left his side. His nephew Eamonn Keane would drop in, as well as his friend Pádraig Kelly, who sang him songs. Although he knew he was dying, he never discussed the final parting. He wasn't afraid of death, never fearful of what lay beyond. He was I'd say respectful of death, and I knew he had the faith to meet it. Other times he'd switch on the television in the room to watch a programme that appealed to him. His body had weakened but his mind, I could see, was as sharp as ever and his wit never deserted him. You had to admire him, he never relented nor capitulated. In fact, in the evenings he went downstairs to meet his old pals in the bar and enjoy their company and their chat.'

*

As he lay in bed, John B.'s children came and went. His son
Conor, a journalist with the *Examiner* in Cork, was particularly
moved by the impact his father's illness was making on his
old friends who had come to say their farewells. 'It was
heartbreaking to watch some of these old and young friends
weep,' Conor recalled, 'but enormously rewarding to see that
my dad had impacted upon their lives to such a degree that
they loved him to the very end. For some of them, it was too
much, and as they climbed the stairs to his bedroom, emotion
overcame them and they left, vainly fighting back the tears,
saying, "I want to remember him the way he was." In fact,
those who could not bear to say goodbye in person phoned
every day to enquire how he was.'

That Wednesday, 29 May, Writers' Week was officially
opened by actress Anna Manahan, one of John B.'s greatest
admirers. She recalled his unique personality and his genius
for words, especially for writing rich dialogue and for
catching vivid, colloquial phrases. He also had the gift of
generosity. Later, the evening was dominated by various
award presentations, yet it seemed to Eileen Battersby that
most of the speakers referred primarily to the man who,
along with Bryan MacMahon, had made Listowel as famous
for literature as for horse-training. Earlier, Anna Manahan
and her theatre friend Phyllis Ryan had visited John B. in
his bedroom and held his hand and said a silent prayer. As
both man and dramatist, he meant an enormous amount
to them both.

It was fitting in a way that John B. was dying as
novelists, poets and playwrights were arriving in the town
for Writers' Week. As night fell over the rooftops, people
still anxiously asked, 'Any news of John B.?' By now, the
news wasn't good; his friends knew his life was ebbing away
in the room above the street. Years before, he had written
'The Street', a poem about Church Street, where he had
been born in July 1928; some local people, including Danny
Hannon, could recite the poem in full. The lines of the
fourth verse seemed appropriate at this poignant time:

A golden mellow peace forever clings
Along the little street
There are so many lasting things
Beyond the wall of strife
In our beleaguered life
There are so many lovely songs to sing
Of God and His eternal love that rings
Of simple people and of simple things.

32

THE CURTAIN FALLS

Outside north Kerry and a circle of close friends elsewhere, many people were unaware that John B. was dying. It was generally believed that he was going about his creative work as usual. There was no denying, however, that when the announcement came early on that Friday morning, 31 May, the reaction throughout the country was a mixture of genuine shock and sadness.

In the case of John A. Murphy, Emeritus Professor of Irish History at UCC, this was certainly true. Murphy admitted that he was shocked by the news, as he was about to set out for Writers' Week, an event that had afforded him an opportunity to renew his friendship with the playwright and his wife Mary once a year. He was glad that, when he had opened Writers' Week a year before, he had paid public tribute to John B. in the audience. The playwright was rooted in Listowel, and this was the key to his success. As Murphy now reflected on the writer's life and times, his abiding memory was of happy occasions in John B.'s bar in William Street and of that extraordinary man contributing good singing in that sweet, expressive voice of his. All he could add was a farewell to his favourite Kerryman.

The news on the radio recalled Mícheál MacLiammóir's words on his seventieth birthday, when he wistfully said, 'You must remember that every time the curtain falls at the end of a play, we actors die a little. We die a little.' That morning, in another sense, his words could embrace dramatists, for had not the curtain fallen symbolically on Keane, who had given actors the lines to say on many inspiring theatrical occasions? It would have been easy to succumb to a sense of deep melancholia but somehow such a feeling seemed at that moment to be out of place. Deep sympathy, yes, but melancholia, no. The truth was, you wanted to remember his anecdotal exuberance as well as his suffering, and above all, his sheer love of life and people.

Joe Dowling is director of the Guthrie Theatre in Minneapolis and first learned of the playwright's death on the internet. The company was rehearsing the world première of Arthur Miller's new play, *Resurrection Blues*, and thoughts of how John B. Keane was to Ireland what writers like Miller were to America went through his mind. 'I felt that Keane was a man who reflected a sense of the real Ireland that cut through a veneer of respectability and civilisation that ignored primal influences on Irish society,' Dowling recalled. 'For me, his greatest achievement was to place on the Irish stage such dynamic characters as the Bull McCabe, Maggie Poplin, Mena in *Sive* and so many others who tell the story of a rural Ireland so often forgotten before John B. imagined them and gave them a stature. He was to rural Ireland what Seán O'Casey was to a generation of Dubliners.'

Dowling himself was very proud of his small part in the amazing career of the Listowel writer. 'When I became artistic director of the Abbey Theatre,' he said, 'it came as a great surprise to me that the Abbey had ignored this major voice in dramatic literature for a long time. No Keane play had been presented in the new national theatre since it was built in 1966. We rectified this with a production, directed by Paul Brennan, of *The Field*, with Joe Lynch as the Bull McCabe, and shortly afterwards, *The Man from Clare*, directed by Pat Laffan. I still remember the huge hug John B. gave me on the opening night of *The Field* in the Abbey foyer. He was delighted to have his work seen at the national theatre and I am delighted that I had the chance to right a serious wrong. The last play I programmed before my resignation in 1985 was a new production of *Sive*, to be directed by Ben Barnes. Thus started a special relationship in Irish theatre and a flowering of John B. Keane work on Dublin stages.'

Joe Dowling believed that Keane's legacy was twofold. He was a chronicler of an earlier time in Irish life before the Celtic Tiger. He spoke of an Ireland that seemed on the surface to be civilised and developed but, under the surface, was savage and unforgiving. He was a brave writer who was not afraid of telling the truth as he saw it and who could also provide audiences with an uncomplicated laugh. His second great influence was that he paved the way for such writers as Martin McDonagh and Marina Carr. Both these superb young writers owed a debt to John B. Keane and to the way he lifted the stone of Irish life and revealed its secrets.

'It is no cliché to say that we will never see his like again,' Dowling added. 'There is no other John B., but his spirit and his work remain to influence us as we move forward into a new century. *Ar dheis Dé go raibh a anam.*'

*

Barry Cassin was at his home in Balbriggan, County Dublin, when he heard of the playwright's death on an RTÉ news bulletin. It did not come to him as a shock, as he had been forewarned by his daughter Ann Cassin – a newsreader – that Keane was gravely ill and was expected to die at any time. 'My first reaction was that I had lost a friend and at that moment memories crowded in on each other,' Barry Cassin recalled. 'I was very fortunate through Phyllis Ryan to come to direct his plays; she had a very sharp eye for a good play and immediately saw potential in his writing. I had many enjoyable years working with him and I never encountered first nights that generated so much excitement in the theatres in Cork and Dublin. Away from the theatre, he was a most entertaining person, and whenever I visited his Listowel pub there was always a warm welcome from himself and his wife, Mary.'

Cassin remembered now what he called the painful struggle the playwright had experienced to be accepted in the capital. 'Although John never became embittered or betrayed his feeling on the matter, I know that this rejection deeply hurt him,' the director said. 'The fact was that when he began to write, the quality of his work wasn't held in high esteem – far from it – but eventually things changed and he won full recognition. Phyllis Ryan contributed largely in bringing about the change because she had the courage to put on his plays.'

Like most people mourning his death, Cassin felt that one could not be melancholy for long where Keane was concerned. 'As sad as his passing is for all of us in the theatre, amusing episodes still come to mind. For example, once we were discussing play scripts and he turned to me and, with an eyebrow raised, said, "I sent you *Many Young Men of Twenty* a few years ago and you didn't do it." I looked at him and replied, "You're quite right, John. I couldn't do it at that particular time because of commitments, but I did offer it to someone else, who turned it down."' Later, Cassin directed it for Noel Pearson, with Joe Lynch playing the leading role.

Cassin recalled another occasion when he was directing *The Year of the Hiker* at the Gate Theatre and it was agreed that John B. would deliver a few words at the final curtain. He could still hear the playwright tell the audience, 'The acting tonight was magnificent *(a short pause)*, the direction was magnificent *(a longer pause)* and the play was magnificent.' To Cassin, the Kerry playwright had 'put the lid' on all future curtain calls. There was a less happy occasion in the same theatre during a revival of *Sharon's Grave*, when Cassin noted that the director in question had omitted a lot of the wake scene. 'At the time, I considered it a fundamental error of judgement,' he recalled, 'and obviously the producer had no understanding of what a wake meant in the country. I didn't mention it to John, for fear it would upset him.'

*

'Breakfast was abandoned at 8 o'clock in our home in Greystones on that Thursday morning,' recalled the playwright Bernard Farrell, 'when the radio news announcer told me that the odds had beaten John B. And at that moment I realised how much we had lost and then, with gratitude, remembered how much he had given us. And I knew that like many before me and many after me, I would always see him and hear him in the legacy of his wonderfully insightful, brutal, tender and comic plays. But, sadly, that I would never again be able to say to him, "Thank you."'

Throughout his own playgoing life, Farrell had seen John

B. very clearly in his plays – the fighter against the odds, the champion of lost causes, the rebel with a cause, the survivor. So when he heard that Keane wasn't well, he believed that he would somehow survive against those odds too. And for a long time, he did. When Farrell met him some time before in the Abbey Theatre for the presentation of the Gradam Award, Keane had said that he didn't think he would ever write another play. 'I said that I was about to begin one,' Farrell recalled, 'and maybe we should start together and see who finishes first. My thinking was that any writer will move mountains to stay alive and finish a work.

'He was a great mountain-mover and he stayed alive anyway. Whenever we'd meet, I'd ask about his health and he would switch the conversation to enquire about my work. It was the nature of this wonderful man to – shyly and humbly – divert the spotlight away from himself and on to the concerns of others.'

Bernard Farrell recognised this shyness in John B. when he first met him in the early 1960s at the Gas Company Theatre in Dun Laoghaire as part of a very enthusiastic audience emerging from *The Highest House on the Mountain* and exiting through the showrooms. 'Then I spotted him – hiding behind some gas-stoves – desperately trying to be invisible. I pointed and said, "That's John Keane" and, as a stampede of autograph-hunters descended on him, he looked at me the way Jesus must have looked at Judas in the Garden of Gethsemane. I didn't meet him again for twenty years – this time as a fellow playwright. Meeting him over the years, I tried to thank him for his wonderful plays and to confess to his deep influence on my own playwriting career. I also confessed to my Judas role at the Gas Company Theatre and asked whether he remembered it or not. He would laugh heartily and thereafter mercilessly repeat this betrayal whenever we were in impressive company.'

*

Tomás MacAnna, a former artistic director of the Abbey Theatre, first heard of John B.'s death on the Thursday evening television news, but it was not unexpected, as his friend Phyllis

Ryan had the day before telephoned him from Listowel. His mind now immediately went back to the Abbey Company's days in the Queen's Theatre – then its temporary home – where he had designed Keane's *Hut 42* and *The Man from Clare*. His first experience of the young playwright was anything but harmonious, however, as he himself seemed to have been the only adjudicator of drama festivals in the country who put his first play, *Sive*, in second place; this was at the Charleville Festival.

Looking back, it was indeed for playwriting such as Keane's, redolent of his native Kerry's soil, that the Abbey Theatre was first founded. 'I would add that he brought back to the Irish theatre the arts of the storyteller and the folklorist, as only a Kerryman could,' MacAnna recalled. 'All that, and his ear for the spoken word, comparable perhaps to that of Synge or Molloy or Murray, but very much his own, rich and racy as a Kerry stream. I doubt if there is a parish in the country that hasn't enjoyed his plays over and over, and his gift to the profession was always full houses and, as the poet Paddy Kavanagh would say, "Applause, applause."'

MacAnna tried to remember some of the moments he had most enjoyed in Keane's plays. 'Let me say, there's one abiding one, and perhaps the one that will always linger,' he recalled. 'It's that little scene in *The Field* where, awaiting their unsuspecting victim in the darkening twilight, the Bull McCabe and his son talk about the crows, an interlude of rustic philosophy far removed from their grim intentions. It remains vivid in my mind still, with the late Ray McAnally and Robert Carlile in that fine production by Barry Cassin on the dimly lit Olympia stage – the very first staging of the play.'

*

Patrick Mason was rehearsing a revival of Hugh Leonard's *Da* at the Abbey Theatre when the news of Keane's death was conveyed to him. Ireland, he thought, could ill afford to lose a playwright of Keane's imagination and talent. It pleased him enormously that in more recent years John B. had commanded centre stage at the national theatre, where he rightfully belonged. Mason himself had never had the satisfaction of directing Keane's plays; this was something he regretted, because they were at once poetic and earthy, with vivid characterisation. Perhaps the most lasting memory of his work for Mason was Brenda Fricker's portrayal of Big Maggie. He felt that this play, and others of Keane's, would surely appeal to new generations of playgoers.

*

James McGlone was proud of his long association with John B.'s plays and over the years had invited actors from Ireland to play leading parts in his productions. He had an absolute belief in the playwright's flair and talent. Around this time, his own book on former Abbey actress and director Ria Mooney was published in America, and he was looking forward to another visit to Ireland with his wife Virginia. He was in his New Jersey home when he first heard of John B.'s death.

'I pressed the blue button next to the flashing light,' McGlone recalled, 'and a recorded voice said, "Hello, Jim, I don't know if you heard while you were away, but I thought I would tell you anyhow, in case you missed it. John B. died yesterday." Our freshly painted domestic office with its bare walls free of Irish play production photos must have contributed to my muted moment of emptiness, followed almost immediately by an overwhelming feeling of melancholy. It seemed to me that a theatrical era had passed in that unexpected announcement.'

McGlone now remembered that, when first presenting *Sharon's Grave* with his students, he discovered he was in the presence of a naturally gifted playwright. Keane's sure instincts with plot progression, character development, tension and pace could not be learned. He recognised the storyteller's natural talent for drawing his audience into the theatrical event. What became clear to him as he worked on particular scenes was Keane's ability to make common cause with society's vulnerable and discarded people. He must have felt, too, for those Irish women who, like Big Maggie, were subject to drunken and profligate husbands bent on ruining their families and themselves. And the Hiker Lacey, driven from his home by his sister-in-law, returning home to die, and rejected by his own children, summons up the boredom and loneliness of the wanderer with no place to call home.

On a more personal note, McGlone considered John B. to have been a shy man, bred into village life, where only the familiar could be trusted. He had the charm of the raconteur – the physical, embracing warmth that made you feel included while it avoided personal relations – McGlone noted. Best of all, he had the Irishman's trick of creating laughter that covered up deeply felt convictions and sympathies. If you sought to discover his identification with the oppressed, the outcast, the defenceless – in short, those for whom life was a trial – you had to look to his plays. His characters are not victims, McGlone asserted; they are strong and fascinating people caught in situations they have no hope of controlling.

McGlone felt that, in a curious way, Keane's theatrical life seemed to mirror his characters' dilemmas, for he himself was discounted by the urban world of the theatre as a mere entertainer – a kind of naive countryman with little formal sophistication and no serious artistic pretensions. Audiences knew better. They grasped instinctively that the playwright was their chronicler, the man who reflected their con-frontation with the loss of a world that, for all of its hardships and dangers, gave meaning to their lives.

*

Feargal Keane, a BBC news correspondent, had returned to Listowel some years previously for the funeral of his father, the actor Eamonn Keane, and had delivered an eloquent graveside oration. He made no secret of his admiration for his uncle and said, 'John B. had been a good brother to my father. He helped him through illness and always gave his love unconditionally.' The journalist now remembered that, when he had met John B. in Listowel during the previous summer, he had looked 'terribly tired'.

Television viewers in Ireland had by now come to know Feargal Keane through his books and his vivid reporting for the BBC. He had been in Pakistan reporting on the flare-up there with neighbouring India when his cousin Conor Keane contacted him to say that his father was close to death. With that, Feargal made hurried arrangements to get back to Ireland and be at John B.'s bedside. Some time later, Conor Keane contacted him again to say that his father had died. Working with typical journalistic speed, and anxious no doubt to express his true feelings about his uncle, Feargal penned a tribute for the *Irish Times*, in the course of which he looked back nostalgically.

'As a child, I remember John B. as a tall, laughing figure who would dig deep into his pockets for ice-cream money in the summer and fetch out pound notes at Christmas,' he wrote. 'I remember going to the bog with him outside Listowel to foot turf, where he told us stories about the King of the World fighting Fionn MacCool on nearby Cnoc an Óir, or walking in the woods at Gurtenard or along the banks of his beloved Feale river. When I began to read literature, he would quote Keats and Thomas Hardy (two of his favourites) and encourage me to read the classics. Later on, whenever I called, the question would be the same: "Are you writing? And if not, why not?"'

It was John B. who had been instrumental in getting him into the *Limerick Leader,* and at the time he gave him one important piece of advice: 'Don't mind the big fellows. They can look after themselves. Listen out for the small man. He'll tell you the truth.' Feargal Keane was by now generally regarded as a crusading journalist and broadcaster in a world where that species appeared conspicuous by its absence. In this respect, he and John B. were kindred spirits. To quote again from his *Irish Times* tribute: 'With those he regarded as hypocrites or bullies, John B. was uncompromising. He was proud of his culture and Irish identity but loathed cultural absolutism and hectoring nationalism; he was a devout Catholic but never shied away from confronting the darker side of the church in Irish life.'

In case readers might be under the impression that he was painting too pious a picture of his uncle, he asked, 'Is this a secular saint I am describing? Of course not. John B. had flaws like any man, but there wasn't a mean or dishonourable bone in his body. At the heart of his life lay a great love affair. His wife, Mary, was his inspiration and his compass. I know he felt that he would never have achieved his fame without her. I think he also knew that he would never have become the human being he was without her love. I think now of Mary and my cousins, Billy, Conor, John and Joanne, and of the great absence in their lives. Not just a man, more a force of nature.'

*

Although John Spillane knew that John B. was dying – and had visited him for the last time in the Bon Secours Hospital scarcely two weeks before – his passing on that May morning not only hit him hard but affected the staff at Mercier Press, with whom he was most popular. In particular, Mary Feehan, who had edited so many of his works and had come to know him on a personal basis, would treat his passing as though it were that of a relative. Her own and John Spillane's immediate thoughts went out to Mary Keane and the rest of the family, for he was an irreplaceable loss to them, just as he was to Mercier Press. John B. was after all the company's best-selling author, and at the time of his death there was much more he wanted to write. For example, he had discussed the possibility of publishing his poetry, together with the ballads and songs from his various plays, in one volume. He was quite enthusiastic about this project, but it was hard to say how far it had progressed. He spoke to Mary Feehan about his plans to start a new novel based on the characters from the street where he was born, Listowel's Church Street. Again he was enthusiastic about the idea but gave no indication he was working on it. Furthermore, there was the possibility of doing some children's stories.

'We had heard that he was an extremely popular tale-teller to his grandchildren,' recalled John Spillane, 'but unfortunately nothing ever came of this. In fact, his last book for us was A *Christmas Omnibus* in 2001. It was a compilation of all the Christmas stories we had published in three previously published Christmas collections but included a number of stories John B. had written in the previous year. As an author, he was easy to deal with. In fact, the only real disagreement I can remember over the years was when our former managing director, Captain Seán Feehan, and himself failed to see eye to eye on John B.'s English translation of *Dan Pheadaí Aindí*, which we had originally published in Irish. That disagreement resulted in the English translation being published by Brandon rather than Mercier, and a few years after that Brandon also published *The Bodhrán Makers*.'

The two men's differences, according to Mary Feehan, did not last very long, and soon she was as busy as ever editing John B.'s latest manuscripts for publication. Keane declined, however, to undertake publicity tours abroad to publicise his novels and short stories, as he felt uncomfortable about the idea – despite the fact that such tours had become part and parcel of the publishing scene. Unlike most modern authors, John B. did not use a computer at home. It was his habit to post his typed manuscripts or have them collected in Listowel. John Spillane remembers that when John B. came to Cork to collect his royalty cheque, he would bring a group of the Mercier staff out and wine and dine them in great style in the late, lamented Oyster Tavern. After the closure of the Oyster, he transferred his allegiance to Jury's Hotel in the city. Later on, when he had curtailed his travelling, he would always entertain a few of them to a "royalty" dinner in the Three Mermaids in Listowel.

Doing business with the playwright was different, Spillane remembered, from working with other Mercier authors and playwrights. For one thing, it invariably concluded with a lively dinner, good wine and storytelling. This was something that in the past had drawn Captain Feehan and Keane closer together, or, as John B. used to say, 'Seán and myself are kindred brethren.' After the Captain's death, John Spillane had a lot of dealings with John B. and visited Listowel fairly regularly. 'I can say that these sessions were some of the most enjoyable elements of my time in Mercier,' he recalled. 'They were never too long and always ended up cheerfully. Indeed, some of the sessions would be conducted walking the beach in Ballybunion, and on one famous occasion at about five in the afternoon we stopped in the hotel there for a drink before we went back to Listowel. John B. got talking with some women who were on holiday and had dropped in for a drink and in no time at all he got the mother-and-father of a sing-song going at that hour of the day.'

The more Spillane reflected on Keane's passing, the more he realised the huge loss he was to them all at Mercier. Over the years, his books had sold millions of copies, and Spillane was quite confident that they would go on selling. At Mercier, they would miss his visits, however. 'The thing is, everybody looked forward to shaking his hand and having a word with him,' Spillane recalled. 'He was more than an author, he was our friend. We will all miss him greatly.'

*

Meanwhile, all that Thursday morning friends and well-wishers from many parts of the country as well as abroad were phoning the Keane home with their condolences. As Feargal Keane recalled, 'All of these people sounded stunned. John B. was part of their hinterland too. Not the same intimate presence he'd represented in my life, but a part of their cultural memory. I will miss him in so many ways, but along with grief, I feel a fierce pride in him. That was a man, all right. That was a man.'

The popular playwright, who was aged seventy-three, had passed away peacefully at 7.45 AM on Thursday, 30 May, surrounded by Mary, his wife, and the children, Billy, Conor, John and Joanne. 'He died a happy man, with his family tending to his every need,' recalled Conor Keane, 'and he told us he had no regrets and was ready to meet his maker. These were not just empty words to console us but John B., as usual, telling the truth as he saw it.' Later the death notice specified, 'Family flowers only' and suggested donations to Listowel Hospice. Among those who telephoned the Keane home was President Mary McAleese. In a brief tribute later, she stated that John B.'s genius had been his ability to observe and reflect so accurately the wonders of life around him and that his work had given him an accurate insight into human strengths and frailties. Whether on the amateur drama circuit or on the national and international stages, his plays had a universal appeal that would endure for many years to come.

Unsurprisingly, at lunchtime that day there were queues outside the local St John's Theatre for the Lartigue Theatre Company's production of *One Way Ticket*, a Keane play that had not been staged for thirty years. Joe Murphy, director of St John's, felt that this was the way the people wanted to express their grief, and that such an attitude was very understandable. They would also get an opportunity to show their sorrow on the following day, Friday, when the playwright's remains were removed to O'Carroll's funeral home in Listowel.

According to Tony Guerin, the town had seldom if ever experienced such an outpouring of public sympathy for one of its own. 'I was glad to be present and to see for myself the esteem in which John B. was held by rich and poor, young and old,' he recalled. ''Twas heartening for all of us who loved him and realised what he had brought to the town. We won't see his like again.'

As for the Keane family, it was noticeable before long that Peg Schuster was particularly grief-stricken over the death of her favourite brother. They had always been very close and, as his theatrical triumphs grew, her late husband, John, and she shared in John B.'s success and were always happy to host first-night parties at their home in Dublin. He was a vital presence and his wit and humour cheered them both on many an occasion. 'I will miss him greatly,' Peg said, still numbed by his death. But then all the family would have treasured memories, including Michael Keane, who grew up with John B. in Listowel and knew him perhaps better than most of the family. Denis Keane, too, who put on John B.'s plays in Dublin, and like Peg and John Schuster seemed to be always at his big first nights in the Olympia, Gaiety or Abbey Theatres. For Joanne Keane, John B.'s only daughter and the youngest of the family, his death would leave a deep void. They got on very well together, and when she got married in the late 1990s she found his support – as, indeed, that of her mother – tremendous. Likewise, her brothers Billy, Conor and John had come to admire their father as an individual and as a writer.

They delighted in his successes, appreciated his wisdom and, above all, never ceased to be amazed by his genuine love of life and people.

At this time, a Dublin company was touring with *The Chastitute*, and that Friday night the troupe was scheduled to stage the play at the Dean Crowe Hall, Athlone, scene in the late 1950s of Keane's triumph with *Sive* in the All-Ireland Drama Festival. Earlier in the day, the producer, Edward Farrell, a friend of Keane's for more than twenty years, had been telephoned by a member of the Keane family in Listowel to tell him that it was their wish that the show go on that night. Farrell made it known that the performance would be a tribute to John B., and added, 'Just to hear people laugh is the best tribute that can be paid to him. He made many people laugh with the language in his plays.' In a personal tribute, Mick Lally, a leading member of the cast, said that the dramatist would be principally remembered because of the exceedingly vibrant characters he had created.

The print and broadcast media, meanwhile, gave intensive coverage to John B.'s passing. It was to be expected, because, apart from the tremendous news value of the story, he had always been generous with his time when called on by television and radio presenters; indeed, he had sometimes acted as an unpaid guide when they visited Listowel, showing them historic places and introducing them to knowledgeable locals. The media would miss him in the future, as there were few writers and playwrights who were so generous with their time. Furthermore, newspaper editors – especially those working on papers to which Keane had been a contributor – would be saddened by his passing. He would no longer be around when news desks looked for a comment on some social or cultural issue of the day. That Friday evening, queues gathered outside O'Carroll's funeral parlour to pay their own tribute.

33

A Dignified Farewell

Saturday 1 June dawned brightly in a town where many hearts were heavy. People awakened to the sad realisation that it was a day like no other in their lives. To his friends, who had admired John B.'s energy, vitality and zest for life, it was a day they had believed would not come in the playwright's early seventies; now that it was an unwelcome reality, they, like everyone else, wanted to give the great man a fitting farewell. In theatrical circles, it was the last act in the drama, except that on this occasion he would not be called on for a curtain speech. It was enough that he had an appreciative audience.

Barry Cassin had set out by car the previous day for Listowel and stayed overnight with a relative in Ennis. Next morning, he crossed to Kerry by Shannon Ferries, arriving in Listowel around 10 o'clock, in ample time to join the many mourners. Nóra Relihan had warned him to get to the church early, as it was sure to be crowded. Already most of the mourners were present, among them President McAleese and her husband, Martin. Soon they would be joined by politicians, well-known footballers – past and present – theatrical personalities, media people and locals. Up to twenty-five priests, led by Bishop Murphy of Kerry, were in the sacristy, with Father Kieran O'Shea as chief concelebrant. The Gospel reading was the Sermon on the Mount – John B.'s favourite passage from the Scriptures. Father O'Shea said that the writer had built his life around that sermon and was constantly speaking of the need for forgiveness. He added that John B. was a devoted family man and a religious person with an extraordinary devotion to the sacrament of penance. The priest said that he had once assured Keane that *Sive* must have been performed in every parish in the country. John B. replied, 'You know, I

329

think the Catholic Church in Ireland only began with *Sive*.'

The music for the occasion was carefully chosen, with sixth-class pupils from a local school singing 'Sweet Listowel' and Anna Manahan, who over the years had memorably spoken many of the dramatist's lines from his plays, reciting his best-known poem, 'The Street'. It was then the turn of Billy Keane to thank President McAleese for her presence in the church, and also to express the family's gratitude to Tony Guerin, a close family friend, and others who had supported them and sent messages of sympathy.

With more than a hint of his famous father's histrionics, he told the congregation, 'Don't be too sad this morning, because that wasn't Dad's way. He didn't believe that death was the end. He was convinced that there was something after.' Billy Keane went on to pay special tribute to the people of Listowel for honouring his father while he was still alive, by such gestures as dedicating a room in the Writers' Centre to him and naming a new road in the town after him. He then explained the route the funeral cortège would follow, lightening the mood by adding that it would stop outside his father's pub. 'You see, my father never went on a long journey without stopping,' he remarked. 'We decided that he would be buried in Listowel cemetery at the back left-hand side of the graveyard. You'll find him at left corner-back, buried between two football fields.'

After sustained applause from the congregation, Billy Keane turned in the direction of his mother and, in a personal tribute, said she had been the driving force behind his late father, adding with feeling, 'He would not have written a line without you. But don't be under any illusions about retirement. You've a lot of pints to fill yet and you'll join him one day, but it won't be until ten years after you receive the hundred-euro cheque from Mrs McAleese for reaching the century.' He also referred warmly to the special bonds between the Keane family and another famous Listowel writer, Bryan MacMahon.

Mary Keane, with her family around her that morning in church, was bearing up bravely to the ordeal, even if it was hard to imagine that for once she was without John B. beside her. For on the big moments of their lives they were usually seen happily together. In silence, and looking a little drawn, she had listened to the warm tributes paid to the man she had married all those years ago, and she had ensured that his funeral was planned and carried through in the way he would have wanted. Like the congregation that filled the church to overflowing, she was pleased with everything about the ceremony, including her eldest son Billy's apt words, as well as Father O'Shea's moving homily. Afterwards, outside the church, she was soon surrounded by friends and other well-wishers, some of whom had travelled a distance and wanted to sympathise with her. Barry Cassin was among those who had a quiet word with her. He had been greatly impressed by the whole ceremony and considered it a worthy tribute to John B. and absolutely fitting for the occasion. 'I thought the choir sang beautifully,' he noted. 'Father O'Shea delivered his homily with a nice mixture of solemnity and humour, and I have to say that Anna Manahan recited "The Street" most touchingly. But I'll most of all remember Billy Keane's words and the way he said them. He reminded me of his father by his wit and gestures and the way he captured the mood of the occasion. Until Father O'Shea spoke about his deep faith, I did not know that John B. was such a religious man.'

To Tony Guerin, the funeral was simply an extension of the playwright's life. It was a dignified farewell, the kind he would have wanted. It was good, too, he said, to see the MacMahon family strongly represented, for Bryan MacMahon, like John B., loved Listowel and its people and had taught generations of them. Everywhere Guerin looked, he saw people who had meant something in John B.'s life, from the small person to the big person; the size of the gathering was a reflection of their genuine regard for him. Fine Gael, the party for which he greatly cared, was represented by two former Taoisigh, Liam Cosgrave and Garret Fitzgerald, and Michael Noonan, a former leader of the party. From Tralee had come former Tánaiste Dick Spring, and from Cork, MEP Brian Crowley. Rugby star Mick Galwey was photographed alongside celebrated Kerry footballers, while Ronnie Drew and Paddy Reilly represented show business and Patrick Bergin the film world. It seemed that every facet of Irish life was there to mourn Keane's passing.

All business premises in Listowel had closed for the funeral and crowds stood silently on the footpaths as the large cortège slowly made its way through the town, stopping briefly outside the Keane family pub before proceeding down the John B. Keane Road to the old cemetery. The graveside oration was given by Danny Hannon, a champion of Keane's plays for nearly forty years and a man who seldom, if ever, missed first nights. He had travelled abroad with Keane, had experienced his wit and temperament, and could now say that the playwright was restless, ambitious, opinionated, provocative – and an approachable genius and national treasure. Everyone in the town of Listowel, he said, considered their cup filled to overflowing if they could shake John B.'s hand and have a chat with him, because he was a man of great grace, manners and personal charm.

'Although we gather here today to mourn the passing of a close friend and an illustrious writer,' Hannon said, 'we have also come to celebrate the life of a spirited, charismatic and generous man who will forever occupy a special niche in the hearts and minds of Irish people everywhere. This is the town he cherished above all others; he loved its people, cherished its streets and laneways where he walked. He was at his most joyful whenever the town was dressed in festive regalia for the races, the wren boys, Writers' Week, the Fleadh Cheoil. But he not only enjoyed these events, he also contributed hugely to their success by his involvement in their committees, and worked tirelessly for their promotion. Furthermore, how many times have you and I been asked by visitors the location of John B.'s pub? Long may it continue to be a shrine, where tumult and confusion and singing will reverberate to the memory of the great man.'

Hannon spoke quietly to the silent gathering about the art of John B. Keane and why it could not be contemplated at a distance. 'In my view,' he said, 'it needs to be lived and loved at close quarters, because, although much of what he wrote about was universal, its roots are deep in north Kerry. You will not stray too far from this place here today before you encounter those whimsical Keane specialities the lovesick farmer, the successful TD, the country postman and the Irish parish priest, and if you do, you'll be glad that here was an

Irish writer who laid it all down on the page for posterity.

'So we thank the man for leading us on this journey along the scenic route through his beloved Kerry landscape, one that he ruled over like a benevolent king, sharing our dreams, teasing our ambitions and mocking our vanities; or as he often said to me, "Danny, these are the joys and small sorrows of married life." Be sure of one thing this day: the sun will never set on the empire of John B. Keane. Always on a stage, in a theatre somewhere, there will be one of his plays in progress. I should add that two things always got under his skin: one was an overdose of solemnity, and the other was long-winded speakers, and I might now be sailing dangerously close to the wind on both of these counts, so thank you for listening to me.'

*

There were others who had enjoyed John B.'s friendship and were members of what might be described as his sporting, political or literary club. Jimmy Deenihan was a prominent member of this club and had talked to the playwright at his bedside during the final days of his illness. He could thank John B. for introducing him to politics and pointing the way to a seat in Dáil Éireann on a Fine Gael ticket. For his part, Deenihan would recall, 'I consider myself very fortunate and privileged to have developed a close personal friendship with John B. over the past forty years. There was always a family friendship between the Deenihans and the Keanes – my father, Mick, knew John B. through north Kerry football and their involvement in the Fine Gael organisation. To my father, he was a hero and his plays and articles were a source of constant discussion in our house. Later on, John B. followed my progress as a county footballer and later advised me about my career prospects. When I was being urged to enter politics, I remember him saying to me, "Jimmy, it's not a nice game – a lot rougher than football – your own can be the cruellest to you – but if you go forward for election, I will give you my full support because I know that you will give it your best, your almighty best."'

Deenihan got that support, and over the years – and even a short time before Keane died – the playwright canvassed for him at general elections. Keane supported some major projects Deenihan initiated in the area. But as Deenihan would thoughtfully add, 'I was not the only one to benefit from his talent and friendship: many of the country's actors owe their success to him. He has left us with a legacy of literature and vibrant characters that will survive while the word is spoken. He remained deep-rooted in his native Listowel and north Kerry all of his life. It is from here that he derived his inner strength. He was never one of them, he was always one of us.'

Gabriel Fitzmaurice, writer and poet, was another notable voice to explore John B.'s roots in relation to his writing. He had first heard of Keane at the age of seven in 1959, when *Sive* was considered a local wonder because it depicted his own people and held a mirror up to them. They looked at themselves and were not displeased. To Fitzmaurice, it was a measure of the playwright's genius that he could tell the truth, the whole truth – much of it unpalatable – about rural Ireland and continue to live there. More than that, he was revered, even loved, by his own people.

The legacy of John B. Keane locally and nationally, he believed, was that there were still poets, playwrights, novelists, short-story writers and balladeers writing in the townlands, towns and villages of Ireland. For his Ireland hadn't died with him. As he passed on, he passed on his Ireland to the next generation. It was now up to them to make of it what they would. As Keane created and inhabited his world, he had given them the freedom to imagine their own. 'Keane didn't create the conscience of his race,' added Fitzmaurice. 'He created dramas. Dramas particular to his native place; dramas large as life that would touch the hearts and minds of audiences beyond his parish, beyond his county, beyond his country. Indeed I have it on the authority of Thom Steinbeck, son of John Steinbeck and himself a distinguished author, that his father was a fan of John B. Keane and regarded him as one of the greatest Irish writers.'

To Fitzmaurice, Keane had looked into the heart of darkness and made peace with it. Like all true peace, however,

334

this had not petered out into a maudlin or 'happy' ending. In fact, his peace meant that he could coexist with the ugliness, the loneliness, the violence, the harshness of rural life, knowing that it could be redeemed by the love he held for his place and its people. John B.'s true successors would be those who had the courage, like him, to accuse and to redeem; to write for their own people; to hold up that mirror in which they observed themselves, good and evil, and not retreat from the truth in cleverality or caricature.

Seldom, if ever, had the death of an Irish writer commanded so much space on the air and in print. All that weekend of early June, copious tributes were paid to him; a few of them were perhaps over-sentimental, but most were searching. One important voice was unavoidably missing, that of Brendan Kennelly. The poet and playwright was indisposed and unavoidably absent, but he was personally represented at the obsequies in Listowel. Few people, as we have seen, admired John B. more than the irrepressible Kerryman, and everyone knew he would have been there for the funeral if it had been at all possible. In conversation, Kennelly's infectious laugh would ring out when John B. made a particularly witty or pungent comment. The two men spoke the same racy language, enjoyed much the same cultural pursuits, and Kennelly always made a point of dropping in to the pub in William Street on his way home at holiday time to see his people in his native Ballylongford.

Kennelly's friendship stretched beyond John B. himself: it embraced Mary and the family, and before that, Eamonn Keane, on whose death he wrote an evocative poetic tribute. No doubt he was already thinking of appropriate lines that would best fit the legendary John B.'s demise. Needless to say, other Irish writers of stature were happy to add their voices to the tributes. In this regard, Hugh Leonard was to say, 'Keane was a gentleman in the most profound sense. He had a very great genius for combining richness of language with internal energy, which is the essence of theatre. He put the town of Listowel on a world map. Among his dramatic forebears was Dion Boucicault; his heirs include Marina Carr . . . We really are going to miss him.'

Anthony Cronin, in the course of his tribute, made the relevant point: 'Except for a short period spent working at various jobs in Northampton in the early 1950s, John B. never left Listowel. This too is an unusual pattern among Irish writers. Most of those writers who come from small towns are glad to shake the dust off their feet. If they return, it is usually only in memory, and often simply a probing of wounds. For his part, John B. helped to make Listowel a place of considerable note, in which his own presence was strong.'

'We salute the fallen chieftain and everyone at the Abbey Theatre offers heartfelt sympathy to his wife, Mary, and children,' was how Ben Barnes, the company's artistic director, described the popular playwright's passing. He had attended the Requiem Mass and was impressed by the dignity of the occasion. In the past, he had visited Listowel to have pre-production conversations with John B., and had always found him cordial and cooperative. 'What should never be forgotten about him,' Barnes added, 'is his great personal courage in standing up for what he believed in when it was neither popular nor profitable. He was a man who was fearless when principles were at stake.'

On a theatrical level, he said that Big Maggie Polpin and the Bull McCabe stood alongside Juno, Molly Bloom and Pegeen Mike among the great characters of twentieth-century Irish drama and literature. The greatest actresses of successive generations, from Marie Keane to Marie Mullen, and including Joan O'Hara, Maureen Toal, Brenda Fricker and Anna Manahan, had brought Keane's brilliant matriarch to life on the stages of Ireland, just as Ray McAnally, Niall Tóibín and Richard Harris had given them memorable Bull McCabes on stage and screen. 'There are few people of whom it can be said,' noted Barnes, 'his like will not be seen again. But that is the truth, and we won't.'

Tomas MacAnna believed that Keane's plays would always be a lively and vital part of the Irish theatre. They would bring images of Irish life, in his time and ours, to our stages, amateur and professional, for many years to come, much more vividly and in a more abiding way than any history book or commentary. His plays were the very essence of folk art and perhaps, one might say, everyday folklore, MacAnna said.

Although Gay Byrne was unable to be at the funeral, he remembered the playwright with the warmest feelings. John B. had after all been a colourful, if provocative, panellist on the popular *Late Late* television show, where he was introduced to a wider audience. 'I enjoyed talking to John B.,' commented Byrne, 'for he always had something interesting to say. I admired his sharp wit and great inventiveness, and his way with words was guaranteed to go down well with the *Late Late* audiences.' It was known that Gay Byrne and his friends never made the journey from Dublin to Kerry for the Rose of Tralee without calling in on the playwright in his Listowel pub for a drink. As the presenter said, 'I always think of John B. in warm terms. I am greatly saddened by his death.'

Everyone, it seemed, wanted to be associated with tributes to the playwright, and their sentiments came across as genuine and sincerely meant. President McAleese was particularly forthcoming in her comments to the media and was obviously deeply touched by the playwright's passing. Likewise, the veteran actor Éamon Kelly, who had appeared in every Keane production at the Abbey Theatre, had made some perceptive remarks about him before his own death in November 2001. John B.'s greatest talent was the stage, he said. He was one of the last storytellers of the stage, and people were interested in his stories. His dialogue was always humorous and witty, and he was a great man to draw characters which were funny and outgoing. Kelly's own favourite Keane role was Pats Bocock in *Sive*. 'It is the tale of two travellers, a father and son, and they are like a Greek chorus in the play,' Kelly noted. 'They used to bring the house down.'

It was no surprise that John B.'s charm and wit appealed to women, and he loved their company. This affection was reciprocated, with many actresses expressing the belief over the years that their careers would have died a death had it not been for the playwright and the wealth of female characters in his plays. 'John B. really gets under the skin of women,' remarked Brenda Fricker. 'Himself and Shakespeare are among the few who have written well for women.' Although she admired Keane as a playwright, she added that there was also a deep joy in knowing him as a man. 'He was one of those people,' she continued, 'if you saw him coming into the room, your life brightened up. We will all miss him.'

Richard Harris, a biblical-looking Bull McCabe in the screen version of *The Field*, recalled that Keane had a wonderful common touch and that was what made him so special. Niall Tóibín, a notable Bull McCabe on stage and a lifelong friend of the playwright, described him as 'a giant of a man' and said his legacy would enhance still further his worldwide reputation. Druid Theatre Company's Garry Hynes, who was preparing a new production of *Sive*, called the playwright 'a giant and a gentleman of Irish theatre.' And prize-winning novelist John McGahern, who was at Writers' Week at the time of Keane's death, said that he had met John B. some years previously and had found him to be a man of great courtesy and charm, and someone who, through his writings, gave enormous pleasure to many people. Keane was a great loss to writing and his own community, McGahern noted.

*

The provincial press has unfailingly played a key role throughout Irish history in recording for posterity the passing of outstanding political, religious and literary figures in their own hinterlands, and researchers have often been grateful to editors for their foresight. In regard to the death of John B. Keane, it was no different. For example, the *Kerryman* newspaper rose to the occasion and produced an exemplary weekend supplement that must have greatly pleased the Keane family. The supplement, which had many pages in colour and was tastefully designed, was a worthy tribute to the great man. It also caught the mood of the occasion; in fact, the newspaper group's owner, Dr A. J. O'Reilly, penned his own eloquent appreciation of the playwright. In a sense, O'Reilly said, John B. Keane was an intensely contemporary writer, whose writings would continue to be relevant fifty years from now, when other writers of today and yesterday may be talked about but not read and listened to.

'I was always gladdened to meet John B.,' he added. 'I feel that his words and his thoughts have blessed us all. He will live on for longer than most playwrights. His observations on our country, our people and our lives tell us where we came from, who we are and, importantly, what we can be.'

The Listowel writer was also remembered by the film world, especially those associated with the screening of his play *The Field*. Producer Noel Pearson echoed what was in the minds of many people in show business – that, regrettably, he hadn't seen John B. Keane as much as he would have liked in recent years. As Pearson put it, 'Time flies and you keep meaning to get down to Listowel but something always seemed to postpone it.' The producer went on to say that he would always remember Keane's honesty and directness – virtues that were, as they all knew, increasingly rare in the world in which they lived. He felt that, as an artist, Keane was grossly under-estimated in Ireland for a very long time.

In Pearson's view, the playwright was not someone who suffered fools easily in relation to either his work or his determined approach to the world. 'John, as I came to know, had a short fuse when it was called for,' Pearson continued, 'and I saw that on a few occasions. I often recall the two of us in deep discussion during the filming of *The Field*, and if someone came over for a few words, he would be the soul of civility. If, however, that person came back once too often, you'd get to see another side of John B. I think his wife, Mary, was a huge influence on him, not alone as his perfect partner, which was clear for all to see, but as a woman who kept his feet on the ground at all stages. As for Keane, details were important to him and he expected standards to be as high as his own.'

As the director of *The Field*, Jim Sheridan recalled that John B. was a huge help to him in the welcome and hospitality he had extended to him on his visit to Listowel. 'Naturally, I was very cautious at first about taking on the job of filming a work so obviously close to his heart,' the director said. 'Yet I imagine he wondered privately about what the end product would become. Film, by its nature, is a very different creature to theatre, and you would expect the author to be nervous and apprehensive, but in credit to him, he never complained and never said anything negative, which I will be eternally gratefully for. John B. was a hugely charming man – one of the most charming I have ever met.'

As Gabriel Fitzmaurice argued, John B. Keane bequeathed the nation more than his plays. He highlighted the importance of place – in his case, Listowel – and, like another native writer, Bryan MacMahon, enriched its heritage and gave it a dimension that few, if any, other Irish town could hope to match. In a word, John B. injected character into the very streets and rivers, demonstrated the magical power and beauty of language, and remained rooted there, letting outsiders come to him. No longer it seemed need poets and writers leave their own villages and towns to become famous. Listowel Writers' Week was another extension of his philosophy, and again this attracted people from all parts to taste the town's unique blend of culture and sociability. Danny Hannon had talked of the John B. pub as a place of entertainment where people could not only drink their pints and small ones but recite poetry, sing songs and ballads, and tell stories. In this, Keane had set an example that might be followed by myriad dull pubs around the country.

*

It is appropriate, therefore, to bring down the curtain on this epic drama in Listowel and reflect on the words of John B.'s lifelong neighbour Ned O'Sullivan, for in our view they must represent the wistful feelings of all Keane admirers. 'Last Thursday,' O'Sullivan wrote in the *Kerryman*, 'Philomena Walsh, a great old Listowel character, came into the shop and said to me, "John B. is gone from us. We're only an ordinary town now." I agreed that Listowel was undoubtedly diminished by the passing of our hero, as Troy was by the death of Hector, but Philomena, you are surely wrong. Listowel will never be an ordinary town, for we'll have the spirit of John B. Keane watching over us as long as the bodhrán beats, as long as the curlew cries and as long as there is love. And that is forever.'

Bibliography of John B. Keane's Work

Published Plays

Sive, Progress House, 1959.

Sharon's Grave, Progress House, 1960.

Many Young Men of Twenty, Progress House, 1961.

The Highest House on the Mountain, Progress House, 1961.

The Year of the Hiker, Mercier Press, 1963.

The Field, Mercier Press, 1966.

Rain at the End of the Summer, Progress House, 1967.

Hut 42, Proscenium Press, 1968.

The Man from Clare, Mercier Press, 1969.

Big Maggie, Mercier Press, 1969.

Moll, Mercier Press, 1971.

The One-Way Ticket, Performance Publishing, 1972.

The Change in Mame Fadden, Mercier Press, 1973.

Values, Mercier Press, 1973.

The Crazy Wall, Mercier Press, 1974.

The Buds of Ballybunion, Mercier Press, 1976.

The Chastitute, Mercier Press, 1981.

Three Plays: Sive, The Field, Big Maggie (revised texts), Mercier Press, 1990.

Three Plays: Sharon's Grave, The Crazy Wall, The Man from Clare (revised texts), Mercier Press, 1995.

Three Plays: Many Young Men of Twenty, Moll (revised text), *The Chastitute*, Mercier Press, 1999.

Three Plays: The Year of the Hiker (revised text), *The Change in Mame Fadden, The Highest House on the Mountain*, Mercier Press, 2001.

The Street and Other Poems, Progress House, 1961.
Strong Tea, Mercier Press, 1963.
Self-Portrait, Mercier Press, 1964.
Letters of a Successful TD, Mercier Press, 1967.
Letters of an Irish Parish Priest, Mercier Press, 1972.
The Gentle Art of Matchmaking, Mercier Press, 1973.
Letters of an Irish Publican, Mercier Press, 1974.
Letters of a Love-Hungry Farmer, Mercier Press, 1974.
Letters of a Matchmaker, Mercier Press, 1975.
Letters of a Civic Guard, Mercier Press, 1976.
Irish Short Stories, Mercier Press, 1976.
Death Be Not Proud, Mercier Press, 1976.
Is the Holy Ghost Really a Kerryman? Mercier Press, 1976.
Dan Pheaidí Aindí, Mercier Press, 1977 (English version: *Man of the Triple Name*, Brandon, 1984).
Letters of a Country Postman, Mercier Press, 1977.
Unlawful Sex and Other Testy Matters, Mercier Press, 1978.
Letters of a Minister of State, Mercier Press, 1978.
Stories from a Kerry Fireside, Mercier Press, 1980.
More Irish Short Stories, Mercier Press, 1981.
Unusual Irish Careers, Mercier Press, 1982.
Man of the Triple Name, Brandon, 1984.
Owl Sandwiches, Brandon, 1985.
The Bodhrán Makers, Brandon, 1986.
The Power of the Word, Brandon, 1989.
Love Bites and Other Stories, Mercier Press, 1991.
Celebrated Letters (TD, Farmer, Matchmaker, Priest, Minister of State), Mercier Press, 1991.
The Ram of God, Mercier Press, 1991.
Durango, Mercier Press, 1992.
The Contractors, Mercier Press, 1993.
Letters to the Brain, Brandon, 1993.
Christmas Tales, Mercier Press, 1993.
A High Meadow, Mercier Press, 1994.
Innocent Bystanders, Mercier Press, 1994.
Inlaws and Outlaws, Mercier Press, 1995.
The Voice of an Angel, Mercier Press, 1996 (paperback edition: *John B. Keane's Christmas*, 1997).

Under the Sycamore Tree & Other Tales, Mercier Press, 1997. (selection from *Irish Short Stories, More Irish Short Stories, Christmas Tales* and *The Voice of an Angel*; reissued as *The Short Stories of John B. Keane*, 2001).

A Warm Bed on a Cold Night, Mercier Press, 1997.

The Best of John B. Keane: Collected Humorous Writings, Mercier Press, 1999.

A Christmas Surprise, Mercier Press, 1999.

More Celebrated Letters (Publican, Civic Guard, Postman, Brain), Mercier Press, 2000.

The Little Book of John B. Keane, Mercier Press, 2000.

The Short Stories of John B. Keane, Mercier Press, 2001.

A Christmas Omnibus: The Best of John B. Keane, Mercier Press, 2001 (new Christmas stories along with three earlier collections: *Christmas Tales, The Voice of an Angel* and *A Christmas Surprise*).

INDEX